Contents

The Definitive Guide to Lift: A Scala-Based Web Framework

by Derek Chen-Becker, Marius Danciu, and Tyler Weir

Welcome to *The Definitive Guide to Lift: A Scala-Based Web Framework*! We hope that you find reading our work as informative, fun, and exciting as writing it has been for us. This book started out as some informal discussions between the Lift committers about a need for a good guide beyond the documentation contained on the Lift wiki and API documents. At the time, Lift had just passed version 0.7, and the mailing list was still relatively low traffic. In the interim, we've made it all the way to a 1.0 release, and the mailing list now has close to 900 members! In other words, Lift has really taken off.

When we sat down and began to outline the content of this book, we made a decision early on to be as comprehensive as possible. We knew that a lot of people would be reading our book having seen very little, if any, Lift code. We also knew that plenty of people who were comfortable with Lift fundamentals might want to exploit some of the more advanced functionality offered by Lift to make their applications even more appealing. With both of these readers in mind, this book is effectively broken into two parts. Chapters 1 through 6 cover the fundamentals of building a Lift application, from the basics of application architecture to how to handle forms, cookies, database access, and more. Chapters 7 through 13 cover the more advanced aspects of Lift, starting with an in-depth look at how Lift processes requests and moving on to topics like JavaScript, AJAX, Comet, and web services. We realize that writing a book that is accessible to newcomers while being relevant to advanced users is an ambitious goal, but we hope that you feel we've succeeded.

One important note that we want to make before you dive into this book is that Lift leverages a lot of the Scala language's features to provide a powerful API. While we will briefly discuss some of these features in context, this book is not intended to be an introduction to or reference for Scala. However, several other books are available that do an excellent job at that task, notably David Pollak's *Beginning Scala* (Apress, 2009). Since David started the whole Lift project from scratch, you can be sure that his book will be particularly relevant to people wanting to learn Scala so that they can use Lift.

Whether you're a seasoned Liftie or just starting out, we hope that you enjoy reading this book!

Acknowledgements

Derek would like to thank his wife, Debbie, for her patience and support while writing this book. He would also like to thank his two young sons, Dylan and Dean, for keeping things interesting and in perspective.

Tyler would like to thank his family, in particular his wife Laura, for encouraging him.

Marius would like to thank his wife, Alina, for her patience during long weekends and for bearing with his monosyllabic answers while working on this book.

This book would not have been possible without the Lift developers and especially David Pollak; without him, we wouldn't have had this opportunity. Also, a special thanks goes to Tim Perrett for his help with the REST API in Chapter 13. It's been very exciting seeing the Lift community grow so fast and to see Lift come so far in such a short time. We're looking forward to the next release and to seeing even more people on the mailing list!

The folks at Apress have been great to work with and have really helped to get this book into shape. We'd like to thank Candace English for herding proverbial cats to get all of the pieces together and on schedule, as well as Heather Lang for working so hard to translate what we wrote into English. Many thanks to Steve Anglin for getting the whole process started and working hard with us to smooth out the occasional wrinkle.

We would also like to thank the Lift community, as well as the following individuals, for valuable feedback on the content of this book: Adam Cimarosti, Malcolm Gorman, Doug Holton, Hunter Kelly, James Matlik, Larry Morroni, Jorge Ortiz, Tim Perrett, Tim Pigden, Dennis Przytarski, Thomas Sant Ana, Heiko Seeberger, and Eric Williger

Chapter 1: Welcome to Lift

Welcome to Exploring Lift. We've created this book to educate you about Lift, which we think is a great framework for building compelling web applications. Lift is designed to make powerful techniques easily accessible, while keeping the overall framework simple and flexible. It may sound like a cliché, but in our experience, Lift development is fun because it lets you focus on the interesting parts of coding. Our goal for this book is that, by the end, you'll be able to create and extend any web application you can think of.

In this chapter, we'll briefly cover the advantages of using Lift, as well as a small application to get you started. We'll cover a more detailed application in Chapter 2.

Lifting Off!

If you have experience with other web frameworks such as Struts, Tapestry, and Rails, you must be asking yourself, "Why another framework? Does Lift really solve problems any differently or more effectively than the ones I've used before?" Based on our experience (and of others in the growing Lift community), the answer is an emphatic "Yes!"

The creators of Lift have cherry-picked the best ideas from a number of other frameworks, while adding some novel ideas of their own. It's this combination of solid foundation and new techniques that makes Lift so powerful. At the same time, Lift has been able to avoid the mistakes made in the past by other frameworks. In the spirit of configuration by convention, Lift has sensible defaults for everything, while making it easy to customize precisely what you need to—no more and no less. Gone are the days of XML file after XML file providing basic configuration for your application. Instead, a basic Lift application requires only that you add the `LiftFilter` to your `web.xml` file and add one or more lines telling Lift what package your classes sit in (see the bootstrapping section in Chapter 3). The methods you code aren't required to implement a specific interface (called a trait), although Lift does contain support traits that simplify the development of your view code. In short, you don't need to write anything that isn't explicitly necessary for the task at hand. Lift is intended to work out of the box and to make you as efficient and productive as possible.

Implementing the View-First Pattern with Lift

One of the key strengths of Lift is the clean separation of presentation content and logic, based on the concept of View-First composition.

To give an example by way of contrast, one of the original Java web application technologies that's still in use today is JSP, or JavaServer Pages (JSP), which you can learn more about at `http://java.sun.com/products/jsp/`. JSP allows you to mix HTML and Java code directly within the page. While this idea may have seemed good at the start, it has proven to be painful in practice. Putting code in your presentation layer makes debugging and understanding what is going on within a page more difficult and makes life more difficult for the people writing the HTML portion, because the contents aren't proper HTML. While many modern programming and HTML editors have been modified to accommodate this mess, proper syntax highlighting and validation don't make up for the fact that you still have to switch back and forth between one or more files to follow the page flow.

Lift takes the approach that there should be no code in the presentation layer, but that the presentation layer has to be flexible enough to accommodate any conceivable uses. To that end, Lift uses a powerful templating system à la Wicket (see `http://wicket.apache.org/`), to bind user-generated data into the presentation layer. The View First pattern means that we start with an XML template (the View), and then embed, or execute, independent components to fill in the template. The benefits of the View-First approach are that your page components naturally become more modular, which makes modifying pages and reusing page components much simpler.

Lift's templating is built on the XML processing capabilities of the Scala language, and allows things such as nested templates, simple injection of user-generated content, and advanced data binding capabilities. Not only does Scala have extensive library support for XML, but XML syntax is actually part of the language. We'll cover this syntax in more detail as we go through this book. If you're coming from JSP, you'll find that Lift's advanced template and XML processing allows you to essentially write custom tag libraries at a fraction of the cost in time and effort.

Leveraging the Scala Language

Lift has another advantage over many other web frameworks: it's designed specifically to leverage the Scala programming language. Scala is a relatively new language developed by Martin Odersky and his programming language research group at Ecole Polytechnique Fédérale de Lausanne (EPFL) in Switzerland. Martin created the Pizza programming language, which led to the Generic Java (GJ) project that was eventually incorporated into Java 1.5; his home page is at `http://lamp.epfl.ch/~odersky/`. Scala compiles to Java bytecode and runs on the JVM, which means that you can leverage the vast ecosystem of Java libraries just as you would with any other Java web framework.

At the same time, Scala introduces some very powerful features designed to make you, the developer, more productive. Among these features are an extremely rich type system, along with powerful type inference, native XML processing, full support for closures and functions as objects, and an extensive high-level library. The power of the type system and its type inference has led people to call it "the statically typed dynamic language" (see `http://scala-blogs.org/2007/12/scala-statically-typed-dynamic-language.html`). In essence, you can write code as quickly as you could with dynamically typed languages (Python, Ruby, etc.), but you have the compile-time type safety of a statically typed language like Java.

Scala is also a hybrid functional and object-oriented (OO) language, which means you can get the power of the higher-level functional programming (FP) languages (Haskell, Scheme, etc.) while retaining the modularity and reusability of OO components. In particular, the FP concept of immutability is encouraged by Scala, making it well-suited for writing very concurrent program that achieve high throughput scalability. The hybrid model also means that if you haven't touched FP before, you can gradually ease into it. In our experience, Scala allows you to do more in Lift with less lines of code. Remember, Lift is all about making you more productive!

Supporting Advanced Features Easily

Lift strives to encompass advanced features in a very concise and straightforward manner. Lift's powerful support for AJAX and Comet allow you to use Web 2.0 features with very little effort. Lift leverages Scala's Actor library to provide a message-driven framework for Comet updates. In most cases, adding Comet support to a page just involves extending a trait to define the rendering method of your page and adding an extra function call to your links to dispatch the update message. Lift handles all of the backend and page-side coding to effect the Comet polling.

AJAX support includes special handlers for doing AJAX form submission via JSON, and almost any link function can easily be turned into an AJAX version with a few keystrokes. In order to perform all of this client-side goodness, Lift has a class hierarchy for encapsulating JavaScript calls via direct JavaScript, jQuery, or Yahoo User Interface (YUI) library. The nice part is that you can utilize these support classes so that code can be generated for you, reducing or eliminating the need to put JavaScript logic into your templates.

Getting to Know the Lift Community

Lift has a very active community of users and developers. Since its inception in early 2007, the community has grown to hundreds of members from all over the world. The project's leader, David Pollak, whose blog you can read at `http://blog.lostlake.org/`, is constantly attending to the mailing list, answering questions, and taking feature requests. A core group of developers work on the project, but submissions are taken from anyone who makes a good case and can turn in good code. While we strive to cover everything you'll need to know in this book, here are several additional resources available for information on Lift:

- The first place to look is the web site at `http://liftweb.net/`. The web site is maintained by not only David but many active members of the Lift community (including us). Portions of this book are inspired by and borrow from content on the web site, including the wiki portion. In particular, the web site has links to all of the generated documentation not only for the stable branch but for the unstable head, if you're feeling adventurous. The wiki also includes an extensive section of how-to and general articles on advanced topics that cover a wealth of information.

- The mailing list at `http://groups.google.com/group/liftweb` is very active, and if there are things that this book doesn't cover, you can feel free to ask questions there. Plenty of very knowledgeable people are on the list, and they should be able to answer your questions. Please post specific questions about this book to the Lift Book Google Group at `http://groups.google.com/group/the-lift-book`. Anything else that is Lift-specific is fair game for the mailing list.
- Lift has an IRC channel at `irc://irc.freenode.net/lift` that usually has several people on at any given time. It's a great place to chat about issues and ideas concerning Lift.

Creating Your First Lift Application

We've talked a lot about Lift and its capabilities, so now you're ready to try out an application. Before we start, though, we need to take care of some prerequisites:

The Java 1.5 JDK: Lift runs on Scala, which runs on top of the JVM. The first thing you'll need to install is a modern version of the Java SE JVM, available at `http://java.sun.com/`. Recently Scala's compiler was changed to target Java version 1.5. Though 1.4 is still available as a target, we're going to assume you're using 1.5. Examples in this book have only been tested with Sun's version of the JDK, although most likely other versions (e.g., Blackdown or OpenJDK) should work with little or no modification.

Maven 2: Maven is a project management tool that has extensive capabilities for building, managing dependencies, testing, and reporting. We assume that you are familiar with basic Maven usage for compilation, packaging, and testing. If you haven't used Maven before, you can get a brief overview in Appendix A. You can download the latest version of Maven from `http://maven.apache.org/`. Brief installation instructions (enough to get you started) are on the download page at `http://maven.apache.org/download.html`.

A programming editor: This isn't a strict requirement for this example, but when we start getting into coding, having a text editor that's a little more capable than notepad will be helpful. If you'd like a full-blown IDE, with support for things like debugging, continuous compile checking, and so on, plug-ins for common IDEs are available on the Scala web site at `http://www.scala-lang.org/node/91` with support for the following:

- Eclipse, which is available at `http://www.eclipse.org/` is supported. The Scala plug-in developer recommends using the Eclipse Classic version of the IDE.
- To use NetBeans, available at `http://www.netbeans.org`, you must use NetBeans 6.5.

- Using IntelliJ IDEA, which is available at `http://www.jetbrains.com/idea/index.html`, requires using version 8 beta.

If you'd like something more lightweight, the Scala language distribution comes with plug-ins for editors like VIM, Emacs, and jEdit. To access these plug-ins, either you can download the full Scala distribution from `http://www.scala-lang.org/` and use the files under `misc/scala-tool-support`, or you can directly access the latest versions via the Subversion (SVN) interface at `https://lampsvn.epfl.ch/trac/scala/browser/scala-tool-support/trunk/src`. Getting these plug-ins to work in your IDE or editor of choice is beyond the scope of this book, although the scala-tools mailing list (`http://www.scala-lang.org/node/199#scala-tools`) is a good place to ask questions.

Now that we have the prerequisites out of the way, it's time to get started. We're going to leverage Maven's archetypes to do 99 percent of the work for us in this example. If you're unfamiliar with archetypes, an archetype is essentially a project template for Maven that provides prompt-driven customization of basic attributes. First, change to whatever directory you'd like to work in, for example:

```
cd work
```

Next, we use Maven's `archetype:generate` command to create the skeleton of your project:

```
mvn archetype:generate -U \
  -DarchetypeGroupId=net.liftweb \
  -DarchetypeArtifactId=lift-archetype-blank \
  -DarchetypeVersion=1.0 \
  -DgroupId=demo.helloworld \
  -DartifactId=helloworld \
  -Dversion=1.0-SNAPSHOT
```

Maven should output several pages of text. It may stop and ask you to confirm the properties configuration, in which case you can just press Enter. At the end, you should get a message that says `BUILD SUCCESSFUL`. You've now successfully created your first project! Don't believe us? Run it to confirm:

```
cd helloworld
mvn jetty:run
```

Maven should produce more output, ending with

```
[INFO] Starting scanner at interval of 5 seconds.
```

This means that you now have a web server (Jetty, which is provided automatically by Maven) running on port 8080 of your machine. Just go to `http://localhost:8080/`, and you'll see your first Lift page displaying the standard "Hello world!" greeting. With just a few simple commands, we've built a functional (albeit limited) web application.

Let's go into a little more detail and look at exactly how these pieces fit together. First, let's examine the index page. Whenever Lift serves up a request where the URL ends in a forward slash, Lift automatically looks for a file called `index.html` in that directory. Technically, it also searches for some variations on `index.html`, including any localized versions of the page, but we'll cover that later in Chapter 3.

For instance, if you tried to go to `http://localhost:8080/test/`, Lift would look for `index.html` under the `test/` directory in your project. The HTML sources will be located under `src/main/webapp/` in your project directory. Here's the `index.html` file from our Hello World project:

```
<lift:surround with="default" at="content">
  <h2>Welcome to your project!</h2>
  <p><lift:helloWorld.howdy /></p>
</lift:surround>
```

This may look a little strange at first. If you have some XML experience, you may recognize the use of prefixed elements here. If don't know what that is, a prefixed element is an XML element of the following form:

```
<prefix:element>
```

In our case, we have two elements in use: `<lift:surround>` and `<lift:helloWorld.howdy />`. Lift assigns special meaning to elements that use the `lift` prefix; they form the basis of lift's extensive templating support, which we will cover in more detail in Chapter 3. When lift processes an XML template, it does so from the outermost element inward. In our case, the outermost element is

```
<lift:surround with="default" at="content">
```

The `<lift:surround>` element basically tells Lift to find the template named by the `with` attribute (`default`, in our case) and to put the contents of our element inside of that template. The `at` attribute tells Lift where in the template to place our content. In Lift, filling in the blanks like this is called binding, and it's a fundamental concept of Lift's template system. Just about everything at the HTML and XML level can be thought of as a series of nested binds.

Before we move on to the `<lift:helloWorld.howdy />` element, let's look at the default template. You can find it in the `templates-hidden` directory of the web application. Much like the `WEB-INF` and `META-INF` directories in a Java web application, the contents of `templates-hidden` cannot be accessed directly by clients. They can, however, be accessed when they're referenced by a `<lift:surround>` element. Here is the `default.html` file:

```
<html xmlns="http://www.w3.org/1999/xhtml"
    xmlns:lift="http://liftweb.net/">
  <head>
    <title>
      demo.helloworld:helloworld:1.0-SNAPSHOT
```

```
    </title>
    <script id="jquery" src="/classpath/jquery.js"
      type="text/javascript"></script>
  </head>
  <body>
    <lift:bind name="content" />
    <lift:Menu.builder />
    <lift:msgs/>
  </body>
</html>
```

The listing shows a proper XHTML file, with `<html>`, `<head>`, and `<body>` tags. Using a complete file is required, since Lift doesn't add these tags itself. Lift simply processes the XML from each template it encounters. The `<head>` element and its contents are boilerplate; the interesting things happen inside the `<body>` element. There are three elements here:

- The `<lift:bind name=”content” />` element determines where the contents of our `index.html` file are bound (inserted). The `name` attribute should match the corresponding at attribute from our `<lift:surround>` element.
- The `<lift:Menu.builder />` element is a special element that builds a menu based on Lift's SiteMap framework (to be covered in Chapter 5). The SiteMap is a high-level site directory component that not only provides a centralized place to define a site menu but allows you to control when certain links are displayed (based on, say, whether users are logged in or what roles they have) and provides a page-level access control mechanism.
- The `<lift:msgs />` element allows Lift (or your code) to display messages on a page as it's rendered. These could be status messages, error messages, and so on. Lift has facilities to set one or more messages from inside your logic code.

Now, look back at the `<lift:helloWorld.howdy />` element from the `index.html` file. This element (and the `<lift:Menu.builder />` element, actually) is called a snippet, and it's of the form

```
<lift:class.method>
```

In this snippet, `class` is the name of a Scala class defined in our project in the `demo.helloworld.snippets` package, and `method` is a method defined on that class. Lift does a little translation on the class name to change camel case back into title case and then locates the class. In our example, the class is located under

```
src/main/scala/demo/helloworld/snippet/HelloWorld.scala
```

and is shown here:

```
package demo.helloworld.snippet
class HelloWorld {
  def howdy: NodeSeq =
  <span>Welcome to helloworld at
        {new java.util.Date}</span>
}
```

As you can see, the howdy method is pretty straightforward. Lift binds the result of executing the method into the location of the snippet element (in this case, a span). It's interesting to note that a method may itself return other <lift:. . .> elements in its content, and they will be processed as well. This recursive nature of template composition is part of the fundamental power of Lift; it means that reusing snippets and template pieces across your application is essentially free. You should never have to write the same functionality more than once.

Now that we've covered all of the actual content elements, the final piece of the puzzle is the Boot class. The Boot class is responsible for the configuration and setup of the Lift framework. As we stated earlier in the chapter, most of Lift has sensible defaults, so the Boot class generally contains only the extras that you need. The Boot class is always located in the bootstrap.liftweb package and is shown here:

```
package bootstrap.liftweb
import net.liftweb.util._
import net.liftweb.http._
import net.liftweb.sitemap._
import net.liftweb.sitemap.Loc._
import Helpers._
class Boot {
  def boot {
    // where to search snippet
    LiftRules.addToPackages("demo.helloworld")
    // Build SiteMap
    val entries = Menu(Loc("Home", List("index"),
                       "Home")) :: Nil
    LiftRules.setSiteMap(SiteMap(entries:_*))
  }
}
```

There are two basic configuration elements placed in the boot method. The first is the LiftRules.addToPackages method. It tells lift to base its searches in the demo.helloworld package. That means that snippets would be located in the demo.helloworld.snippets package, views (see Chapter 3) would be located in the demo.helloworld.views package, and so on. If you have more than one hierarchy (multiple packages) you can just call addToPackages multiple times. The second item in the Boot class is the SiteMenu setup. Obviously, this is a pretty simple menu in this example, but we'll cover more interesting examples in the SiteMap chapter (Chapter 5).

Conclusion

Now that we've covered a basic example, we hope you're beginning to see why Lift is so powerful and can make you more productive. We've barely scratched the surface on Lift's templating and binding capabilities, but what we've shown here is already a big step. In roughly 10 lines of Scala code and about 30 lines of XML, we have a functional site. If we wanted to add more pages, we've already got our default template set up, so we don't need to write the same boilerplate HTML again. In this example, we're directly generating the content for our `helloWorld.howdy` snippet, but in later examples, we'll show just how easy it is to actually pull content from the template itself into the snippet and modify it as needed.

In the following chapters we'll be covering

- Much more complex templating and snippet binding, including input forms and programmatic template selection
- How to use SiteMap and its ancillary classes to provide a context-aware site menu and access control layer
- How to handle state within your application
- Lift's object relational mapping (ORM) layer, Mapper, which provides a powerful yet lightweight interface to databases
- Advanced AJAX and Comet support in Lift for Web 2.0–style applications

We hope you're as excited about getting started with Lift as we are to show it to you!

Chapter 2: PocketChange

As a way to demonstrate the concepts in this book, we've decided to build an application as an evolutionary example. The application we've picked is an expense tracker, and we're calling it PocketChange.

In this chapter, we'll start by briefly introducing the requirements of PocketChange. Next, we'll define our data model that we'll use to store expense and account information in the database. After that, we'll start coding up some XHTML templates for the user interface, followed by defining the Scala snippets (handling code) that process display logic and user input. Finally, we'll give you a little taste of how easy it is to make PocketChange a Web 2.0 application by adding some AJAX features.

Keeping Track of Your PocketChange

PocketChange, shown in Figure 2-1, will track your expenses, keep a running total of what you've spent, and allow you to organize transaction with tags and visualize the data. During the later chapters of this book, we'll add a few fun features such as AJAX charting and allowing multiple people per account (using Comet to update entries). Above all, we want to keep the interface lean, mean, and clean.

Figure 2-1. The PocketChange Application

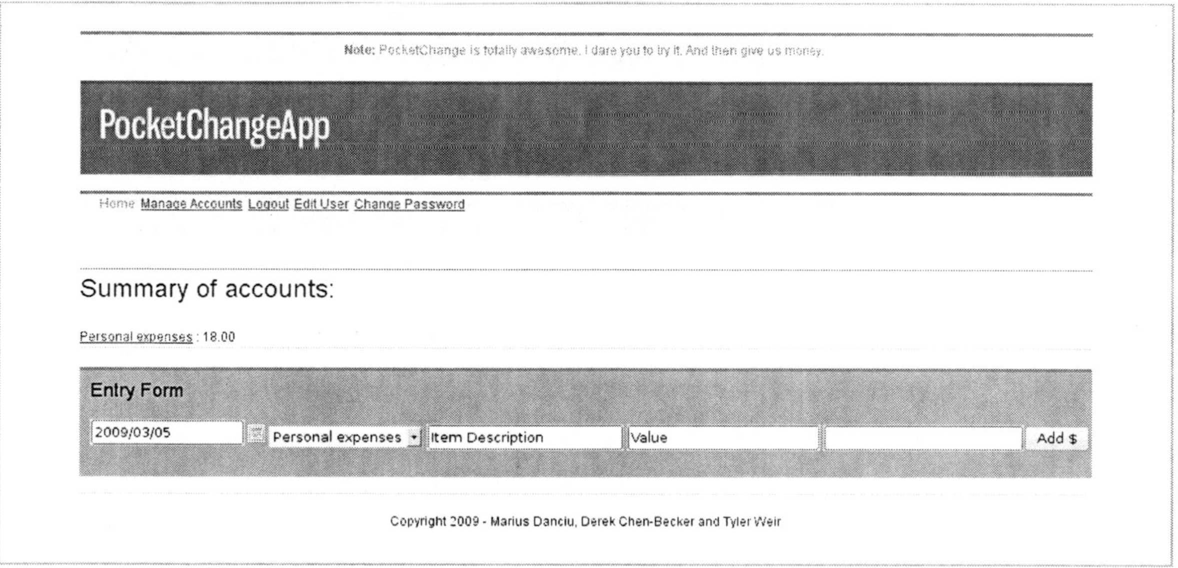

We're going to be using the View First pattern for the design of our application, since Lift's separation of presentation and logic via templating, views, and snippets lends itself to View First so well. For an excellent article on the design decisions behind Lift's approach to templating and logic, read David Pollak's "Lift View First" article on the Lift wiki at `http://wiki.liftweb.net/index.php?title=Lift_View_First`. Note that the example code is somewhat out of date on this page; the interesting part is David's reasoning and decisions that have made Lift so easy to use.

Another important thing to note is that we're going to breeze through the application in this chapter and touch briefly on a lot of details. We'll provide plenty of references to the chapters where things are covered more fully; this chapter is intended to just give you a taste of Lift, so feel free to read ahead if you want more information on how something works.

In addition, full source code for the entire PocketChange application is available at GitHub (`http://github.com/tjweir/pocketchangeapp/tree`). You can pull your own version of the PocketChange git repository with the following command (assuming you have git installed):

```
git clone git://github.com/tjweir/pocketchangeapp.git
```

Note git is freely available at `http://git-scm.com/download`.

Enough chatter, let's go!

Defining the Model

The first step we'll take is to define the database entities that we're going to use for our application. The following items cover base functionality of a categorized expense tracker:

- *User*: Represents a user of the application
- *Account*: Represents a specific expense account (We want to support more than one per user.)
- *Expense*: Represents a specific expense transaction tied to a particular account
- *Tag*: Allows us a to categorize each expense for later searching and reporting

We'll start out with the user, as shown in Listing 2-1. This is taken directly from the `src/main/scala/com/pocketchangeapp/model/User.scala` source file that you can pull from the git repository. We leverage Lift's `MegaProtoUser` (see Chapter 6) class to handle most of what we need for user management. For example, with just the code you see, we define an entire user management function for our site, including sign-up, lost password, and login pages. The accompanying SiteMap (see Chapter 5) menus are generated with a single call to `User.siteMap`. As you can see, we can customize the XHTML that's generated for the user management pages with a few simple `def`s; the customization potential for `MetaMegaProtoUser` is extensive.

Listing 2-1. The PocketChange User Entity

```
package com.pocketchangeapp.model
import _root_.net.liftweb.mapper._
import DB._
import _root_.net.liftweb.util._
import _root_.java.sql.Connection
object User extends User with MetaMegaProtoUser[User] {
  // define the DB table name
  override def dbTableName = "users"
  // Spruce up the forms a bit
  override def loginXhtml =
   <lift:surround with="default" at="content">
    <div id="formBox">{ super.loginXhtml }</div>
   </lift:surround>
  override def signupXhtml(user: User) =
   <lift:surround with="default" at="content">
    <div id="formBox">
     { super.signupXhtml(user) }
    </div>
   </lift:surround>
}
class User extends MegaProtoUser[User] {
  def getSingleton = User // what's the "meta" server
  def accounts : List[Account] =
    Account.findAll(By(Account.owner, this.id))
  def administered : List[Account] =
    AccountAdmin.findAll(By(AccountAdmin.administrator,
      this.id)).map(_.account.obj.open_!)
  def editable = accounts ++ administered
  def viewed : List[Account] =
    AccountViewer.findAll(By(AccountViewer.viewer,
      this.id)).map(_.account.obj.open_!)
  def allAccounts : List[Account] =
    accounts ::: administered ::: viewed
}
```

Note that we've also added a few utility methods to the `User` class to retrieve all of the accounts for a given user (as well as accounts that the user can administer and view). We don't cover the `AccountAdmin` and `AccountViewer` classes in this chapter, although they're defined in the source in GitHub. The functionality that they represent is very similar to other classes we'll be covering here, so you're not missing anything. For simple access to the accounts that a user owns, we use the MetaMapper.findAll method (available in the User singleton, which extends MetaMapper through MetaMegaProtoUser) to do a query by owner ID (see Chapter 6).

Defining the Account entity is a little more involved, as shown in Listing 2-2. Here, we define a class with a Long primary key and some fields associate with the accounts. We also define some helper methods for object relationship joins (see Chapter 6). The Expense and Tag entities (along with some ancillary entities) follow suit, so we won't cover them here.

Listing 2-2. The PocketChange Account Entity

```
package com.pocketchangeapp.model
import java.math.MathContext
import net.liftweb.mapper._
import net.liftweb.util.Empty
class Account extends LongKeyedMapper[Account]
    with IdPK {
  def getSingleton = Account
  object owner extends MappedLongForeignKey(this, User)
  { override def dbIndexed_? = true }
  def admins =
  AccountAdmin.findAll(
    By(AccountAdmin.account, this.id))
  def addAdmin (user : User) =
   AccountAdmin.create
     .account(this).administrator(user).save
  def viewers =
  AccountViewer.findAll(
    By(AccountViewer.account, this.id))
  object is_public extends MappedBoolean(this) {
    override def defaultValue = false
  }
  // The balance has 16 digits and 2 decimal places
  object balance extends MappedDecimal(this,
    MathContext.DECIMAL64, 2)
  def entries = Expense.getByAcct(this, Empty, Empty,
    Empty)
  def tags = Tag.findAll(By(Tag.account, this.id))
  object name extends MappedString(this,100)
  object description extends MappedString(this, 300)
  object externalAccount extends MappedString(this, 300)
  def notes =
    AccountNote.findAll(
      By(AccountNote.account, this.id))
}
object Account extends Account with
```

```
    LongKeyedMetaMapper[Account] {
  def findByName (owner : User,
                  name : String) : List[Account] =
    Account.findAll(By(Account.owner, owner.id.is),
      By(Account.name, name))
}
```

Creating Your First Template

Our next step is to figure out how we'll present this data to the user. We'd like to show a home page on the site that shows either a welcome message or a summary of account balances and a place to enter new expenses if the user is logged in.

Listing 2-3 shows a basic template to handle this functionality. We'll save the template as `index.html`. Did you notice that we have a head element but no body? This is XHTML, so how does this work? This template uses the `<lift:surround>` tag (see Chapter 3) to embed itself into a master template (`/templates_hidden/default.html`); Lift actually does what's called a head merge (see Chapter 3) to include the contents of the head tag in our template within the head element of the master template. The `<lift:HomePage.summary>` and `<lift:AddEntry.addentry>` tags are snippet definitions. Snippets are the Scala code the control the actual page logic behind the scenes; we'll be covering them in the next section

Listing 2-3. The Welcome Template

```
<lift:surround with="default" at="content">
<head>
  <!-- required plugins -->
  <script type="text/javascript"
    src="/scripts/date.js"></script>
  <!--[if IE]>
  <script type="text/javascript"
    src="/scripts/jquery.bgiframe.js">
  </script>
  <![endif]-->
  <!-- jquery.datePicker.js -->
  <script type="text/javascript"
    src="/scripts/jquery.datePicker.js">
  </script>
  <link rel="stylesheet" type="text/css"
    href="/style/datePicker.css" />
</head>
  <lift:HomePage.summary>
    <div class="column span-24 bordered">
    <h2>Summary of accounts:</h2>
      <account:entry>
```

```
        <acct:name /> : <acct:balance /> <br/>
      </account:entry>
    </div>
    <hr />
  </lift:HomePage.summary>
  <div class="column span-24">
    <lift:AddEntry.addentry form="POST">
      <div id="entryform">
        <div class="column span-24"><h3>Entry Form</h3>
          <e:account /> <e:dateOf /> <e:desc />
          <e:value />
          <e:tags/><button>Add $</button>
        </div>
      </div>
    </lift:AddEntry.addentry>
  </div>
  <script type="text/javascript">
    Date.format = 'yyyy/mm/dd';
    jQuery(function () {
      jQuery('#entrydate').datePicker(
      {startDate:'00010101', clickInput:true});
    })
  </script>
</lift:surround>
```

As you can see, there's no control logic at all in our template, just well-formed XML and some JavaScript to activate the jQuery datePicker functionality.

Writing Snippets

Now that we have a template, we need to write the summary and addEntry snippets so that we can actually do something with the site. First, let's look at the summary snippet, shown in Listing 2-4. We've skipped the standard Lift imports (see Listing 3-2) to save space, but we've specifically imported java.util.Date and all of our model classes.

Listing 2-4. The summary Snippet Definition

```
package com.pocketchangeapp.snippet
import ... standard imports ...
import com.pocketchangeapp.model._
import java.util.Date
class HomePage {
 def summary (xhtml : NodeSeq) : NodeSeq =
  User.currentUser match {
  case Full(user) => {
   val entries : NodeSeq = user.allAccounts match {
```

```
      case Nil => Text("You have no accounts set up")
      case accounts => accounts.flatMap({account =>
       bind("acct", chooseTemplate("account", "entry",
                                   xhtml),
            "name" ->
              <a href={"/account/" + account.name.is}>
                {account.name.is}</a>,
           "balance" -> Text(account.balance.toString))
      })
     }
     bind("account", xhtml, "entry" -> entries)
    }
    case _ => <lift:embed what="welcome_msg" />
  }
 }
```

Our first step is to use the `User.currentUser` method (this is part of `MetaMegaProtoUser`) to determine if someone is logged in. If so, we use the `User.allAccounts` method to retrieve a `List` of all of the user's accounts. If the user doesn't have any accounts, we say so by returning an XML `Text` node that will be bound where our tag was placed in the template. If the user does have an account, we map the account information into XHTML using the bind function. For each account, we bind the name of the account where we've defined the `<acct:name>` tag in the template and the balance where we defined `<acct:balance>`. The resulting `List` of XML `NodeSeq` entities is used to replace the `<lift:HomePage.summary>` element in the template. Finally, we match the case where a user isn't logged in by embedding the contents of the welcome template (which may be further processed).

Of course, it doesn't do us any good to display account balances if users can't add expenses, so let's define the `addEntry` snippet. The code is shown in Listing 2-5. This looks different than the `summary` snippet primarily because we're using a `StatefulSnippet` (see Chapter 3). The primary difference is that with a `StatefulSnippet` the same instance of the snippet is used for each page request in a given session, so we can keep the variables around in case we need the user to fix something in the form. The basic structure of the snippet is the same as for our summary: we do some work (we'll cover the `doTagsAndSubmit` function in a moment) and then bind values back into the template. In this snippet, however, we use the `SHtml.select` and `SHtml.text` methods to generate form fields. The `text` fields simply take an initial value and a function (closure) to process the value on submission. The `select` field is a little more complex because we give it a list of options, but the concept is the same.

Listing 2-5. The addEntry Snippet

```
package com.pocketchangeapp.snippet
import ... standard imports ...
import com.pocketchangeapp.model._
import com.pocketchangeapp.util.Util
import java.util.Date
/* date | desc | tags | value */
class AddEntry extends StatefulSnippet {
 def dispatch = {
  case "addentry" => add _
 }
 var account : Long = _
 var date = ""
 var desc = ""
 var value = ""
 var tags = S.param("tag") openOr ""
 def add(in: NodeSeq): NodeSeq =
  User.currentUser match {
   case Full(user) if user.editable.size > 0 => {
    def doTagsAndSubmit(t: String) {
     tags = t
     if (tags.trim.length == 0) {
      error("We're going to need at least one tag.")
     } else {
     /* Get the date correctly, yyyy/mm/dd */
     val entryDate = Util.slashDate.parse(date)
     val amount = BigDecimal(value)
     val currentAccount = Account.find(account).open_!
     /* determine the last serial number and balance
        for the date in question */
     val (entrySerial,entryBalance) =
      Expense.getLastExpenseData(currentAccount,
                                 entryDate)
     val e = Expense.create.account(account)
                  .dateOf(entryDate)
                  .serialNumber(entrySerial + 1)
                  .description(desc)
                  .amount(BigDecimal(value)).tags(tags)
                  .currentBalance(entryBalance + amount)
     e.validate match {
      case Nil => {
       Expense.updateEntries(entrySerial + 1, amount)
       e.save
       val acct = Account.find(account).open_!
       val newBalance = acct.balance.is + e.amount.is
       acct.balance(newBalance).save
```

```
        notice("Entry added!")
        // dpp: remove the statefullness of this snippet
        unregisterThisSnippet()       }
      case x => error(x)
    }
  }
}

val allAccounts =
  user.allAccounts.map(acct => (acct.id.toString,
                                acct.name))
bind("e", in,
     "account" -> select(allAccounts, Empty,
                         id => account = id.toLong),
     "dateOf" -> text(Util.slashDate.format(
                        new Date()).toString,
                       date = _,
                       "id" -> "entrydate"),
     "desc" -> text("Item Description", desc = _),
     "value" -> text("Value", value = _),
     "tags" -> text(tags, doTagsAndSubmit))
 }
case _ => Text("")
 }
}
```

The doTagsAndSubmit function is a new addition; its primary purpose is to process all of the submitted data, create and validate an Expense entry, and then return to the user. This pattern of defining a local function to handle form submission is quite common as opposed to defining a method on your class. The main reason is that by defining the function locally, it becomes a closure on any variables defined in the scope of your snippet function.

Sprinkling a Little AJAX Spice

So far, this code is all pretty standard fare, so let's add a bit of flavor with more advanced functionality. Listing 2-6 shows a template for displaying a table of expenses for the user with an optional start and end date. The Accounts.detail snippet is what we'll be defining later in this section.

Listing 2-6. The Expense Table

```
<lift:surround with="default" at="content">
 <lift:Accounts.detail eager_eval="true">
  <div class="column span-24">
   <h2>Summary</h2>
   <table><tr><th>Name</th><th>Balance</th></tr>
    <tr><td><acct:name /></td>
        <td><acct:balance /></td></tr>
   </table
  <div>
   <h3>Filters:</h3>
   <table><tr><th>Start Date</th>
              <td><acct:startDate /></td>
              <th>End Date</th>
              <td><acct:endDate /></td></tr>
   </table>
  </div>
  <div class="column span-24" >
   <h2>Transactions</h2>
   <lift:embed what="entry_table" />
  </div>
 </lift:Accounts.detail>
</lift:surround>
```

The `<lift:embed />` tag (see Chapter 3) allows you to substitute the contents of another template where `<lift:embed />` tag is placed. In our case, the `entry_table` template is shown in Listing 2-7. This template is really just a fragment that is not intended to be used alone, since it's not a full XHTML document and doesn't surround itself with a master template. It does, however, provide binding sites that we can fill in.

Listing 2-7. An Embedded Expense Table

```
<table class="" border="0" cellpadding="0"
  cellspacing="1"   width="100%">
 <thead>
  <tr>
   <th>Date</th><th>Description</th>
   <th>Tags</th><th>Value</th>
   <th>Balance</th>
  </tr>
 </thead>
 <tbody id="entry_table">
  <acct:table>
   <acct:tableEntry>
    <tr><td><entry:date /></td><td><entry:desc /></td>
        <td><entry:tags /></td><td><entry:amt /></td>
```

```
        <td><entry:balance /></td>
    </tr>
   </acct:tableEntry>
  </acct:table>
 </tbody>
</table>
```

Before we get into the AJAX portion of the code, let's define a helper method, shown in Listing 2-8, to generate the XHTML table entries that we'll be displaying (assuming normal imports). The function basically pulls the contents of the `<acct:tableEntry>` tag (via the `Helpers.chooseTemplate` method explained in Appendix C) and binds each `Expense` from the provided list into it. As you can see in the `entry_table` template, that corresponds to one table row for each entry.

Listing 2-8. The Table Helper Function

```
def buildExpenseTable(entries : List[Expense],
                      template : NodeSeq) = {
 entries.flatMap({ entry =>
  bind("entry", chooseTemplate("acct", "tableEntry",
                               template),
       "date" ->
        Text(Util.slashDate.format(entry.dateOf.is)),
       "desc" -> Text(entry.description.is),
       "tags" ->
        Text(entry.tags.map(_.tag.is).mkString(", ")),
       "amt" -> Text(entry.amount.toString),
       "balance" -> Text(entry.currentBalance.toString))
 })
}
```

The final piece is our `Accounts.detail` snippet, shown in Listing 2-9. We start off with some boilerplate matches to locate the `Account` to be viewed, and then we define some `vars` to hold state. It's important that they're `vars` so that they can be captured by the `entryTable`, `updateStartDate`, and `updateEndDate` closures and the AJAX form fields that we define.

The only magic we have to use is the `SHtml.ajaxText` form field generator (see Chapter 9), which will turn our update closures into AJAX callbacks. The values returned from these callbacks are JavaScript code that will be run on the client side. You can see that, in a short piece of code, we now have a page that will automatically update your `Expense` table when you set the start or end dates!

Listing 2-9. Our Ajax Snippet

```
package com.pocketchangeapp.snippet
import ... standard imports ...
import com.pocketchangeapp.model._
import com.pocketchangeapp.util.Util
class Accounts {
 def detail (xhtml: NodeSeq) : NodeSeq =
  S.param("name") match {
   case Full(acctName) => {
    Account.findByName(User.currentUser.open_!,
                       acctName) match {
    case acct :: Nil => {
     // Some closure state for the Ajax calls
     var startDate : Box[Date] = Empty
     var endDate : Box[Date] = Empty
     // Method defined here to capture the closure
     // vars defined above
     def entryTable =
      buildExpenseTable(Expense.getByAcct(acct,
                          startDate, endDate, Empty),
                        xhtml)
     def updateStartDate (date : String) = {
      startDate = Util.parseDate(date,
                    Util.slashDate.parse)
      JsCmds.SetHtml("entry_table", entryTable)
     }
     def updateEndDate (date : String) = {
      endDate = Util.parseDate(date,
                  Util.slashDate.parse)
      JsCmds.SetHtml("entry_table", entryTable)
     }
     bind("acct", xhtml,
          "name" -> acct.name.asHtml,
          "balance" -> acct.balance.asHtml,
          "startDate" -> SHtml.ajaxText("",
                           updateStartDate),
          "endDate" -> SHtml.ajaxText("",
                         updateEndDate),
          "table" -> entryTable)
    }
   case _ => Text("Could not locate account " +
                  acctName)
   }
  }
  case _ => Text("No account name provided")
 }
```

```
}
```

Conclusion

We hope that this chapter has demonstrated that Lift can be powerful while remaining concise and easy to use. We've shown how you can write templates using standard XML to easily generate web pages. We've also shown how you can use snippets and template composition to keep your logic and presentation modular, and we've demonstrated how simple it is to set up classes that map your data to a database. Finally, we've given you brief taste of how easy Lift makes it to use advanced functionality like AJAX to enable responsive applications.

We're going to continue to expand on this example application throughout this book, so feel free to look back here for a recap of the basics if you get confused later. Now let's dive in!

Chapter 3: Lift Fundamentals

In this chapter, we will cover some of the fundamental aspects of writing a Lift application, including the architecture of the Lift library and how it processes requests. We will cover the rendering pipeline in detail and show you how you can add your own code as a part of that processing.

Entering Lift

The first step in Lift's request processing is intercepting the HTTP request. Originally, Lift used a `Servlet` instance to process incoming requests. This was changed to use a `Filter` instance, because this allows the container to handle any requests that Lift does not (in particular, static content). The filter acts as a thin wrapper on top of the existing `LiftServlet` (which still does all of the work), so don't be confused when you look at the Scala documentation and see both classes. The main thing to remember is that your `web.xml` file should specify the filter and not the servlet, as shown in Listing 3-1.

A full `web.xml` example is shown in Appendix G. In particular, the filter mapping (lines 13–16) specifies that the `Filter` is responsible for everything. When the filter receives the request, it checks a set of rules to see if it can handle it. If the request is one that Lift handles, the filter passes on the request to an internal `LiftServlet` instance for processing; otherwise, it chains the request and allows the container to handle it.

Listing 3-1. LiftFilter Setup in web.xml

```
<?xml version="1.0" encoding="ISO-8859-1"?>
... DTD here ...
<web-app>
  <filter>
    <filter-name>LiftFilter</filter-name>
    <display-name>Lift Filter</display-name>
    <description>The Filter that intercepts lift
                 calls</description>
    <filter-class>net.liftweb.http.LiftFilter
    </filter-class>
  </filter>
  <filter-mapping>
    <filter-name>LiftFilter</filter-name>
    <url-pattern>/*</url-pattern>
  </filter-mapping>
</web-app>
```

Making Standard import Assumptions for This Book

For the sake of saving space, the import statements in Listing 3-2 are assumed for all example code through the rest of this book.

Listing 3-2. Standard import Statements

```
import _root_.net.liftweb.http._
import S._
import _root_.net.liftweb.util._
import Helpers._
import _root_.scala.xml._
```

Bootstrapping in Lift

When Lift starts up, you'll want to set up a number of things before any requests are processed. These include setting up a SiteMap (see Chapter 5), rewriting URLs, performing custom dispatches, and searching classpaths, among other things. The Lift servlet looks for the bootstrap.liftweb.Boot class and executes the boot method in the class. You can also specify your own Boot instance by using the bootloader context parameter, as shown in Listing 3-3.

Listing 3-3. Overriding the Boot Loader Class

```
<web-app>
  <filter>
    ...
    <init-param>
      <param-name>bootloader</param-name>
      <param-value>foo.bar.baz.MyBoot</param-value>
    </init-param>
  </filter>
  ...
</web-app>
```

Your MyBoot class must subclass net.liftweb.http.Bootable and implement the boot method. The boot method will only be run once, so you can place initialization calls for other libraries here as well.

Using LiftRules

Most of your configuration in your Boot class will be done via the LiftRules object, which serves as a common location for almost everything configurable about Lift. Because LiftRules spans such a diverse range of functionality, we're not going to cover it directly; rather, we will mention it as we cover each of the aspects that it controls.

Resolving Classes

As part of our discussion of the Boot class, it's also important to cover a small detail of how Lift determines where to find classes for view and snippet rendering. The LiftRules.addToPackages method tells Lift what Scala packages to look in for a given class. Lift has implicit extensions to the paths you enter; in particular, if you tell Lift to use the com.pocketchangeapp package, Lift will look for view classes under com.pocketchangeapp.view and will look for snippet classes under com.pocketchangeapp.snippet. The addToPackages method should almost always be executed in your Boot class. A minimal Boot class would look like Listing 3-4.

Listing 3-4. Minimal Boot Class

```
class Boot {
  def boot = {
    ...
    LiftRules.addToPackages("com.pocketchangeapp")
    ...
  }
}
```

Rendering in Lift

Before we move on, we want to give a brief overview of the processes involved when Lift transforms a request into a response—the rendering pipeline. We're only going to touch on the major points here; a much more detailed tour of the pipeline is given in Chapter 7. The steps that we'll cover in this chapter follow:

1. Perform any URL rewriting. This is covered in the "Rewriting URLs" section.
2. Execute any matching custom dispatch functions. This is covered in the "Adding Custom Dispatch Functions" section.
3. Locate the template to use for the request. This is handled via three mechanisms:
   - Check the LiftRules.viewDispatch RulesSeq to see if any custom dispatch has been defined. We cover custom view dispatch in the "Adding Custom Dispatch Functions" section.
   - If there is no matching viewDispatch, locate a template that matches and use it. We'll cover templates, and how they're located, in the "Rendering with Templates" section.
   - If no templates match, attempt to locate a view based on matching class name and method dispatch. We'll cover views in the "Rendering with Views" section.

In our experience, views and templates will meet most of your needs, but as we'll demonstrate in later chapters, Lift has plenty of ways to customize the request handling.

The following sections cover each aspect of our rendering steps, but not in order. We'll start with templates, since those are by far the most common mechanism for rendering content in Lift. Next, we'll cover views, which are essentially programmatic templates. Third, we'll examing the various Lift tags for template and view content. After that, we'll take an in-depth look at snippets, which act as a bridge between your template (XML) content and your Scala code. Finally, we'll cover how you can provide highly customized processing of your requests using URL rewriting and custom dispatch functions.

Rendering with Templates

Templates form the backbone of Lift's flexibility and power. A template is an XML file that contains Lift-specific tags, (see "Getting to Know the Lift Tags" section) as well as whatever content you want returned to the user. Lift includes built-in tags for specific actions, and these are of the form `<lift:snippet_name/>`. Lift also allows you to create your own tags, which are called snippets (see the "Using Snippets" section). These user-defined tags are linked directly to Scala methods that can process the XML contents of the snippet tag or generate their own content from scratch. A simple template is shown in Listing 3-5.

Listing 3-5. A Sample Lift Template

```
<lift:surround with="default" at="content">
  <head><title>Hello!</title></head>
  <lift:Hello.world />
</lift:surround>
```

Notice the tags, which in this case are `<lift:surround>` and `<lift:snippet>`, are of the form `<lift:`*`name`*`>`. These are two examples of Lift-specific tags. We'll discuss all of the tags that users will use in the "Getting to Know the Lift Tags" section, but let's discuss the two contained here. We use the built-in `<lift:surround>` tag (see the "surround" section) to make Lift embed our current template inside the default template. We also use the `<lift:snippet>` tag (aliased to `Hello.world`) to execute a snippet that we defined. In this case, we execute the method `world` in the class `Hello` to generate some content.

During template processing, Lift tries to locate a file in the WAR tree that matches the request. Lift tries several suffixes (`html`, `xhtml`, and `htm`, as well as no suffix) and also tries to match based on the client's `Accept-Language` header. The pattern Lift uses follows:

```
<path to template>[_<language, optional>][.<suffix>]
```

Because Lift will implicitly search for suffixes, it's best to leave the suffix off of your links within the web application. If you have a link with an href attribute of "/test/template.xhtml", it will only match that file. However, assume you use "`/test/template`" for the `href` attribute and you have the following templates in your web application:

- /test/template.xhtml
- /test/template_es-ES.xhtml
- /test/template_ja.xhtml

In that case, Lift will use the appropriate template based on the user's requested language if a corresponding template is available. For more information regarding internationalization, please see Appendix D.

In addition to normal templates, your application can make use of hidden templates. These are templates that are located under the /templates-hidden directory of your web application. Technically, Lift hides files in any directory ending in "hidden", but templates-hidden is the de facto standard name. Like in the WEB-XML directory, the contents of the hidden directory cannot be directly requested by clients. They can, however, be used by other templates through mechanisms like the <lift:surround> and <lift:embed> tags (see the "embed" section). If Lift cannot locate an appropriate template based on the request path, it will return a 404 (Not Found) error to the user.

Once Lift has located the correct template, the next step is to process the contents. You need to understand that Lift processes XML tags from the outside in. That means that, in our example Listing 3-5, the <lift:surround /> tag gets processed first. In this case the surround loads the default template and embeds our content at the appropriate location. The next tag to be processed is the <lift:Hello.world/> snippet tag. This tag is essentially an alias for the <lift:snippet /> tag (specifically, <lift:snippet type="Hello:world">) and will locate the Hello class and execute the world method on it. If you omit the "method" part of the type and only specify the class (<lift:Hello> or <lift:snippet type="Hello">), Lift will attempt to call the render method of the class.

As you can see, templates are a nice way of setting up your layout. Once you apply the template, you can write a few methods to fill in the XML fragments that make up your web applications. They provide a simple way to generate a uniform look for your site, particularly if you composite your templates using the <lift:surround /> and <lift:embed /> tags. If you'd like more control or don't need a template for a certain section, you'll want to use a view, which we'll explain in the next section.

Rendering with Views

In our discussion of templates, you saw that, through a combination of an XML file, Lift tags, and Scala code, you can respond to requests made by a user. You can also generate those responses entirely in code using views.

Views are generally used as implicitly defined custom dispatch methods. We'll cover explicit custom dispatch in more depth in the "Adding Custom Dispatch Functions" section. A view is a normal Scala method of type () => scala.xml.NodeSeq. As we showed at the beginning of the

"Rendering in Lift" section, there are two ways that a view can be invoked: the first is by defining a partial function for `LiftRules.viewDispatch`. This allows you to dispatch to a view for any arbitrary request path, but is usually overkill for most use cases. The second way that a view can be invoked is like this: if the first element of the request path matches the class name of the view, the second element is used to lookup the view function depending on what trait the view class implements.

There are two traits that you can use when implementing a view class. One is to extend the `LiftView` trait, and the other is to extend the `InsecureLiftView` trait (both traits are under the `net.liftweb.http` package). As you may be able to tell from the names, we would prefer that you use the `LiftView` trait. `InsecureLiftView` determines method dispatch by turning a request path into a class and method name. For instance, if we have a path `/MyStuff/enumerate`, Lift will look for a class called `MyStuff` in the `view` subpackage (class resolution is covered in the "Resolving Classes" section). If Lift finds the class and it has a method called `enumerate`, Lift will execute the method and return its results to the user. The main issue with this dispatch is that Lift uses reflection to get the method, so it can access any method in the class, even ones that you don't intend to make public. A better way to do it is to use the `LiftView` trait, which defines a `dispatch` partial function. This `dispatch` function maps a string (the method name) to a function that will return a `NodeSeq`.

Listing 3-6 shows a custom `LiftView` class where the path `/ExpenseView/enumerate` will map to the `ExpenseView.doEnumerate` method. Anyone who attempts to go to `/ExpenseView/privateMethod` will get a 404 error, since that path is not defined in the dispatch function.

Listing 3-6. Dispatch in LiftView

```
class ExpenseView extends LiftView {
  override def dispatch = {
    case "enumerate" => doEnumerate _
  }
  def doEnumerate () : NodeSeq = {
    ...
    <lift:surround with="default" at="content">
     { expenseItems.toTable }
    </lift:surround>
  }
}
```

Another difference between custom dispatches and views is that the `NodeSeq` returned from the view method is processed for template tags including surrounds and includes, just like snippets; dispatch methods, on the other hand, expect a `LiftResponse`. That means that you can use the full power of the templating system from within your view, as shown in Listing 3-6's `doEnumerate` method.

Since you can choose to not include any of the predefined template XHTML, you can easily generate any XML-based content such as Atom or RSS feeds using a view.

Getting to Know the Lift Tags

In the earlier sections on templates and views, we briefly touched on some of Lift's built-in tags, namely `snippet` and `surround`. In this section, we'll go into more detail on those and the rest of the Lift tags.

snippet

Here's an example using the `snippet` tag:

```
<lift:snippet form="GET/POST" type="Class:method"
  multipart="true/false" />
<lift:Class.method form="..." multipart="..." />
<lift:Class form="..." multipart="..." />
```

The `snippet` tag is the workhorse of Lift. In our experience, most of the functionality of your web applications will be handled via snippets. They're so important that we're going to cover their mechanism separately in the "Using Snippets" section. In this section, however, we'll cover the specifics of the `snippet` tag.

The most important part of the tag is the class and method definition. There are three ways to specify this:

- *The* `type` *attribute*: The value should be *`ClassName`*`:`*`method`* for the particular snippet method you want to have handle the tag.
- *A tag suffix of* `Class.method`: This is the same as specifying the `type="`*`Class:method`*`"` attribute.
- *A tag suffix of just* `Class`: This will use the `render` method of the specified class to handle the tag.

Classes are resolved as specified in the "Resolving Classes" section. Listing 3-7 shows three equivalent `snippet` tags.

Listing 3-7. Snippet Tag Equivalence

```
<lift:snippet type="MyClass:render" />
<lift:MyClass.render />
<lift:MyClass />
```

The `form` and `multipart` attributes are optional. If `form` is included, an appropriate form tag will be emitted into the XHTML using the specified submission method. The `multipart` attribute is a

Boolean value that specifies whether a generated form tag should be set to use multipart form submission; this is most typically used for file uploads (see Chapter 4).

surround

The `<lift:surround />` tag follows:

```
<lift:surround with="template_name" at="binding">
...children...
</lift:surround>
```

It surrounds the child nodes with the named template. The child nodes are inserted into the named template at the binding point specified by the `at` parameter (we'll cover the `<lift:bind />` tag in a subsequent section) Typically templates that will be used to surround other templates are incomplete by themselves, so we usually store them in the `<app root>/templates-hidden` subdirectory so that they can't be accessed directly. Having said that, it's not required that the templates be in any specific location (except for `WEB-INF`, obviously). The most common usage of surround is so that you can use a master template for your site CSS, menu, and so on. An example use of `surround` is shown in Listing 3-8. We'll show you its master template counterpart in the section on the `<lift:bind />` tag. One more note is that the surrounding template name can either be a fully qualified path (e.g., `/templates-hidden/default`) or just be the base filename (`default`). In the latter case, Lift will search all subdirectories of the application root for the template.

Listing 3-8. Surrounding Your Page

```
<lift:surround with="default" at="content">
  <p>Welcome to PocketChange!</p>
</lift:surround>
```

Note that you can use multiple surrounding templates for different functionality, and surrounds can be nested. For example, you might want to have a separate template for your administrative pages that adds a menu to your default template. In that case, your `admin.html` could look like Listing 3-9. As you can see, we've named our bind in the `Admin` template to also be `"content"` so that we keep things consistent for the rest of our templates.

Listing 3-9. Adding an Admin Menu

```
<lift:surround with="default" at="content">
  <lift:Admin.menu />
  <lift:bind name="content" />
</lift:surround>
```

Caution You cannot have a hidden template with the same name as a subdirectory of your web application context directory. For example, if you had an `admin.html` template in `/templates-hidden`, you could not also have an `admin` directory.

bind

Here's the `<lift:bind />` tag's usage:

```
<lift:bind name="binding_name" />
```

The `<lift:bind />` tag is the counterpart to the `<lift:surround />` tag; it specifies where in the surrounding template the content will be placed. An example is shown in Listing 3-10.

Listing 3-10. Binding in Templates

```
<html>
  <body>
  <lift:bind name="content" />
  </body>
</html>
```

embed

This is how we use `<lift:embed />`:

```
<lift:embed what="template_name" />
```

The `<lift:embed />` tag allows you to embed a template within another template. This can be used to compose your pages from multiple smaller templates, and it allows you to access templates from JavaScript commands (see Chapter 8). Like the `<lift:surround />` tag, the template name can either be the base filename or a fully qualified path.

Note If you use the `<lift:embed />` tag to access templates from within a `JsCmd` (typically an Ajax call), any JavaScript code in the embedded template won't be executed. This includes, but is not limited, to Comet widgets.

comet

Here is the usage of the `<lift:comet />` tag:

```
<lift:comet type="ClassName" name="optional" />
```

The <lift:comet /> tag embeds a Comet actor into your page. The class of the Comet actor is specified by the type attribute. The name attribute tells Lift to create a unique instance of the Comet actor; for example, you could have one Comet actor for site updates and another for administrative messages. The contents of the tag are used by the comet actor to bind a response. Listing 3-11 shows an example of a comet binding that displays ledger entries as they're added. Comet is covered in more detail in Chapter 9.

Listing 3-11. A Ledger Entry in Comet

```
<div class="ledgerUpdates">
  <lift:comet type="LedgerMonitor">
    <ul><ledger:entries>
      <li><entry:time/> : <entry:user /> :
          <entry:amount /></li>
    </ledger:entries></ul>
  </lift:comet>
</div>
```

As we mentioned in the <lift:embed /> tag section, mixing Comet with AJAX responses can be a bit tricky because of the embedded JavaScript that Comet uses.

Merging HTML Headings

Another feature of Lift's template processing is the ability to merge the HTML <head /> tag from within a template. In Listing 3-5, notice that we've specified a <head /> tag inside the template. Without merging, this <head /> tag would show up in the default template where our template gets bound. Lift is smart about this, though: it takes the contents of the head tag and merges them into the outer template's <head /> tag. This means that you can use a <lift:surround /> tag to keep a uniform default template but still change the title of the page, add in scripts or special CSS, and so on. For example, if you have a table in a page that you'd like to style with jQuery's TableSorter, you would add a <head /> tag as shown in Listing 3-12.

Listing 3-12. Merging Headings

```
<lift:surround with="default" at="foo">
<head>
  <script src="/scripts/tablesorter.js"
          type="text/javascript" />
<head>
...
</lift:surround>
```

And just for this snippet, you'll import TableSorter.

Providing User Feedback

Feedback for the user—error messages for issues, status messages for update, and general notifications—is important for modern applications. Lift provides a unified model for such messages that can be used for static pages as well as for AJAX and Comet calls. We cover the messaging support in Appendix B.

Using Snippets

A snippet is a function that takes a single `scala.xml.NodeSeq` argument and is expected to return a `NodeSeq`.

Caution It's important to explicitly specify the return type of your snippet methods as `NodeSeq`. Failure to do so sometimes means that Lift can't locate the snippet method, in which case, the snippet may not execute!

The argument passed to the method is the XML contents of the `snippet` tag. Because Lift processes from the outside in, the contents are not processed before being passed to the snippet method unless you specify the `eager_eval` attribute (see the "Using Eager Evaluation" section). As an example, let's say we wanted a snippet that would output the current balance of our ledger. Listing 3-13 shows what our snippet method looks like.

Listing 3-13. A Simple Snippet

```
import scala.xml.{NodeSeq,Text}
class Ledger {
  def balance (content : NodeSeq) : NodeSeq =
    Text(currentLedger.formattedBalance)
}
```

We simply return an XML Text node with the formatted balance. Note that the XML that a snippet returns is further processed from the outside in, so if your snippet instead looked like Listing 3-14, the `lift:Util.time` snippet will be processed after our snippet method returns.

Listing 3-14. Returning Tags from a Snippet

```
import scala.xml.{NodeSeq,Text}
class Ledger {
  def balance (content : NodeSeq) : NodeSeq =
    <p>{currentLedger.formattedBalance}
      as of <lift:Util.time /></p>
}
```

This hierarchical processing of template tags makes Lift so flexible. If you already have some JavaServer Pages (JSP) experience, you'll be glad to know that Lift is designed to let you write your own tag libraries, except much more powerful and much simpler to use than the standard JSP/servlet model.

Binding Values in Snippets

So far, we've only shown our snippets generating complete output and ignoring the input to the method. Lift actually provides some very nice facilities for using the input `NodeSeq` within your snippet to help keep presentation and controller code separate. First, remember that the input `NodeSeq` consists of the child elements for the snippet tag in your template. For example, assume we have the snippet in Listing 3-15.

Listing 3-15. Snippet Tag Children

```
<lift:Ledger.balance>
  <ledger:balance /> as of <ledger:time />
</lift:Ledger.balance>
```

In this case, the `Ledger.balance` method receives the following as its input parameter:

```
<ledger:balance /> as of <ledger:time />
```

This is perfectly correct XML, although it may look a little strange if you haven't used prefixed elements in XML before. The key is that Lift allows you to selectively bind, or replace, these elements with data inside your snippet. The `net.liftweb.util.Helpers.bind` method takes three arguments:

- The prefix of the elements you wish to bind, `ledger` in our example
- The `NodeSeq` that contains the elements you wish to bind
- One or more `BindParam` elements that maps the element name to a replacement value.

Note Technically, the bind method is overloaded and can even fill in values for the <lift:bind /> tag, but this is advanced usage, and we're not going to cover that here.

While you can create your own BindParam instances by hand, we generally recommend importing Helpers._, which among other things contains an implicit conversion from Pair to BindParam. With this knowledge in hand, we can change our previous definition of the balance method to the one shown in Listing 3-16.

Listing 3-16. Binding the Ledger Balance

```
class Ledger {
  def balance (content : NodeSeq ) : NodeSeq =
    bind ("ledger", content,
          "balance" ->
            Text(currentLegdger.formattedBalance),
          "time" -> Text((new java.util.Date).toString))
}
```

As you can see in Listing 3-16, we actually gain a line of code over our previous effort, but the trade-off makes it far simpler for us to change the layout just by editing the template.

Choosing Between Stateless and Stateful Snippets

The life cycle of a snippet by default is stateless. That means that for each request, Lift creates a new instance of the snippet class to execute; any changes you make to instance variables will be discarded after the request is processed. If you want to keep some state around you have a couple of options:

- Store the state in a cookie (see the "Using Cookies" section). This can be useful if you have data that you want persisted across sessions. The downside is that you have to manage the cookie as well as deal with any security implications for the data in the cookie, since it's stored on the user's machine.
- Store the state in a SessionVar (see the "Storing Session and Request States" section). This is a little easier to manage than using cookies, but you still have to handle adding and removing the session data if you don't want it around for the duration of the session. Like a cookie, a SessionVar is also global, which means that it will be the same for all snippet instances
- Use a StatefulSnippet subclass. This is ideal for small, conversational state, such as a form that spans multiple pages or multiple variables that you want to be able to tweak individually within a page.

Using a StatefulSnippet is very similar to a normal snippet, with the addition of a few mechanisms. First, the StatefulSnippet trait defines a dispatch method of type PartialFunction[String, NodeSeq => NodeSeq]. This lets you define which methods handle which snippets. Because the def dispatch in the base DispatchSnippet can be overridden with a var, it also lets you redefine this behavior as a result of snippet processing.

Another key to using StatefulSnippets is that, when you render a form, a hidden field is added to that form that causes the same instance to be used on the page that is the target of the form submission. If you need to link to a different page but would like the same snippet instance to handle snippets on that page, use the StatefulSnippet.link method (instead of SHtml.link). Likewise, if you need to redirect to a different page, the StatefulSnippet trait defines a redirectTo method. In either of these cases, a function map is added to the link or redirect, respectively, that causes the instance to be reattached.

As an example of when you might use a stateful snippet, consider a graph that shows your spending for some time period and allows you to specify criteria for selecting the data to graph. Say you've changed the time span from the default 1 month to 3 months. Now, you'd like to limit the expense categories to show only food. More than likely, you'll want the application to respect the change in time span as well. This is a case where keeping a bit of state around will allow you to do this. Using a StatefulSnippet instance greatly simplifies writing the snippet, because you can keep all of your pertinent information around as instance variables instead of having to insert and extract them from every request, link, and so on.

Using Eager Evaluation

As we mentioned in the "Binding Values in Snippets" section, Lift processes the contents of a snippet tag after it processes the tag itself. If you want the contents of a snippet tag to be processed before the snippet, then you need to specify the eager_eval attribute on the tag:

```
<lift:Hello.world eager_eval="true">
...
</lift:Hello.world>
```

This is especially useful if you're using an embedded template (see the <lift:embed /> tag section); without the eager_eval attribute, your snippet just sees the <lift:embed /> tag, but with eager_eval set to true, you can put bindable common snippet content into a single embedded template instead of copying it between templates.

Rewriting URLs

Now that we've gone over templates, views, and snippets, as well as discussing how a request is dispatched to a Class.method, we can discuss how to intercept requests and handle them any way we want. URL rewriting is the mechanism that allows you to modify the incoming request so that it dispatches to a different URL. It can be used, among other things, to allow you to

- Use user-friendly, bookmarkable URLs like `http://www.example.com/budget/2008`.
- Use short URLs similar to `http://tinyurl.com` instead of long, hard-to-remember ones.
- Use portions of a URL to determine how a particular snippet or view responds. For example, you could make it so that a user's profile is displayed via a URL like `http://someplace.com/user/derek` instead of having the user name sent as part of a query string.

The mechanism is fairly simple to set up. We need to write a partial function from a `RewriteRequest` to a `RewriteResponse` to determine if and how we want to rewrite particular requests. Once we have the partial function, we modify the `LiftRules.rewrite` configuration to hook into Lift's processing chain. The simplest way to create a partial function is with Scala's pattern-matching expressions, which will allow us to selectively match on some or all of the request information. It is important to understand that the Lift session is not created at the point when the rewrite functions run; that means that you generally can't set or access properties in the `S` object. `RewriteRequest` is a case object that contains three items: the parsed path, the request type, and the original `HttpServletRequest` object.

The parsed path of the request in a `ParsePath` case class instance. The `ParsePath` class contains

- The parsed path as a `List[String]`
- The suffix of the request (e.g., `html` or `xml`)
- Whether the path is absolute, i.e. starts with a slash (/)
- Whether the path ends in a slash (/)

The latter three properties are useful only in specific circumstances, but the parsed path is what lets us work magic. The path of the request is defined as the parts of the URI between the context path and the query string. Table 3-1 shows examples of parsed paths for a Lift application under the `myapp` context path.

Table 3-1. ParsePath Examples

REQUESTED URL PATH	PARSED PATH
`/home?test_this=true`	`List("home")`
`/user/derek`	`List("user", "derek")`
`/view/item/14592`	`List("view","item","14592")`

The RequestType basically maps to the five HTTP methods: GET, POST, HEAD, PUT, and DELETE. These are represented by the corresponding case classes (GetRequest, PostRequest, and so on), with an UnknownRequest case class to cover anything strange.

The flexibility of Scala's matching system is what really makes this powerful. With matching on Lists in particular, we can match parts of the path and capture others. For instance, for our second example, we'd like to rewrite the /account/<account name> path so that it's handled by the /viewAcct template, as shown in Listing 3-17. In this case, we provide two rewrites so that someone could specify an optional tag for filtering the account view.

Listing 3-17. A Simple Rewrite Example

```
...standard Lift imports...
class Boot {
  def boot {
    LiftRules.rewrite.append {
      case RewriteRequest(
             ParsePath(List("account", acctName),
                       _,_,_),_,_) =>
             RewriteResponse(List("viewAcct"),
               Map("name" -> acctName))
      case RewriteRequest(
             ParsePath(List("account", acctName, tag),
                       _,_,_),_,_) =>
             RewriteResponse(List("viewAcct"),
               Map("name" -> acctName,
                   "tag" -> tag))
    }
  }
}
```

The RewriteResponse simply contains the new path to send. It can also take a Map that contains parameters that will be accessible via S.param in the snippet or view. As we stated before, the LiftSession (and therefore most of S) isn't available at this time, so the Map is the only way to pass information on to the rewritten location. Technically, a rewrite results in a 302 (Moved Temporarily) result code that forwards the client to a new request. Because of that, even if you could set data in LiftSession or S, the data would disappear when the redirect occurs.

We can combine the ParsePath matching with the RequestType and HttpServletRequest to be very specific with our matches. For example, say we wanted to support a RESTful interface through an existing template. REST (representational state transfer) is a technique for performing actions over HTTP, similar in concept to mechanisms like SOAP or XML-RPC, but using HTTP's native commands. A good explanation of REST is at http://www.ics.uci.edu/~fielding/pubs/dissertation/rest_arch_style.htm, and we'll cover a REST API in Chapter 13. If we wanted to support the REST DELETE verb, we could redirect the request as shown in Listing 3-18.

We'll go into more detail about how you can use this in the following sections. In particular, SiteMap (see Chapter 5) provides a mechanism for doing rewrites combined with menu entries.

Listing 3-18. A Complex Rewrite Example

```
val rewriter = {
  case RewriteRequest(
         ParsePath(List("txservice", txid),
                   _, _, _),
         DeleteRequest,
         httpreq)
         if isMgmtSubnet(httpreq.getRemoteHost()) =>
      RewriteResponse(List("deleteTx"),
                      Map("txid"->txid))
}
LiftRules.rewrite.append(rewriter)
```

Adding Custom Dispatch Functions

Once the rewriting phase is complete (whether we pass through or are redirected), the next phase is to determine if there should be a custom dispatch for the request. A custom dispatch allows you to handle a matching request directly by a method instead of going through the template lookup system. Because a custom dispatch bypasses templating, you're responsible for the full content of the response. A typical use case would be a web service returning XML or a service to return, say, a generated image or PDF. In that sense, the custom dispatch mechanism allows you to write your own pseudo-servlets without all the mess of implementing the interface and configuring them in web.xml.

Custom dispatch, like rewriting, is realized via a partial function. In this case, it's a function of type PartialFunction[Req,()=> Box[LiftResponse]] that will do the work. The Req is similar to the RewriteRequest case class; it provides the path as a List[String], the suffix of the request, and the RequestType. If you attach the dispatch function via LiftRules.dispatch, you'll have full access to the S object and LiftSession. If you use LiftRules.statelessDispatchTable instead, these aren't available. The result of the dispatch should be a function that returns a Box[LiftResponse]. If the function returns Empty, Lift returns a 404 (Not Found) response.

As a concrete example, let's look at returning a generated chart image from our application. There are several libraries for charting, but we'll take a look at JFreeChart (available at http://www.jfree.org/jfreechart/) in particular.

First, let's write the method in Listing 3-19, which will chart our account balance history.

Listing 3-19. Charting Method

```
... standard Lift imports ...
import org.jfree....jfreechart imports...
object Charting {
  def history (accountName : String) :
      Box[LiftResponse] = {
    // Query, set up chart, etc...
    balanceChart = ...
    val buffered =
      balanceChart.createBufferedImage(width,height)
    val chartImg = ChartUtilities.encodeAsPNG(buffered)
    Full(InMemoryResponse(chartImage,
                   List(Content-Type -> image/png),
                   Nil,
                   200))
  }
}
```

Once we've set up the chart, we use the `ChartUtilities` helper class from JFreeChart to encode the chart into a PNG byte array. We can then use Lift's `InMemoryResponse` to pass the encoded data back to the client with the appropriate `Content-Type` header. Now, we just need to hook the request into the dispatch table from the `Boot` class, as shown in Listing 3-20. In this case, we want state so that we can get the current user's chart, so we use `LiftRules.dispatch`.

Listing 3-20. Hooking dispatch into Boot

```
class Boot {
  def boot {
    ...
    LiftRules.dispatch.append {
      case Req(List("graph", acctName, "history"),
              _, _) =>
        () => Charting.history(acctName)
    }
    ...
  }
}
```

As you can see, we capture the `acctName` parameter from the path and pass it into our chart method. This means we can use a URL like `http://foo.com/graph/MyAcct/history` to obtain the image. Since the dispatch function has an associated Lift session, we can also use the `S.param` method to get query string parameters, in case we wanted to allow someone to send an optional width and height:

```
val width = S.param("width").map(_.toInt) openOr 400
val height = S.param("height").map(_.toInt) openOr 300
```

Or you can use a slightly different approach:

```
val width = S.param("width").dmap(400)(_.toInt)
val height = S.param("height").dmap(300)(_.toInt)
```

In the preceding code, `dmap` is identical with the `map` function except the first argument is the default value applicable in case that the `Box` is `Empty`. Realistically, we need to do some error handling in case a noninteger parameter is passed here, but we don't show that in this example. A number of other `ListResponse` subclasses are available to meet your needs, including responses for XHTML, XML, Atom, JavaScript, CSS, and JSON. We cover these in more detail in Chapter 7.

Using HTTP Redirects

HTTP redirects are an important part of many web applications. In Lift, you can send a redirect to the client in one of two ways:

- Call `S.redirectTo`. When you do this, Lift throws an exception and catches it later on, so any of your code following the redirect is skipped. If you're using a `StatefulSnippet` (see the "Choosing Between Stateless and Stateful Snippets" section), use `this.redirectTo` so that your snippet instance is used when the redirect is processed.
- When you need to return a `LiftResponse` you can just return a `RedirectResponse` or a `RedirectWithState` response.

The `RedirectWithState` allows you to specify a function to be executed when the redirected request is processed. You can also sent Lift notices (see the sections on `S.notice`, `S.warning`, and `S.error` in Appendix B) that would be rendered in the redirected page, as well as cookies to be set on the redirect. Similarly, there is an overloaded version of `S.redirectTo` that allows you to specify a function to be executed when the redirect is processed.

Using Cookies

Cookies are described briefly at http://java.sun.com/products/servlet/2.2/javadoc/javax/servlet/http/Cookie.html, are useful when you want data persisted across user sessions. A cookie is essentially a token of string data that is stored on the user's machine. While cookies can be quite useful, you should be aware of a few things:

- The user's browser may have cookies disabled, in which case you need to be prepared to work without cookies or tell the user to enable them for your site.
- Cookies are relatively insecure; there have been a number of browser bugs related to data in cookies being read by viruses or other sites. For more details on cookie security issues, see http://www.w3.org/Security/Faq/wwwsf2.html (see Question 10) and http://www.cookiecentral.com/faq/.

- Cookies are easy to fake, so you need to ensure that you validate any sensitive cookie data.

Using Cookies in Lift is very easy. In a stateful context, everything you need is covered by a few methods on the S object:

- `addCookie`: This method adds a cookie to be sent in the response.
- `deleteCookie`: This one deletes a cookie (technically, adds a cookie with a `maxage` of 0 so that the browser removes it). You can either delete a cookie by name or with a `Cookie` object.
- `findCookie`: This method looks for a cookie with a given name and returns a `Box[Cookie]`. Empty means that the cookie doesn't exist.
- `receivedCookies`: This method returns a `List[Cookie]` of all of the cookies sent in the request.
- `responseCookies`: And this method returns a `List[Cookie]` of the cookies that will be sent in the response.

If you need to work with cookies in a stateless context, many of the `ListResponse` classes (see Chapter 7) include a `List[Cookie]` in their constructor or apply arguments. Simply provide a list of the cookies you want set, and they'll be sent in the response. If you want to delete a cookie in a `LiftResponse`, you have to do it manually by adding a cookie with the same name and a `maxage` of 0.

Storing Session and Request States

Lift provides a very easy way to store per-session and per-request data through the `SessionVar` and `RequestVar` classes. In keeping with Lift's goals of combining simplicity with flexibility, these classes provide the following:

- Type-safe access to the data they hold
- A mechanism for providing a default value if the session or request doesn't exist yet
- A mechanism for cleaning up the data when the variable's life cycle ends

Additionally, Lift provides easy access to HTTP request parameters via the `S.param` method, which returns a `Box[String]`. Note that HTTP request parameters (sent either via `GET` or `POST`) differ from `RequestVars` in that query parameters are string values sent as part of the request. `RequestVars`, by contrast, use an internal per-request map so that they can hold any type and are initialized entirely in code. At this point, you might be wondering what `RequestVars` can be used for; a typical example would be sharing state among different snippets, since there is no connection between snippets other than at the template level.

SessionVars and RequestVars are intended to be implemented as singleton objects so that they're accessible from anywhere in your code. Listing 3-21 shows an example definition of a RequestVar used to hold the number of entries to show per page. We start by defining the object as extending the RequestVar. You must provide the type of the RequestVar so that Lift knows what to accept and return. The constructor argument is a by-name parameter that must evaluate to the var's type. In our case, we attempt to use the HTTP request variable pageSize, and if that isn't present or isn't an integer, we default to 25.

Listing 3-21. Defining a RequestVar

```
class Accounts {
  object pageSize extends
    RequestVar[Int](S.param("pageSize"
    ).map(_.toInt) openOr 25)
  ...
}
```

Accessing the value of the RequestVar is handled via the is method, as shown in Listing 3-22. You can also set the value using the apply method.

Listing 3-22. Accessing the RequestVar

```
query.setMaxResults(Accounts.pageSize.is)
// Change the value
Accounts.pageSize(50)
```

In addition to taking a parameter that defines a default value for setup, you can also handle cleaning up the value when the variable ends it life cycle. Listing 3-23 shows an example of opening a socket and closing it at the end of the request. You can see that we provide a function to the registerGlobalCleanupFunc method. The parameter for the cleanup function is a Box[LiftSession] for RequestVar and LiftSession for SessionVars, and these can be used to get access to the function without needing the S object. Also remember that you're responsible for handling any exceptions that might be thrown during either default initialization or cleanup.

Listing 3-23. Defining a Cleanup Function

```
object mySocket extends RequestVar[Socket](
  new Socket("localhost:23")
) {
  registerGlobalCleanupFunc {
    (ignore) => this.is.close
  }
}
```

The information we've covered here is equally applicable to SessionVars; the only difference between them is the scope of their respective life cycles.

Gathering a Few More Useful Objects

In addition to what we've covered so far, a few more objects are important to understand. We're going to cover these in detail in later sections, but we want to briefly mention each one here just so you're aware of them.

S object

The `S` object represents the state of the current request. As such, it is used to retrieve information about the request and modify information that is sent in the response. Among other things, it can be used for notices (see Appendix B), cookie management (see section "Using Cookies"), localization/internationalization (see Appendix D), and redirection (see section "Using HTTP Redirects").

SHtml

The `SHtml` object's main purpose is to define HTML-generation functions, particularly those having to do with form elements. We cover forms in detail in Chapter 4. In addition to normal form elements, `SHtml` defines functions for Ajax and JSON form elements (see Chapters 9 and 8, respectively).

Conclusion

In this chapter, we explored how Lift gets from a request to a response, using a combination of templates, views, custom dispatch and rewriting. We also covered how to manage state in your snippets and in a session. These techniques form the basis for almost all of your Lift applications. In the next few chapters, we'll be going into more detail on

- How forms are constructed and processed in Lift (using templates and snippets).
- How you can leverage the SiteMap framework in Lift to add navigation and security to your application.
- How to use Lift's Mapper framework to store and retrieve data from a database.

We've covered a lot of material, and we still have a lot more to go. Hopefully, this chapter provides a firm basis to start from when exploring the rest of this book.

Chapter 4: Forms in Lift

In this chapter, we're going to discuss the specifics of how you generate and process forms with Lift. Besides standard GET/POST form processing, Lift provides AJAX forms (see Chapter 9) as well as JSON form processing (see Chapter 8), but we're going to focus on standard HTML form tags here. We're going to assume that you have a general knowledge of basic HTML form tags as well as how CGI form processing works.

Practicing Form Fundamentals

Let's start with the basics of Lift form processing. A form in Lift is usually produced via a snippet that contains the additional `form` attribute. As we mentioned in Chapter 3, this attribute takes the values GET and POST and makes the snippet code embed the proper form tags around the snippet HTML. Code Listing 4-1 shows the expense-entry form in PocketChange (`src/main/webapp/index.html`) that we will be discussing throughout this section.

Code Listing 4-1. An Example Form Template

```
<div class="column span-24">
 <lift:AddEntry.addentry form="POST"
    multipart="true">
  <div class="column span-24">
  <h3>Entry Form</h3>
   <div id="entryform">
    <table>
     <tr>
      <td>Account</td>
      <td>Date</td>
      <td>Description</td>
      <td>Value</td>
      <td>Receipt Image</td>
      <td>Tags</td>
      <td></td>
     </tr>
     <tr>
      <td><e:account /></td>
      <td><e:dateOf /></td>
      <td><e:desc /></td>
      <td><e:value /></td>
      <td><e:receipt /></td>
      <td><e:tags /></td>
      <td><button>Add Expense</button></td>
     </tr>
    </table>
```

```
    </div>
   </div>
  </lift:AddEntry.addentry>
 </div>
```

The first thing to understand about Lift's form support is that you don't generally use the HTML tags for form elements directly. Rather, you use generator functions on the `net.liftweb.http.SHtml object`; the main reason for this is that it allows Lift to set up all of the internal plumbing so that you keep your code simple. Additionally, we use Lift's binding mechanism (see Chapter 3) to attach the form elements in the proper location. In our example in Listing 4-1, we have bindings for a description field, an amount, and a submit button.

Our next step is to define the form snippet itself. Corresponding to our expense-entry template is Listing 4-2 (taken from PocketChange, `/src/main/scala/com/pocketchange/snippet/AddEntry.scala`). This shows our add method with a few vars to hold the form data and a binding to the proper form elements. In this case, we're using a `StatefulSnippet`, so we specify the vars as class members instead of local to the add function.

Listing 4-2. An Example Form Snippet

```
... standard Lift imports...
import _root_.scala.xml.NodeSeq
class AddEntry extends StatefulSnippet {
...
var account : Long = _
var date = ""
var desc = ""
var value = ""
var tags = S.param("tag") openOr ""
var fileHolder : Box[FileParamHolder] = Empty

def add(in: NodeSeq): NodeSeq = User.currentUser match {
 case Full(user) if user.editable.size > 0 => {
  def doTagsAndSubmit(t: String) {
   tags = t
   if (tags.trim.length == 0)
    error("We're going to need at least one tag.")
   else {
    // Get the date correctly, comes in as yyyy/mm/dd
    val entryDate = Util.slashDate.parse(date)
    val amount = BigDecimal(value)

    val currentAccount = Account.find(account).open_!

    // We need to determine the last serial number
```

```
    // and balance for the date in question
    val (entrySerial,entryBalance) =
     Expense.getLastExpenseData(currentAccount,
                                entryDate)

    val e =
     Expense.create.account(account)
      .dateOf(entryDate).serialNumber(entrySerial + 1)
      .description(desc).amount(BigDecimal(value))
      .tags(tags).currentBalance(entryBalance + amount)

    // Add the receipt if it's the correct type
    val receiptOk = fileHolder match {
     case Full(FileParamHolder(_,mime,_,data))
           if (mime.startsWith("image/")) => {
       e.receipt(data).receiptMime(mime)
       true
      }
     case Full(_) => {
       S.error("Invalid receipt attachment")
       false
     }
     case _ => true
    }

    (e.validate,receiptOk) match {
     case (Nil,true) => {
      Expense.updateEntries(entrySerial + 1, amount)
      e.save
      val acct = Account.find(account).open_!
      val newBalance = acct.balance.is + e.amount.is
      acct.balance(newBalance).save
      notice("Entry added!")
      // remove the statefullness of this snippet
      unregisterThisSnippet()
     }
     case (x,_) => error(x)
    }
   }
  }
  bind("e", in,
   "account" -> SHtml.select(
    user.editable.map(acct => (acct.id.toString,
                               acct.name)),
    Empty,
    id => account = id.toLong),
   "dateOf" -> SHtml.text("", date = _) %
```

```
      ("id" -> "entrydate") %
      ("maxlength" -> "10") %
      ("size" -> "10"),
    "desc" -> SHtml.text("", desc = _),
    "value" -> SHtml.text("", value = _),
    "receipt" -> SHtml.fileUpload(fh => fileHolder = Full(fh)),
    "tags" -> SHtml.text(tags, doTagsAndSubmit))
  }
  case _ => Text("")
}
...
}
```

Another simpler example, just to illustrate a different approach, is given in Listing 4-3.

Listing 4-3. A Simpler Form Snippet

```
... standard Lift imports...
import _root_.scala.xml.NodeSeq
def add (xhtml : NodeSeq) : NodeSeq = {
  def processEntry () = {
   S.notice("Entry is " + desc + ", " + amount)
  }
  var desc = ""
  var amount = "0"
  bind("e", xhtml,
       "description" -> SHtml.text(desc, desc = _),
       "amount" -> SHtml.text(amount, amount = _),
       "submit" -> SHtml.submit("Process",
                                processEntry))
```

First, you may be wondering why we use vars defined inside the method. Normally, these vars would be locally scoped (stack-based) and would be discarded as soon as the method returns. The beauty of Scala and Lift is that the argument to each of the SHtml functions is actually a function itself. Because these functions (also known as closures) reference variables in the local scope, Scala transforms them to heap variables behind the scenes. Lift, in turn, adds the function callbacks for each form element into its session state, so that when the form is submitted, the appropriate closure is called, and the state is updated. This is also why we define the processEntry function inside of the add method: by doing so, the processEntry function has access to the closure variables. In our example, we're using the wildcard shorthand to define our functions; our description processing function could also be defined as follows:

```
newDesc => description = newDesc
```

One important thing to remember, however, is that each new invocation of the add method in our simple snippet (for each page view) will get its own unique instance of the variables that we've defined. That means that if you want to retain values between submission and re-

rendering of the form, you'll want to use RequestVars (see Chapter 3) or the StatefulSnippet approach we've used for PocketChange. The drawback to using StatefulSnippets is that they're more heavyweight and require more explicit management of state than RequestVars when you're moving from page to page.

As an example, you might use RequestVars if you want to do form validation and retain submitted values if validation fails, as shown in Listing 4-4. In this case, we set an error message (see Appendix B). Since we don't explicitly redirect, the same page is loaded (the default action for a page in Lift is the page itself), and the current request var value of description is used as the default value of the text box.

Listing 4-4. Using RequestVar with Forms

```
... standard Lift imports...
import _root_.scala.xml.NodeSeq
object description extends RequestVar("")
object amount extends RequestVar("0")
def add (xhtml : Group) : NodeSeq = {
  def processEntry () =
    if (amount.toDouble <= 0) {
      S.error("Invalid amount")
    } else {
      // ... process Add ...
      redirectTo(...)
    }
  bind("entry", xhtml,
       "description" ->
         SHtml.text(description.is, description(_)),
  ...
}
```

The next thing to look at is how the form elements are generated. We use the SHtml helper object to generate a form element of the appropriate type for each variable. In our case, we just want text fields for the description and amount, but SHtml provides a number of other form element types, which we'll be covering later in this section.

Generally, an element generator takes an argument for the initial value as well as a function to process the submitted value. Usually both of these arguments will use a variable, but there's nothing stopping you from doing something like this:

```
"description" ->
    SHtml.text("", println("Description = " + _))
```

Finally, our submit function executes the partially applied processEntryAdd function, which, through access to the variables we've defined, can do whatever it needs to do when the submit button is clicked.

Now that we've covered the basics of forms, we're going to go into a little more detail for each form element generator method on SHtml. All three variants of the a method as well as the ajax* methods are specific to Ajax forms, which are covered in detail in Chapter 9. The json* methods are covered in Chapter 8. We'll be covering the fileUpload method in detail in the "Uploading Files" section.

One final note before we dive in is that most generator methods have an overloaded definition with a trailing asterisk (e.g., hidden_*); these are generally equivalent to the version without an asterisk, except that where a function argument would be required, they take one of Lift's internal AFuncHolder instances. In other words, you probably shouldn't use these versions.

checkbox

The checkbox method generates a check box form element, taking an initial Boolean value as well as the function (Boolean)=>Any, which is called when the check box is submitted. If you've done a lot of HTML form processing, you might wonder how this actually occurs, since an unchecked check box is not actually submitted as part of a form. Lift works around this by adding a hidden form element for each check box with the same element name but with a false value, to ensure that the callback function is always called.

Because more than one XML node is returned by the generator, you can't just use the % metadata mechanism to set attributes on the check box element.

Note The % metadata mechanism is actually part of the Scala XML library. Specifically, scala.xml.Elem has a % method that allows the user to update the attributes on a given XML element. We suggest reading more about this in the Scala API documents, or in the Scala XML docbook at http://burak.emir.googlepages.com/scalaxbook.docbk.html.

Instead, Lift provides a checkbox_id generator; it takes an additional Box[String] parameter that will add an id attribute to the form element. Additionally, both overloads for checkbox take a final varargs sequence of Pair(String,String) so that you can provide any other attributes you'd like. For example, Listing 4-5 shows a check box with an id of "snazzy" and a special CSS class.

Listing 4-5. A checkbox Example

```
class ExampleSnippet {
  def checkboxSnippet (...) = {
    bind(..., "check" ->SHtml.checkbox_id(false, if (_) frobnicate(),
               Full("snazzy"), "class" -> "woohoo"))
  }
}
```

hidden

The `hidden` method generates a hidden form field. Unlike the HTML hidden field, the `hidden` tag is not intended to hold a plain value; rather, in Lift it takes a function argument of type `()=>Any` that is called when the form is submitted. As with most of the other generators, it also takes a final `varargs` sequence of `Pair[String,String]` attributes to be added to the XML node. Listing 4-6 shows an example of using a hidden field to log information.

Listing 4-6. A hidden Example

```
class ExampleSnippet {
  def hiddenInput (...) = {
  bind(..., "hidden" -> SHtml.hidden(() => println("Form was submitted")))
  }
}
```

link

The `link` method generates a standard HTML link to a page (an <a> tag, or anchor) but also ensures that a given function is executed when the link is clicked.

The first argument is the web context relative link path; the second argument is the `()=>Any` function that will be executed when the link is clicked, and the third argument is a `NodeSeq` that will make up the body of the link. You may optionally pass one or more `Pair[String,String]` attributes to be added to the link element.

Listing 4-7 shows using a link to load a ledger entry for editing from within a table. In this case, we're using a `RequestVar` to hold the entry to edit, so the `link` function is a closure that loads the current ledger entry. This combination of `link` and `RequestVars` is a common pattern for passing objects between pages.

Listing 4-7. A link Example

```
class ExampleSnippet {
  object currentExpenseEntry extends
    RequestVar[Box[Expense]](Empty)
  def list (xhtml : Group) : NodeSeq = {
    ...
    entries.flatMap({entry =>
     bind("entry",
      chooseTemplate("ledger", "entries", xhtml),
      ...
      "edit" ->
       SHtml.link("/editLedger",
        () => currentExpenseEntry(Full(entry)),
        Text("Edit")))
    })
  }
}
```

text and password

The text and password methods generate standard text and password HTML form input fields. While both take string default values and (String)=>Any functions to process the return, the password HTML input type masks typed characters and doesn't allow copying the value from the box on the client side. Listing 4-8 shows an example of using both text and password for a login page.

Listing 4-8. An Example Using text and password

```
class ExampleSnippet {
  def login(xhtml : Group) : NodeSeq = {
    var user = ""; var pass = "";
    def auth () = { ... }
    bind("login", xhtml,
         "user" ->
           SHtml.text(user, user = _, "maxlength" -> "40")
         "pass" -> SHtml.password(pass, pass = _)
         "submit" -> SHtml.submit("Login", auth))
  }
}
```

textarea

The textarea method generates a text area HTML form element. Generally, the functionality mirrors that of text, although you can add attributes to control text area width and height, as shown in Listing 4-9.

Listing 4-9. A textarea Example

```
class ExampleSnippet {
  def textAreaSnippet (...) = {
    var noteText = ""
    val notes = SHtml.textarea(noteText,
                  noteText = _,
                  "cols" -> "80",
                  "rows" -> "8")
  }
}
```

submit

The submit method generates the form submission element (typically a button). It requires two parameters: a string value to use as the button label and a ()=>Any function that can be used to process your form results.

One important thing to note about submit is that form elements are processed in the order that they appear in the HTML document. This means that you should put your submit element last in your forms, any items after the submit element won't have been set by the time the submit function is called.

Listing 4-8 shows how a submit function is used to process a login. When the submit button is clicked, the form will be submitted, the user and pass variables will be updated, and then the auth function will be called.

multiselect

Up to this point, we've covered some fairly simple form elements; multiselect is a bit more complex in that it doesn't just process single values. Instead, it allows you to select multiple elements out of an initial Seq and process each selected element individually.

Listing 4-10 shows using a multiselect to allow the user to select multiple tags for an expense entry. A Tag entity has an id synthetic key as well as a string name value. The first thing we do is map the collection of all categories into pairs of (value, display) strings. The value is what will be returned to our processing function, while the display string is what will be shown in the select box for the user.

Next, we turn the current entry's categories into a Seq of just value strings; we also set up a Set variable to hold the returned values.

Finally, we do our form binding. In this example, we use a helper function, loadTag (not defined here) that takes a String representing a tag's primary key and returns the Tag entity. We then use this helper method to update the Set that we created earlier. Note that the callback function will be executed for each selected item in the multiselect, which is why the callback takes a String, instead of Set[String], argument. This is also why we have to use our own set to manage the values. Depending on your use case, you may or may not need to store the returned values in a collection.

Listing 4-10. Using multiselect

```
... standard Lift imports...
import scala.collection.mutable.Set
class ExampleSnippet {
  def editExpense (xhtml : NodeSeq) : NodeSeq = {
  ...
  val possible =
    allTags.map(c => (c.id.toString, c.name))
  val current =
    currentEntry.tags.map(c => c.id.toString)
  val updated = Set.empty[Tag]
  def updateExpense () = { ... }
  def loadTag(id : String) : Tag = { ... }
  bind ("entry", xhtml, "tags" ->
  SHtml.multiselect(possible, current,
  updated += loadTag(_)),
  Shtml.submit("Save", updateExpense))
  }
}
```

radio

The radio method generates a set of radio buttons that take String values and return a single String (the selected button) on form submission. The values are used as labels for the radio buttons, so you may need to set up a Map to translate these back into useful values.

The radio method also takes a Box[String] that can be used to preselect one of the buttons. The value of the Box must match one of the option values, or if you pass Empty, no buttons will be selected.

Listing 4-11 shows an example of using radio to select a color. In this example, we use a Map from color names to the actual color values for the translation. To minimize errors, we use the keys property of the Map to generate the list of options.

Listing 4-11. Using radio for Colors

```
... standard Lift imports...
import java.awt.Color
class MySnippet {
  def chooseColor(xhtml : NodeSeq) : NodeSeq = {
    var myColor : Color = _
    val colorMap = Map("Red" -> Color.red,
                       "White" -> Color.white,
                       "Blue" -> Color.blue)
    val colors = SHtml.radio(colorMap.keys.toList,
                     Empty,
                     myColor = colorMap(_))
    ...
  }
}
```

select

The select method is very similar to the multiselect method except that only one item may be selected from the list of options. That also means that the default option is a Box[String] instead of a Seq[String]. As with multiselect, you pass a sequence of (value,display) pairs as the options for the select and process the return with a (String)=>Any function. Listing 4-12 shows an example of using a select to choose an account to view.

Listing 4-12. A select Example

```
class ExampleSnippet {
  def viewAccount (...) = {
    var selectedAccount : Account = _
    val accounts = User.accounts.map(
                     acc => (acc.id.toString, acc.name))
    val chooseAccount = SHtml.select(accounts,
                          Empty,
                          selectedAccount = loadAccount(_))
    ...
  }
}
```

An important thing to note is that Lift will verify that the value submitted in the form matches one of the options that was passed in. If you need to dynamically update the list, you'll need to use untrustedSelect (see the "untrustedSelect" section).

selectObj

One of the drawbacks with the select and multiselect generators is that they deal only in strings. If you want to select objects, you need to provide your own code for mapping from the strings. The selectObj generator method handles all of this for you. Instead of passing a sequence of value and display string pairs, you pass in a sequence of object and display string pairs.

Similarly, the default value is a Box[T], and the callback function is (T)=>Any, where T is the type of the object (selectObj is a generic function). Listing 4-13 shows a reworking of our radio example from Listing 4-11; in this listing, you can select colors directly.

Listing 4-13. Using selectObj for Colors

```
...standard Lift imports...
import java.awt.Color
class MySnippet {
  def chooseColor(xhtml : NodeSeq) : NodeSeq = {
    var myColor : Color = _
    val options = List(Color.red, Color.white,
                       Color.blue).map(
                    color => (color, color.toString))
    val colors = SHtml.selectObj(options, Empty,
                   myColor = _)
    ...
  }
}
```

untrustedSelect

The untrustedSelect generator is essentially the same as the select generator, except that the value returned in the form isn't validated against the original option sequence. This can be useful if you want to update the selection on the client side using JavaScript. The example in Listing 4-12 would essentially be the same for untrustedSelect, other than using the SHtml.untrustedSelect method as a form element generator.

Uploading Files

File uploads are a special case of form submission that allow the client to send a local file to the server, which is accomplished by using multipart forms. You can enable multipart form submission by setting the multipart attribute on your snippet tag to true. In Listing 4-1, we added the multipart attribute to the tag, and this is how we adding in a binding location for a receipt image to be uploaded:

```
<lift:AddEntry.addentry form="POST"
   multipart="true">
...
 <e:receipt />
...
</lift:AddEntry.addentry>
```

In Listing 4-2, we showed how to utilize a `net.liftweb.http.FileParamHolder` variable. The `FileParamHolder` case class contains information about the uploaded file, including the filename, MIME type, and the actual byte contents of the file. Unlike some other web frameworks, Lift doesn't store the file on the local system and then give you the filename; instead, Lift reads the whole file into memory and gives you the array of bytes to work with. Usually, reading the whole file into memory isn't an issue, since the web server itself will have meaningful limits on `POST` sizes. The relevant section of the snippet for file upload handling is shown in Listing 4-14.

Listing 4-14. Modifications to the addEntry Snippet for File Uploads

```
// In the class body
var fileHolder : Box[FileParamHolder] = Empty

// In the processing function
    // Add the receipt if it's the correct type
    val receiptOk = fileHolder match {
     case Full(FileParamHolder(_,mime,_,data))
           if (mime.startsWith("image/")) => {
       e.receipt(data).receiptMime(mime)
       true
      }
     case Full(_) => {
       S.error("Invalid receipt attachment")
       false
     }
     case _ => true
    }

...

// in the form bind:
   "receipt" -> fileUpload(fh => fileHolder = Full(fh)),
```

The `SHtml.fileUpload` callback function won't be called unless a file is sent with the upload, so we need to test (with the match) to see if we even receive a file. We use the match to further validate that the uploaded file has an image MIME type, and we return a Boolean flag from the match so that we can combine it with the `Mapper` validation to determine how to handle the form submission.

Conclusion

In this chapter, we've covered the foundations of form handling in Lift. The primary mechanism for form handling in Lift is using closures to tie form elements back to processing functions and variables that we define in our snippets. The callback approach that Lift takes to form processing simplifies the code path that a developer must work with when dealing with user input by handling many of the underlying request details. In addition to simple form elements like text input and check boxes, we've covered how to provide a set of options that the user can choose from using `radio`, `select`, `selecObj`, `multiselect`, or `untrustedSelect` elements. Finally, we covered the special topic of File upload handling in forms.

In later chapters, we'll expand on this functionality to include things like AJAX and Comet forms, as well as JSON and JavaScript.

Chapter 5: SiteMap

SiteMap is a very powerful part of Lift that does essentially what it says: provides a map (menu) for your site. Of course, if it only generated a set of links on your pages, we wouldn't have a whole chapter dedicated to it. In addition to basic menu generation functionality, SiteMap also provides

- Access control mechanisms that deal not only with whether a menu item is visible but whether the page it points to is accessible
- Grouping of menu items so that you can easily display portions of menus where you want them
- Nested menus so you can have hierarchies
- Request rewriting (similar to URL rewriting that we covered in Chapter 3)
- State-dependent computations for things like page titles, page-specific snippets, and so on

The beauty of SiteMap is that it's very easy to start out with the basic functionality and expand it as needed as you grow.

Defining SiteMap

Let's start with our basic menu for PocketChange. To keep things simple, we'll just define four menu items at the beginning:

- The home page, which will display either the user's entries or a welcome page, depending on whether the user is logged in or not
- Login and registration links if the user isn't logged in, and a logout link otherwise
- A view/edit profile link if the user is logged in
- A help page

We'll assume that we have the corresponding pages—index, login, logout, and profile—written and functional. We'll also assume that the help pages reside under the `help` subdirectory to keep things neat, and that the entry to help is `/help/index`.

Creating the Link Class

The `net.liftweb.sitemap.Loc.Link` class is a fundamental part of menu definitions. It contains two parameters, a `List[String]` of path components and a Boolean value that controls whether prefix matching is enabled. The path components represent the portion of the URI following your web context, split on the slash character (/). Listing 5-1 shows how you would use Link to represent the /utils/index page.

Listing 5-1. Link Path Components

```
val myUtilsIndex =
  new Link("utils" :: "index" :: Nil, false)
```

Prefix matching allows the path components you specify to match any longer paths as well. Following our first example, if you wanted to match anything under the utils directory (say, for access control), you would set the second parameter to true, as shown in Listing 5-2.

Listing 5-2. Link Prefix Matching

```
val allUtilPages = new Link("utils" :: Nil, true)
```

Using ExtLink

The ExtLink object can be used to create a Link instance using your own full link URL. As its name implies, it would usually be used for an external location. Listing 5-3 shows a menu item that points to a popular web site.

Listing 5-3. ExtLink

```
val goodReference =
  Menu(Loc("reference",
           ExtLink("http://www.liftweb.net/"),
           "LiftWeb"))
```

Creating Menu Entries

Menu entries are created using the net.liftweb.sitemap.Menu class, and its corresponding Menu object. A menu, in turn, holds a net.liftweb.sitemap.Loc trait instance, which is where most of the interesting things happen. A menu can also hold one or more child menus, which we'll cover in the "Using Nested Menus" section.

Note that the Loc object has several implicit methods that make defining Locs easier, so you generally want to import those methods into your scope. The simplest way is to import net.liftweb.sitemap.Loc._, but you can import specific methods by name if you prefer. A Loc can essentially be thought of as a link in the menu and contains four basic items:

- *The* Loc *name*: This must be unique across your SiteMap, because it can be used to look up specific menu items if you customize your menu display (see the "Using Menu" section).
- *The* Loc*'s link*: Usually, this will refer to a specific page, but Lift allows a single Loc to match based on prefix as well (see the "Creating the Link Class" section).

- *The menu item text*: This what will be displayed to the user. You can use a static string or you can generate it with a function (see the "Controlling the Menu Text" section).
- `LocParam` *parameters*: This optional set of parameters control behavior and appearance of the menu item. These parameters are covered in the "Customizing the Display," "Controlling Access with Menus," "Miscellaneous Menu Functionality", and "Rendering Specific Pages" sections.

For our example, we'll tackle the help page link first, since it's the simplest (it's a static link, essentially). The definition is shown in Listing 5-4. We're assuming that you've imported the `Loc` implicit methods to keep things simple; we'll cover instantiating the classes directly in later sections of this chapter.

Listing 5-4. Defining the Help Menu

```
val helpMenu = Menu(Loc("helpHome",
                        ("help" :: "" :: Nil) -> true,
                        "Help"))
```

For our example, we've named this menu item `helpHome`. The second parameter is a `Pair[List[String],Boolean]`, which converts directly to a `Link` class with the given parameters. In our case, by passing in `true`, we're saying that anything under the help directory will also match. If you just use a `List[String]`, the implicit conversion is to a `Link` with prefix matching `disabled`. The final parameter, `"Help"`, is the text for the menu link.

Note SiteMap won't allow access to any pages that don't match any menu entries, so by enabling prefix matching, we're allowing full access to all of the help files without having to specify a menu entry for each.

Using Nested Menus

The `Menu` class supports child menus simply by passing them in as final constructor parameters. For instance, if we wanted to have an About menu under Help, we could define the menu as shown in Listing 5-5.

Listing 5-5. Defining a Nested Menu

```
val aboutMenu =
  Menu(Loc("about", "help" :: "about" :: Nil, "About"))
val helpMenu =
  Menu(Loc(...as defined above...), aboutMenu)
```

When the menu is rendered, it will have a child menu for About. Child menus are only rendered by default when the current page matches their parent's Loc. That means that, for instance, the following links would show an About child menu item:

```
/help/index
/help/usage
```

But the following links would not show About:

```
/index
/site/example
```

We'll cover how you can customize the rendering of the menus in the "Using Menu section."

Setting the Global SiteMap

Once you have all of your menus items defined, you need to set them as your SiteMap. As usual, we do this in the Boot class by calling LiftRules.setSiteMap method, as shown in Listing 5-6. The setSiteMap method takes a SiteMap object that can be constructed using your menu items as arguments.

Listing 5-6. Setting the SiteMap

```
class Boot {
  def boot {
    ...
    LiftRules.setSiteMap(
      SiteMap(homeMenu, profileMenu, ...))
    ...
  }
}
```

When you're dealing with large menus, and in particular when your model objects create their own menus (such as MegaProtoUser, in Chapter 6), it can be more convenient to define a List[Menu] and set that, as shown in Listing 5-7.

Listing 5-7. Using List[Menu] for SiteMap

```
val menus = Menu(Loc("HomePage", "", "Home"),...) ::
            ...
            Menu(...) :: Nil
LiftRules.setSiteMap(SiteMap(menus : _*))
```

The key to using List for your menus is to explicitly define the type of the parameter as _* so that it's treated as a set of varargs instead of a single argument of type List[Menu].

Customizing the Display

There are many cases where you may want to change the way that particular menu items are displayed. For instance, if you're using a Menu item for access control in a subdirectory, you may not want the menu item displayed at all. We'll discuss how you can control whether or not your Menu item appears, what text will be displayed for the menu item, as well as how you can perform custom on-demand rendering of the entire menu, individual menu items, or groups of menu items in this section.

Using the Hidden LocParam

The Hidden LocParam does exactly what it says: it hides the menu item from the menu display and leaves the rest of the menu functionality fully operable. A typical example, shown in Listing 5-8, is to restrict access to a particular subdirectory based on some condition. We'll cover the If LocParam in the "Using If Clauses" section.

Listing 5-8. Hidden Menus

```
val receiptImages =
  Menu(Loc("receipts",
           ("receipts" :: Nil) -> true,
           "Receipts",
           Hidden, If(...)))
```

Note that, in this example, we've used the implicit conversion from Pair[String,Boolean] to Link to make this Menu apply to everything under the receipts directory.

Controlling the Menu Text

The LinkText class defines the function that will return the text to display for a given menu item. As we've shown, this can easily be set using the implicit conversion for String=>LinkText from Loc. As an added bonus, the implicit conversion actually takes a by-name String for the parameter; that means you can just as easily pass in a function to generate the link text as a static string. For example, with our profile link we may want to make the link say "<username>'s profile". Listing 5-9 shows how we can do it by defining a helper method.

Listing 5-9. Customizing Link Text

```
def profileText = User.shortName + "'s profile"
val profileMenu = Menu(Loc("Profile",
                           "profile" :: Nil,
                           profileText, ...))
```

Of course, if you want, you can construct the `LinkText` instance directly; just pass in a constructor function that returns a `NodeSeq`. The function that you use with `LinkText` takes a type-safe input parameter, which we'll discuss in more detail in the "Using Type-Safe Parameters" section.

Using Menu

So far, we've covered the Scala side of things. The other half of the magic is the special `<lift:Menu />` tag. This tag handles the rendering of your menus into XHTML. The `<lift:Menu />` tag uses a built-in snippet (technically, `net.liftweb.builtin.snippet.Menu`) to handle several rendering functions. The most common use method is the `<lift:Menu.builder />` snippet tag. This snippet renders your entire menu structure as an unordered list (`<ul>` in XHTML). Listing 5-10 shows an example of using the `Menu` tag to build the default menu (yes, it's that easy).

Listing 5-10. Rendering with <lift:Menu.builder />

```
<div class="menu">
  <lift:Menu.builder />
</div>
```

Of course, Lift offers more customization on this snippet than just emitting some XHTML. By specifying some prefixed attributes on the tag itself, you can add attributes directly to the menu elements. The following prefixes are valid for attributes:

- `ul`: Adds the specified attribute to the `<ul>` (unordered list) element that makes up the menu
- `li`: Adds the specified attribute to each `<li>` (list item) element for the menu
- `li_item`: Adds the specified attribute to the current page's menu item
- `li_path`: Adds the specified attribute to the current page's breadcrumb path, which is the set of menu items leading to this one

The suffix of the attributes can be anything and will be passed directly through. For instance, we can add CSS classes to our menu and elements fairly easily, as shown in Listing 5-11. Notice that we also add a little JavaScript to our current menu item.

Listing 5-11. Using Attributes with <lift:Menu.builder />

```
<lift:Menu.builder
  li:class="menuitem"

  li_item:onclick=
    "javascript:alert('Already selected!');" />
```

In addition to rendering the menu itself, the Menu class has a few other tricks. The <lift:Menu.title /> snippet tag can be used to render the title of the page, which, by default, is the name parameter of the Loc for the menu (the first parameter). If you write your own Loc implementation (see the "Writing Your Own Loc" section), or you use the Title LocParam (see the "Setting the Title" section), you can override the title to be whatever you'd like. Listing 5-12 shows how you use <lift:Menu.title /> to render the title as Home Page.

Code Listing 5-12. Rendering the Menu Title

```
// In Boot:
val MyMenu =
  Menu(Loc("Home Page", "index" :: Nil, "Home"))
// In template (or wherever)
<title><lift:Menu.title /></title>
```

The next snippet in the Menu class is item. The <lift:Menu.item /> snippet tag allows you to render a particular menu item by specifying the name attribute (matching the first parameter to Loc). Like Menu.builder, it allows you to specify additional prefixed attributes for the link to be passed to the emitted item. Because it applies these attributes to the link itself, the only valid prefix is a. Additionally, if you specify child elements for the snippet tag, it will be used instead of the default link text. Listing 5-13 shows an example using our Home Page item defined in Listing 5-12; we've added some replacement text as well as specifying a CSS class for the link. The final snippet that the Menu class provides is the Menu.group method. We're going to cover the use of Menu.group in detail the "Categorizing with LocGroup" section.

Listing 5-13. Rendering an Individual Menu Item

```
<lift:Menu.item name="Home Page"
  a:class="homeLink">
  <b>Go Home</b>
</lift:Menu.item>
```

Controlling Access with Menus

So far, we've covered how to control the display side of menus, so now we can cover some of the plumbing behind the scenes. One important function of menus is that they control access to the pages in your app; if no Menus match a given request then the user gets a 404 (Not Found) error. Other than this binary control of "matches=>display" and "doesn't match=>don't display", SiteMap provides for arbitrary access checks through the If and Unless LocParams.

Using If Clauses

The If LocParam takes a test function, ()=>Boolean, as well as failure message function, ()=> LiftResponse, as its arguments. When the Loc that uses the If clause matches a given path, the test function is executed, and if `true` is returned, the page is displayed normally. If the function evaluates to `false`, the failure message function is executed and its result is sent to the user.

There's an implicit conversion in `Loc` from a `String` to a response, which converts to a `RedirectWithState` instance (see Chapter 7). The redirect is to the location specified by `LiftRules.siteMapFailRedirectLocation`, which is the root (/) of your web application context by default. If you want, you can change this in `LiftRules` for a global setting, or you can provide your own `LiftResponse`. Listing 5-14 shows a revision of the profile menu that we defined in Listing 5-9, extended to check whether the user is logged in. If the user isn't logged in, we redirect to the login page.

Listing 5-14. Using the If LocParam

```
val loggedIn = If(() => User.loggedIn_?,
                  () => RedirectResponse("/login"))
val profileMenu = Menu(Loc("Profile",
                           "profile" :: Nil,
                           profileText, loggedIn))
```

Using the Unless LocParam

The `Unless LocParam` is essentially the mirror of `If`. The exact same rules apply, except that the page is displayed only if the test function returns `false`. The reason that there are two classes to represent this behavior is that it's generally clearer when a predicate is read as "working" when it returns `true`.

Page-specific rendering with SiteMap is an advanced technique that provides a lot of flexibility for making pages render differently depending on state.

Working with the Template LocParam

Generally, the template that will be used for a page is derived from the path of the request. The `Template LocParam`, however, allows you to completely override this mechanism and provide any template you want by passing in the function `()=> NodeSeq`. Going back to our example menus (see the "Defining SiteMap" section), we'd like the welcome page to show either the expense entries for a logged-in user or a plain welcome screen otherwise. One approach to this is shown in Listing 5-15. In this example, we create a `Template` instance that generates the appropriate template and then bind it into the home page menu `Loc`.

Listing 5-15. Programmatic Template Selection

```
val homepageTempl = Template({ () =>
  <lift:surround with="default" at="content">
  { if (User.loggedIn_?) {
      <lift:Entries.list />
    } else {
      <lift:embed what="welcome" />
    }
  }
  </lift:surround> })
val homeMenu = Menu(Loc("Home Page",
                        "" :: Nil,
                        "Home Page", homepageTempl))
```

Working with the Snippet and LocSnippets Parameters

Besides overriding the template for a page render (admittedly, a rather coarse approach), SiteMap has two mechanisms for overriding or defining the behavior of specific snippets: the `Snippet` and `LocSnippets` `LocParams`.

The first, `Snippet`, allows you to define the dispatch for a single snippet based on the name of the snippet. Listing 5-16 shows how we could use `Snippet` to achieve the same result for the home page rendering as we just did with the `Template` parameter. All we need to do is use the `<lift:homepage />` snippet on our main page, and the snippet mapping will dispatch based on the state.

Listing 5-16. Using the Snippet LocParam

```
val homeSnippet = Snippet("homepage",
  if (User.loggedIn_?) {
    Entries.list _
  } else {
    Utils.welcome _
  })
val homeMenu = Menu(Loc("Home Page",
                        "" :: Nil,
                        "Home Page", homeSnippet))
```

The `LocSnippets` trait extends the concept of `Snippet` to providing a full dispatch partial function. This allows you to define multiple snippet mappings associated with a particular `Loc`. To simplify things, Lift provides a `DispatchLocSnippets` trait that has default implementations for the `apply` and `isDefinedAt` methods; that means you only need to provide a `dispatch` method implementation for it to work. Listing 5-17 shows an example of using `DispatchLocSnippets` for a variety of snippets.

Listing 5-17. Using LocSnippets

```
val entrySnippets = new DispatchLocSnippets {
  def dispatch = {
    case "entries" => Entries.list _
    case "add" => Entries.newEntry _
  }
}
```

Setting the Title

As we mentioned in the "Using Menu" section, the Title LocParam can be used to provide a state-dependent title for a page. The Title LocParam simply takes a function (T)=> NodeSeq, where T is a type-safe parameter (we'll cover this in the "Using Type-Safe Parameters" section). Generally, you can ignore it if you want, as we do in Listing 5-18.

Listing 5-18. Customizing the Title

```
val userTitle = Title({
  if (User.loggedIn_?) {
    Text(User.name + "'s Ledger")
  } else {
    Text("Welcome to PocketChange")
  }})
val homeMenu = Menu(Loc("Home Page",
                        "" :: Nil,
                        "Home Page", homepageTempl,
                        userTitle))
```

Testing a Request

Test is intended to be used to ensure that a given request has the proper parameters before servicing. With Test, you provide a function, (Req)=> Boolean, that is passed the full Req object. Note that the test is performed when the SiteMap tries to locate the correct menu, as opposed to If and Unless, which are tested after the proper Loc has been identified. Returning false means that this Loc doesn't match the request, so SiteMap will continue to search through your Menus to find an appropriate Loc. As an example, we could check to make sure that a given request comes from Opera with the code in Listing 5-19.

Listing 5-19. Testing the Request

```
val onlyOpera = Test(req => req.isOpera)
val operaMenu =
  Menu(Loc("Opera", "opera" :: Nil, "Only Opera",
           onlyOpera))
```

Categorizing with LocGroup

The LocGroup parameter allows you to categorize your menu items. Using the Menu.group snippet (mentioned in the "Using Menu" section) allows you to render the menu items for a specific group in place. First, to set up the groups for a Menu item, simply add a LocGroup parameter with one or more String arguments for the group names, as shown in Listing 5-20.

Listing 5-20. Categorizing Your Menu

```
val siteMenu = Menu(Loc(...,LocGroup("admin", "site")))
```

In your templates, you would then specify the binding of the menu as shown in Listing 5-21. As you can see, we've also added a prefixed attribute to control the CSS class of the links (a is the only valid prefix), and we've added some body XHTML for display. In particular, the <menu:bind /> tag controls where the menu items are rendered. If you don't provide body elements, or if you provide body elements without the <menu:bind /> element, your body XHTML will be ignored and the menu will be rendered directly.

Listing 5-21. Binding a Menu Group

```
<div class="site">
  <lift:Menu.group group="site"
    a:class="siteLink">

    <li><menu:bind /></li>
  </lift:Menu.group>
</div>
```

Writing Your Own Loc

As we've shown, a lot of functionality is available for your Menu items. If you need more control, the Loc trait offers functionality, like rewriting, that doesn't have a direct correspondence in a LocParam element. The basic definition of a Loc implementation covers a lot of the same things. The following vals and defs are abstract, so you must provide them:

- def name: This is the name that can be used to retrieve the menu via Menu.item.
- def link: This represents the actual link. You can use the implicit conversions from List[String] or Pair[List[String],Boolean], or you can create the Link object yourself.
- def text: This represents the text that will be displayed to the user. You can use the implicit conversion from String, or you can provide your own LinkText instance.
- def params: This one must return a List[LocParam] that is used to control behavior, as we've shown in the previous sections.

- `def defaultParams`: This is used for type-safe rewriting, which we'll cover in the "Using Type-Safe Parameters" section.

These essentially mirror the parameters that are required when you use `Loc.apply` to generate a `Loc`. We'll be writing our own `Loc` class in the next section to demonstrate the functionality. Because this will directly overlap things that already exist in PocketChange, we'll start a new `custom-loc` branch in git so that you can see real, working code. If you already have the code for PocketChange checked out (see Chapter 2), you can work with the new branch with the following command:

```
git checkout -track -b custom-loc origin/custom
```

You can then switch back and forth between the branches with the commands:

```
git checkout master
git checkout custom-loc
```

Knowing the Corresponding Functions

Table 5-1 lists the `LocParams` and their corresponding methods in `Loc`, with notes concerning any differences in definition or usage. If you prefer to use the `LocParams` instead, just define the `params` method on `Loc` to return a list of the `LocParams` you want.

Table 5-1. LocParam Methods in Loc

LocParam	Loc Method	Notes
`Hidden`	Not applicable	To make your `Loc` hidden, add a `Hidden` `LocParam` to your `params` method return value
`If` and `Unless`	`testAccess`	You need to return an `Either` to indicate success (`Left[Boolean]`) or failure (`Right[Box[LiftResponse]]`).
`Template`	`calcTemplate`	Return a `Box[NodeSeq]`.
`Snippet` and `LocSnippets`	`snippets`	`snippets` is a `PartialFunction[String, Box[ParamType]), NodeSeq => NodeSeq]`, which lets you use the type-safe parameter to control behavior.
`Title`	`title`	You can override `def title` or `def title(in: ParamType)` depending on whether you want to use type-safe parameters.

Table 5-1 (Continued)

Test	doesMatch_?	It's your responsibility to make sure that the path of the request matches your Loc, since this method is what SiteMap uses to find the proper Loc for a request.
LocGroup	inGroup_?	There's nothing special here.

Using Type-Safe Parameters

One of the nice features of Loc is that it allows you to rewrite requests in a type-safe manner. What this means is that we can define a rewrite function on our Loc instance that returns not only a standard RewriteResponse but also a parameter that we can define to pass information back to our menu to control behavior. The reason that this is type safe is that we define our Loc on the type of the parameter itself. For instance, let's expand the functionality of our application so that we have a page called acct that shows just the expense entries for a given account. We would like this page to normally be visible to only the owner of the account, but owners should be able to share this information publicly if they choose.

The first thing we need to do is modify our Account Mapper entity for public viewing. We already have an is_public MappedBoolean on the Account class to control whether outside users can view, but using the current Long ID of the entity as the lookup key would make browsing public account pages much too simple, so we'll add a MappedUniqueId field. Listing 5-22 shows this change.

Listing 5-22. Modifying the Account Class

```
class Account extends LongKeyedMapper[Account] with IdPK {
  ...

  // 32 chars should be plenty to keep things unique
  object stringId extends MappedUniqueId(this,32)
}
```

We also need to update our account management page to allow the user to control whether or not the account is public. This isn't shown here, but if you're interested, you can find the changes in src/main/scala/com/pocketchangeapp/snippet/Accounts.scala, in the manage method.

The next step is to define our type-safe parameter class as shown in Listing 5-23.

Listing 5-23. Defining AccountInfo

```
abstract class AccountInfo
case object NoSuchAccount extends ExpenseInfo
case object NotPublic extends ExpenseInfo
case class FullAccountInfo(account :
Account,
                          entries : List[Expense])  extends AccountInfo
```

We define a few case classes and objects to indicate various conditions. The `FullAccountInfo` holds the account itself as well as a list of entries so that we can match on whether the account has entries (shown in Listing 5-26). Now that we have our parameter type, we can start to define our `Loc`, as shown in Listing 5-24.

Listing 5-24. Defining a Type-Safe Loc

```
//... default imports ...

// Additional imports:
import _root_.scala.xml.{NodeSeq,Text}

import _root_.net.liftweb.sitemap._
import Loc._

import _root_.net.liftweb.mapper._

import _root_.com.pocketchangeapp.model._
import _root_.com.pocketchangeapp.snippet.Accounts

object AccountLoc extends Loc[AccountInfo] {
  // Default to "not here"
  def defaultParams = Full(NoSuchAccount)

  // We don't want to show this page in the menu
  def params = List(Hidden)

  // Required to provide the next three (abstract),
  // but not used
  val link = new Link[AccountInfo](List("account"))
  val name = "Account"
  val text = LinkText[AccountInfo](i => Text("Account"))
...
}
```

Since our Account instance now has a unique string ID, we would like to use URL rewriting so that we can access a ledger via /acct/<unique_id>. This allows someone to send a link to other people to view and bookmark. Our rewrite function, shown in Listing 5-25, handles two things: locating the correct ledger and checking to make sure that the account (if found) is public. With custom Locs, we return a Pair for our rewrite function instead of just the RewriteResponse. The second element of the pair is the type-safe parameter (AccountInfo in our case) that will be passed to other methods within our custom Loc. This allows you to centralize the decisions on how your page will behave under different conditions.

Listing 5-25. The Rewrite Function

```
class AccountLoc extends Loc[AccountInfo] {
...
override def rewrite = Full({
 case RewriteRequest(
  ParsePath(List("acct", aid), _, _, _), _, _) => {
   Account.findAll(By(Account.stringId, aid)) match {
    case List(account) if account.is_public.is == true => {
     (RewriteResponse("account" :: Nil),
      FullAccountInfo(account, account.entries))
    }
    case List(account) => {
     (RewriteResponse("account" :: Nil),
      NotPublic)
    }
    case _ => {
     (RewriteResponse("account" :: Nil),
      NoSuchAccount)
    }
   }
 }
})
}
```

Now that we've defined the transformation from a URL to a parameter, we need to define the behaviors based on that parameter. The account page will show a list of expense entries only if the account is located and is public. For this example, we'll use a single template, and we'll change the snippet behavior based on our parameter, as shown in Listing 5-26.

Listing 5-26. Defining Snippet Behavior

```
object AccountLoc extends Loc[AccountInfo] {
...
override def snippets = {
  case ("entries", Full(NoSuchAccount)) =>
    {ignore : NodeSeq =>
     Text("Could not locate the requested account")}
  case ("entries", Full(NotPublic)) =>
    {ignore : NodeSeq =>
     Text("This account is not publicly viewable")}
  case ("entries",
        Full(FullAccountInfo(account, List()))) =>
    {ignore : NodeSeq =>
     Text("No entries for " + account.name.is)}
  case ("entries",
        Full(FullAccountInfo(account, entries))) =>
    Accounts.show(entries) _
}
}
```

In this example, we simply return some text if the `Account` can't be located, isn't public, or doesn't have any `Expense` entries. Remember that this function needs to return a snippet function, which is why we need to include the `ignore` parameter as part of our closures. If our `Account` does have entries, we return a real snippet method defined in our `Accounts` object. In our template, we simply use an `entries` snippet tag, as shown in Listing 5-27.

Listing 5-27. Our Public Template

```
<lift:surround with="default" at="content">
<lift:entries  eager_eval="true">
  <h1><lift:Menu.title /></h1>
  <lift:embed what="entry_table" />
</lift:entries>
</lift:surround>
```

We're using our embedded table template for the body of the table along with the `eager_eval` attribute so that we can use the same markup for all occurrences of our expense table display.

We can also define the title of the page based on the parameter, as shown in Listing 5-28.

Listing 5-28. Defining the Title

```
object AccountLoc extends Loc[AccountInfo] {
...
override def title(param : AccountInfo) =
  param match {
    case FullAccountInfo(acct, _) =>
      Text("Expense summary for " + acct.name.is)
    case _ => Text("No account")
  }
}
```

This title can be accessed using the built-in `<lift:Menu.title />` tag.

Conclusion

As we've shown in this chapter, SiteMap offers a wide range of functionality to let you control site navigation and access. You can customize the display of your individual items using the `LinkText` `LocParam` as well as the functionality of the built-in `Menu` builder and item snippets. You can use the `If` and `Unless` `LocParams` to control access to your pages programmatically, and you can use the `Test` `LocParam` to check the request before it's even dispatched. Page-specific rendering can be customized with the `Template`, `Snippet`, and `LocSnippet` `LocParams`, and you can group menu items together via the `LocGroup` `LocParam`. Finally, you can consolidate all of these functions by writing your own `Loc` trait subclass directly and gain the additional benefit of type-safe URL rewriting. Together these offer a rich set of tools for building your web site exactly how you want.

Chapter 6: Mapper and Record

In our experience, most web applications want to store user data somewhere. Once you start working with user data, though, you start dealing with issues like coding input forms, and validation and persistence to handle the data. That's where the Mapper and Record frameworks come in. These frameworks provide scaffolding for all of your data-manipulation needs. Mapper is the original Lift persistence framework and is closely tied to JDBC for its storage. Record is a new refactorization of Mapper that is backing-store agnostic at its core, so it doesn't matter whether you want to save your data to JDBC, Java Persistence API (JPA), or even something like XML. With Record, selecting the proper driver will be as simple as hooking the proper traits into your class.

Note The Record framework is relatively new to Lift. The plan is to move to Record as the primary ORM framework for Lift sometime after version 1.0. Because Record is still under active design and development, and because of its current moving-target status, this chapter will focus mostly on Mapper. We will, however, provide a few comparative examples of Record functionality to give you a general feel for the flavor of the changes. In any case, Mapper will not go away even when Record comes out, so you can feel secure that any code using Mapper will be viable for quite a while.

Introducing Mapper and MetaMapper

Let's start by discussing the relationship between the `Mapper` and `MetaMapper` traits (and the corresponding `Record` and `MetaRecord` traits). `Mapper` provides the per-instance functionality for your class, while `MetaMapper` handles the global operations for your class and provides a common location to define per-class static specializations of things like field order, form generation, and HTML representation. In fact, many of the `Mapper` methods actually delegate to methods on `MetaMapper`.

In addition to `Mapper` and `MetaMapper`, the framework includes a third trait, `MappedField`, which provides the per-field functionality for your class. The `MappedField` trait lets you define the individual validators as well as things transform filters and filed name. In `Record`, the trait is simply called `Field`, and it adds some functionality like tab order and default error messages for form input handling. Typically, you don't use `MappedField` directly and instead use one of its subclasses that corresponds to a particular type. We'll be covering these subclasses later in this chapter.

Adding Mapper to Your Project

Since Mapper is a separate module, you need to add a dependency to your pom.xml file to access it (see Appendix A for an overview of Maven), as shown in Listing 6-1.

Listing 6-1: The Mapper pom.xml Dependency

```
<dependency>
  <groupId>net.liftweb</groupId>
  <artifactId>lift-mapper</artifactId>
  <!-- or 1.1-SNAPSHOT, etc, to match your project -->
  <version>1.0</version>
</dependency>
```

You'll also need the following import in any Scala code that uses Mapper:

```
import _root_.net.liftweb.mapper._
```

Setting Up the Database Connection

The first step you need to get out of the way is defining the database connection. We do this by defining an object called DBVendor (you can call it whatever you want). This object extends the net.liftweb.mapper.ConnectionManager trait and must implement two methods: newConnection and releaseConnection. You can make this as sophisticated as you want, with pooling, caching, and so on, but for now, Listing 6-2 shows a basic implementation to set up a PostgreSQL driver.

Listing 6-2. Setting Up the Database

```
... standard Lift and Mapper imports...
import _root_.java.sql._ // for Connection, DriverManager

object DBVendor extends ConnectionManager {
  Class.forName("org.postgresql.Driver")
  def newConnection(name : ConnectionIdentifier) = {
    try {
      Full(DriverManager.getConnection(
           "jdbc:postgresql://localhost/mydatabase",
           "root", "secret"))
    } catch {
      case e : Exception => e.printStackTrace; Empty
    }
  }
  def releaseConnection (conn : Connection) {
    conn.close
  }
}
```

```
class Boot {
  def boot {
    ...
    DB.defineConnectionManager(DefaultConnectionIdentifier, DBVendor)
  }
}
```

You should note a few items about Listing 6-2:

- The `name` parameter for `newConnection` can be used if you need to have connections to multiple distinct databases. One specialized case of this is when you're doing database sharding (horizontal scaling). Multiple database usage is covered in more depth in the "Using Multiple Databases" section.
- The `newConnection` method needs to return a `Box[java.sql.Connection]`. Returning `Empty` indicates failure.
- The `releaseConnection` method exists so that you have complete control over the life cycle of the connection. For instance, if you were doing connection pooling yourself, you would return the connection to the available pool rather than closing it.
- The `DB.defineConnectionManager` call is what binds our manager into Mapper. Without it, your manager will never get called.

Constructing a Mapper-Enabled Class

Now that we've covered some basic background, we can start constructing some Mapper classes to get more familiar with the framework. We'll start with a simple example of a class for an expense entry from our PocketChange application with the following fields:

- Date
- Description, with a maximum length of 100 characters
- Amount, a decimal value with a precision of 16 digits and 2 decimal places
- A reference to the account that owns the entry

Given these requirements, we can declare our class as shown in Listing 6-3.

Listing 6-3. The Expense Class in Mapper

```
import _root_.net.liftweb.mapper._
import _root_.java.math.MathContext
class Expense extends LongKeyedMapper[Expense]
  with IdPK
{
  def getSingleton = Expense
  object dateOf extends MappedDateTime(this)
  object description extends MappedString(this,100)
  object amount extends MappedDecimal(this,
    MathContext.DECIMAL64, 2)
  object account extends MappedLongForeignKey(this, Account)


}
```

For comparison, the Record version is shown in Listing 6-4. This example shows some functionality that hasn't been ported over to Record from Mapper; among other things, the `IdPK` trait and foreign key fields (many to one mappings) are missing. The other minor differences are that the `getSingleton` method has been renamed to `meta`, and the `Field` traits use different names under the Record framework (i.e., `DateTimeField` versus `MappedDateTime`).

Listing 6-4. The Expense Class in Record

```
import _root_.java.math.MathContext
import _root_.net.liftweb.record._
class Expense extends KeyedRecord[Expense,Long] {
  def meta = Expense
  def primaryKey = id
  object id extends LongField(this)
    with KeyField[Long,]
  object dateOf extends DateTimeField(this)
  object description extends StringField(this, 100)
  object amount extends DecimalField(this,
    MathContext.DECIMAL64, 2)
  object account extends LongField(this)
}
```

As you can see in Listing 6-3, we've set `Expense` to extend the `LongKeyedMapper` and `IdPK` traits, and we've added the fields required by our class. We would like to provide a primary key for our entity. While a synthetic primary key is not strictly necessary, having one often helps with create, read, update, and delete (CRUD) operations. The `LongKeyedMapper` trait accomplishes two objectives: it tells Lift that we want a primary key defined and that the key should be a `long`. Basically, `LongKeyedMapper` acts as a shortcut for using the `KeyedMapper[Long,Expense]` trait. When you use the `KeyedMapper` trait, you need to provide an implementation for the primaryKeyField def, which must match the type of the KeyedMapper trait and be a subtype of IndexedField.

The IdPK trait handles the implementation, but note that IdPK currently only supports Long keys. Mapper supports both indexed Longs and Strings, so if you want Strings, you'll need to explicitly use KeyedMapper[String,. . .] and provide the field definition yourself. It's possible to use some other type for your primary key, but you'll need to roll your own (see the "Defining Custom Field Types" section). Technically, Int indexes are supported as well, but there is no corresponding trait for an Int foreign key. Without a built-in trait, if you use an Int for the primary key, you may not be able to do a relationship with other objects (see the "Creating Object Relationships" section) unless you write your own.

Record is a little more flexible in primary key selection, since it uses, in effect, a marker trait (KeyField) to indicate that a particular field is a key field. One thing to note is that in the Mapper framework, the table name for your entity defaults to the name of the class (Expense in our case). If you want to change this, you just need to override the dbTableName def in your MetaMapper object.

Looking at these examples, you've probably noticed that the fields are defined as objects rather than instance members (vars). The basic reason for this is that the MetaMapper needs access to fields for its validation and form functionality; it is more difficult to cleanly define these properties in the MetaMapper if it had to access member vars on each instance since a MetaMapper instance is itself an object. Also note that MappedDecimal is a custom field type, which we'll cover in section see the "Defining Custom Field Types" section.

Note We are working on adding MappedDecimal to the core library soon after Lift 1.0. To tie all of this together, we need to define a matching LongKeyedMetaMapper object as the singleton for our entity, as shown in Listing 6-5. The Meta object (whether MetaMapper or MetaRecord) is where you define most behavior that is common across all of your instances. In our examples, we've decided to give the Meta object and instance class the same name; we don't feel that this is unclear, since the two together are what really define the ORM behavior for a type.

Listing 6-5. Expense Meta Object

```
object Expense extends Expense with
    LongKeyedMetaMapper[Expense] {
  override def fieldOrder = List(dateOf, amount, description)
  ...
}
```

In our case, we're simply defining the order that fields will be displayed in XHTML and forms by overriding the fieldOrder method. The default behavior is an empty list, which means no fields are involved in display or form generation; generally, you will want to override fieldOrder, since this is not very useful. If you don't want a particular field to show up in forms or XHTML output, simply omit it from the fieldOrder list.

Since fields aren't actually instance members, operations on them are slightly different that a regular var. The biggest difference is that we set fields using the apply method. In addition, field access can be chained so that you can set multiple field values in one statement, as shown in Listing 6-6.

Listing 6-6. Setting Field Values

```
myEntry.dateOf(new Date).description("A sample entry")
myEntry.amount(BigDecimal("127.20"))
```

The underlying value of a given field can be retrieved with the is method (value method in Record) as shown in Listing 6-7.

Listing 6-7. Accessing Field Values in Record

```
// mapper
val tenthOfAmount = myEntry.amount.is / 10
val formatted = String.format("%s : %s",
                              myEntry.description.is,
                              myEntry.amount.is.toString)
// record
if (myEntry.description.value == "Doughnuts") {
  println("Diet ruined!")
}
```

Creating Object Relationships

Often, it's appropriate to have relationships between different entities. The archetypal example of this is the parent-child relationship. In SQL, a relationship can be defined with a foreign key that associates one table to another based on the primary key of the associated table. As we showed in Listing 6-3, there is a corresponding MappedForeignKey trait, with concrete implementations for Long and String foreign keys. Once we have this defined, accessing the object via the relationship is achieved by using the obj method on the foreign key field. With the foreign key functionality, you can easily do one-to-many and many-to-one relationships (depending on where you put the foreign key). One-to-many relationships can be achieved using helper methods on the "one" side that delegate to queries. We'll cover queries in a moment, but Listing 6-8 shows examples of two sides of the same relationship.

Listing 6-8. Accessing Foreign Objects

```
class Expense extends LongKeyedMapper[Expense]
  with IdPK
{
 ...
  object account extends
  MappedLongForeignKey(this, Account)
  def accountName =
    Text("My account is " +
      account.obj.map(acctacct.openOr("unknown"))
}

class Account ... {
  ...
  def entries =
  Expense.findAll(
    By(Expense.account, this.id))
}
```

If you want to do many-to-many mappings, you'll need to provide your own join class with foreign keys to both of your mapped entities. An example would be if we wanted to have tags (categories) for our expense entries and wanted to be able to have a given entry have multiple tags (e.g., you purchase a book for your mother's birthday, so it has the tags `Gift`, `Mom`, and `Books`). First we define the `Tag` entity, as shown in Listing 6-9.

Listing 6-9. Tag Entity

```
class Tag extends LongKeyedMapper[Tag] with IdPK {
  def getSingleton = Tag
  object name extends MappedString(this,100)
}
object Tag extends Tag with LongKeyedMetaMapper[Tag] {
  override def fieldOrder = List(name)
}
```

Next, we define our join entity, as shown in Listing 6-10. It's a `LongKeyedMapper` just like the rest of the entities, but it only contains foreign key fields to the other entities.

Listing 6-10. Join Entity

```
class ExpenseTag extends LongKeyedMapper[ExpenseTag] with IdPK
{
  def getSingleton = ExpenseTag
  object tag extends MappedLongForeignKey(this,Tag)
  object expense extends
    MappedLongForeignKey(this,Expense)
}
object ExpenseTag extends ExpenseTag with
  LongKeyedMetaMapper[ExpenseTag]
{
  def join (tag : Tag, ex : Expense) =
    this.create.tag(tag).expense(ex).save
  ...
}
```

To use the join entity, you'll need to create a new instance and set the appropriate foreign keys to point to the associated instances. As you can see, we've defined a convenience method on our `Expense` metaobject to do just that. To make the many-to-many accessible as a field on our entities, we can use the `HasManyThrough` trait, as shown in Listing 6-11.

Listing 6-11. HasManyThrough for Many-to-Many Relationships

```
class Expense ... {
  private object extends HasManyThrough(this, Tag,
    ExpenseTag, ExpenseTag.tag, ExpenseTag.expense)
}
```

A similar field could be set up on the `Tag` entity to point to entries. It's important to note a few items:

- The only way to add new entries is to directly construct the instances and save them (either directly or via a helper method). You can't make any modifications via the `HasManyThrough` trait.
- Although the field is defined as a query, the field is actually lazy and only runs once. That means if you query it and then add some new instances, they won't show up in the field contents.

If you want a way to retrieve the joined results such that the method call pulls fresh from the database each time, you can instead define a helper join method as shown in the "Making Joins a Little Friendlier" section.

Indexing

Adding indexes to a database often helps improve performance. Mapper makes it easy to do most simple indexing simply by overriding the dbIndexed_? def on the field. Listing 6-12 shows how we would add an index to our Expense.account field.

Listing 6-12. Indexing a Field

```
class Expense ... {
  object account extends ... {
    override def dbIndexed_? = true
  }
}
```

Mapper provides for more complex indexing via the MetaMapper.dbIndexes def combined with the Index, IndexField, and BoundedIndexField case classes. Listing 6-13 shows some examples of how we might create more complex indices.

Listing 6-13. More Complex Indices

```
object Expense extends ... {
  // equivalent to the previous listing
  override def dbIndexes =
    Index(IndexField(account)) :: Nil
  /* equivalent to
    "create index ... on transaction_t
 (account, description(10))"
   */
  override def dbIndexes =
    Index(IndexField(account),
    BoundedIndexField(description,10)) :: Nil
}
```

Mapping Schemas

The Mapper framework makes it easy not only to define domain objects but also to create the database schema to go along with those objects. The Schemifier.schemify method does all of the work for you; you simply pass in the MetaMapper objects that you want the schema created for, and it does the rest.

Listing 6-14 shows how we could use Schemifier to set up the database for our example objects. The first argument controls whether an actual write will be performed on the database; if false, Schemifier will log all of the Data Definition Language (DDL) statements that it would like to apply, but no changes will be made to the database. The second argument is a logging function (logging is covered in Appendix E). The remaining arguments are the MetaMapper objects that you would like to have schemified. You need to be careful and remember to include all objects; otherwise, tables won't be created.

Listing 6-14. Using Schemifier

```
Schemifier.schemify(true, Log.infoF _, User,
 Expense , Account, Tag, ExpenseTag)
```

As we mentioned in the "Constructing a Mapper-Enabled Class" section, you can override the default table name for a given `Mapper` class via the `dbTableName def` in the corresponding `MetaMapper`. The default table name is the name of the `Mapper` class, except when the class name is also an SQL reserved word; in this case, `_t` is appended to the table name. You can also override individual column names on a per-field basis by overriding the `dbColumnName def` in the field itself. Like tables, the default column name for a field will be the same as the field name as long as it's not an SQL reserved word, in which case `_c` is appended to the column name. Listing 6-15 shows how we could make our `ExpenseTag.expense` field map to `expense_id`.

Listing 6-15. Setting a Custom Column Name

```
class ExpenseTag ... {
  object expense extends ... {
    override def dbColumnName = "expense_id"
  }
}
```

Performing Persistence Operations on an Entity

Now that we've defined our entity, we probably want to use it in the real world to load and store data. There are several operations on `MetaMapper` that we can use:

- `create`: This operation creates a new instance of the entity.
- `save`: This one saves an instance to the database.
- `delete_!`: This deletes the given entity instance.
- `count`: This operation returns the number of instances of the given entity. An optional query criteria list can be used to narrow the entities being counted.
- `countByInsecureSql`: This operation is similar to count, except a raw SQL string can be used to perform the count. The count value is expected to be in the first column and row of the returned result set. An example follows:

```
Expense.countByInsecureSql("select count(amount) from " +
     "Expense where amount > 20", ...)
```

There are also quite a few methods available for retrieving instances from the database. Each of these methods comes in two varieties: one that uses the default database connection and one that allows you to specify the connection to use (see the "Using Multiple Databases" section). The latter typically has DB appended to the method name. The query methods on MetaMapper follow:

- findAll: This method retrieves a list of instances from the database. It is overloaded to take an optional set of query criteria parameters; these will be covered in detail in their own section, "Querying for Entities."
- findAllByInsecureSqlfindAllByPreparedStatement: This method is similar to findAllByInsecureSQL except that prepared statements are used, which usually means that the driver will handle properly escaping arguments in the query string.
- findAllFields: This allows you to do a normal query returning only certain fields from your Mapper instance. For example, if you only wanted the amount from the table, you would use this method. Note that any fields that aren't specified in the query will return their default values; generally, this method is only useful for read access to data, because saving any retrieved instances could overwrite real data.
- findMap*: These methods provide the same functionality as the findAll methods but take an extra function argument that transforms an entity into a Box[T], where T is an arbitrary type. An example would be getting a list of descriptions of our Expenses:

  ```
  Expense.findMap(entry =>
    Full(entry.description.is))
  ```

The KeyedMetaMapper trait adds the find method, which can be used to locate a single entity based on its primary key. In general, these operations will be supported in both Record and Mapper. However, because Record isn't coupled tightly to a JDBC backend, some of the find methods may not be supported directly, and additional persistence methods may not be available in Mapper. For this reason, this chapter will deal specifically with Mapper's persistence operations.

Creating a Mapper Instance

Once we have a MetaMapper object defined, we can use it to create objects using the create method. You generally don't want to use the new operator because the framework has to set up internal data, such as field owner, for the instance. This is important to remember, since nothing will prevent you from creating an instance manually; you may just get errors when you go to use the instance. The join method in Listing 6-10 shows an example of create usage.

Saving a Mapper Instance

Saving an instance is as easy as calling the save method on the instance you want to save. Optionally, you can call the save method on the Meta object, passing in the instance you want to save. The save method uses the saved_? and clean_? flags to determine whether an insert or update is required to persist the current state to the database, and returns a Boolean to indicate whether the save was successful or not. The join method in Listing 6-10 shows an example of saving.

Deleting a Mapper Instance

There are several ways to delete instances. The simplest way is to call the delete_! method on the instance you'd like to remove. An alternative is to call the delete_! method on the Meta object, passing in the instance to delete. In either case, the delete_! method returns a Boolean indicating whether the delete was successful or not. Listing 6-16 shows an example of deleting instances.

Listing 6-16. A Deletion Example

```
if (! myExpense.delete_!)
  S.error("Couldn't delete the expense!")
//or
if (! (Expense delete_! myExpense)) S.error(...)
```

Another approach to deleting entities is to use the bulkDelete_!! method on MetaMapper.This method allows you to specify query parameters to control which entities are deleted. We will cover query parameters in the "Querying for Entities" section (an example is in Listing 6-23).

Querying for Entities

A variety of MetaMapper methods are available for querying for instances of a given entity. The simplest method is findAll called with no parameters. This bare findAll returns a List of all of the instances of a given entity loaded from the database. Note that each findAll. . . method has a corresponding method that takes a database connection for sharding or multiple database usage (see sharding in the "Using Multiple Databases" section). Of course, for all but the smallest datasets, pulling the entire model to get one entity from the database is inefficient and slow. Instead, the MetaMapper provides flag objects to control the query.

The ability to use fine-grained queries to select data is a fundamental feature of relational databases, and Mapper provides first-class support for constructing queries in a manner that is not only easy to use but type safe. This means that you can catch query errors at compile time instead of runtime. The basis for this functionality is the QueryParam trait, which has several concrete implementations that are used to construct the actual query. `QueryParam` can be broken up into two main groups:

- **Comparison**: These are typically items that would go in the where clause of an SQL query. They are used to refine the set of instances that will be returned
- **Control**: These are items that control things like sort order and pagination of the results.

Although Mapper provides a large amount of the functionality in SQL, some features are not covered directly. In some cases, we can define helper methods to make querying easier, particularly for joins (see the "Making Joins a Little Friendlier" section).

Using Comparison QueryParams

The simplest `QueryParam` to refine your query is the `By` object and its related objects. `By` is used for a direct value comparison of a given field, essentially an `=` operator in SQL. For instance, Listing 6-17 shows how we can get all of the expenses for a given account.

Listing 6-17. Retrieving All Expenses by Account ID

```
val myEntries = Expense.findAll(
  By(Expense.account, myAccount.id))
```

Note that we specify the account primary key (`id`) on the right side, because the type of `Expense.account` is really `Long`, not `Account`, so we need to match the type. Besides `By`, the other basic clauses follow:

- `NotBy`: Select entities whose queried field is not equal to the given value.
- `By_>`: Select entities whose queried field is greater than the given value.
- `By_<`: Select entities whose queried field is less than the given value.
- `ByList`: Select entities whose queried field is equal to one of the values in the given `List`. This corresponds to the `field IN (x,y,z)` syntax in SQL.
- `NullRef`: Select entities whose queried field is `null`.
- `NotNullRef`: Select entities whose queried field is not null.
- `Like`: Select entities whose queried field is like the given string. As in SQL, the percent sign is used as a wildcard.

In addition to the basic clauses, there are some slightly more complex ways to control the query. The first of these is `ByRef`, which selects entities whose queried field is equal to the value of another query field on the same entity. A contrived example would be if we define a tree structure in our table and root nodes are marked as having themselves as parents, as shown in Listing 6-18.

Listing 6-18. An Example of ByRef

```
// select all root nodes from the forest
TreeNode.findAll(ByRef(TreeNode.parent,TreeNode.id))
```

The related NotByRef tests for inequality between two query fields.

Getting slightly more complex, we come to the In QueryParameter, which is used just like an IN clause with a subselect in an SQL statement. As an example, let's say we wanted to get all of the entries that belong to tags that start with the letter "c". Listing 6-19 shows the full breakdown.

Listing 6-19. Using In

```
val cExpenses = ExpenseTag.findAll(In(ExpenseTag.tag,
     Tag.id,
     Like(Tag.name, "c%"))
  ).map(_.expense.obj.open_!)
.removeDuplicates
```

We use the ByRef parameters to do the join between the many-to-many entities on the query. Related to In is InRaw, which allows you to specify your own SQL subquery for the IN portion of the where clause. An example in Listing 6-20 shows how we could use this to find the Tags for Expense entries made in the last 30 days.

Listing 6-20. Using InRaw

```
def recentTags = {
  val joins = ExpenseTag.findAll(
    InRaw(ExpenseTag.expense,
      "select id from Expense where dateOf" +
      " > (CURRENT_DATE - interval '30 days')",
      IHaveValidatedThisSQL("dchenbecker",
                            "2008-12-03"))
  joins.map(_.tag.obj.open_!)
.removeDuplicates
}
```

In Listing 6-20, things are starting to get a little hairy. InRaw allows us to specify only the subquery for the IN clause, so we have to do some postprocessing to get unique results. If you want to do this in the query itself, you'll have to use the findAllByInsecureSql or findAllByPreparedStatement methods, which are covered in the "Performing SQL-Based Queries" section. The final parameter for InRaw acts as a code audit mechanism that says that someone has checked the SQL to make sure it's safe to use. Since the query fragment is added to the master query as-is, no escaping or other filtering is performed on the string. That means that if you take user input you need to be very careful about it, or you run the risk of an SQL injection attack on your site.

The next QueryParam we'll cover is BySql, which lets you use a complete SQL fragment that gets put into the where clause. An example of this would be if we want to find all expense entries within the last 30 days, as shown in Listing 6-21. The IHaveValidatedThisSQL case class is required as a code audit mechanism to make sure someone has verified that the SQL used is safe.

Listing 6-21. Using BySql

```
val recentEntries = Expense.findAll(
  BySql("dateOf >" +
        " (CURRENT_DATE - interval '30 days')",
        IHaveValidatedThisSQL("dchenbecker",
                              "2008-12-03"))
```

The trade-off with using BySql is that you need to be careful with what you allow into the query string. BySql supports parameterized queries, as shown in Listing 6-22, so use those if you need to have dynamic queries. In addition to making the queries safe from SQL injection, parameterized queries can improve performance due to query plan caching and reduced parsing overhead.

Listing 6-22. Parameterized BySql

```
val amountRange = Expense.findAll(
  BySql("amount between ? and ?",
        lowVal,
        highVal))
```

As we mentioned in the "Deleting a Mapper Instance" section, we can use the query parameters to effect bulk deletes in addition to querying for instances. This is accomplished using the QueryParam classes to constrain what you want to delete. Obviously, these control parameters, but the compiler won't complain. Listing 6-23 shows an example of deleting all entries older than a certain date.

Listing 6-23. Bulk Deletion

```
def deleteBefore (date : Date) =
  Expense.bulkDelete_!!(
    By_<(Expense.dateOf, date))
```

Using Control QueryParams

Now that we've covered the selection and comparison QueryParams, we can start to look at the control parameters. The first one that we'll look at is OrderBy. This operates exactly like the order-by clause in SQL and allows you to order on a given field in either ascending or descending order. Listing 6-24 shows an example of ordering our Expense entries by amount.

The Ascending and Descending case objects are in the net.liftweb.mapper package. The OrderBySql case class operates similarly except you provide your own SQL fragment for the ordering, as shown in the example. Again, you need to validate this SQL.

Listing 6-24. OrderBy Clause

```
val cheapestFirst =
  Expense.findAll(
    OrderBy(Expense.amount,Ascending))
// or
val cheapestFirst =
  Expense.findAll(
    OrderBySql("amount asc"),
    IHaveValidatedThisSQL("dchenbecker", "2008-12-03"))
```

Pagination of results is another feature that people often want to use, and Mapper provides a simple means for controlling it with two more QueryParam classes: StartAt and MaxRows, as shown in Listing 6-25. In this example, we take the offset from a parameter passed to our snippet, with a default of zero.

Listing 6-25. Pagination of Results

```
val offset = S.param("offset").map(_.toLong) openOr 0
Expense.findAll(StartAt(offset), MaxRows(20))
```

An important feature of the methods that take QueryParams is that they can take multiple parameters, as shown in Listing 6-25. A more complex example is shown in Listing 6-26. In this example we're doing a query using a Like clause, ordering on the date of the entries, and paginating the results—all in one statement!

Listing 6-26. Multiple QueryParams

```
Expense.findAll(
  Like(Expense.description, "Gift for%"),
  OrderBy(Expense.dateOf,Descending),
  StartAt(offset),
  MaxRows(pageSize))
```

Another useful QueryParam is the Distinct case class, which acts exactly the same way as the DISTINCT keyword in SQL. The final control QueryParam that we'll cover is PreCache. It's used when you have a mapped foreign key field on an entity. Normally, when Mapper loads your main entity, it leaves the foreign key field in a lazy state, so that the query to get the foreign object isn't executed until you access the field. This can obviously be inefficient when you have a whole lot of entities loaded that you need to access, so the PreCache parameter forces Mapper to preload the foreign objects as part of the query. Listing 6-27 shows how we could use this to fetch an Expense entry as well as the account for the entry.

Listing 6-27. Using PreCache

```
def loadExpensePlusAccount (id : Long) =
  Expense.findAll(By(Expense.id, id),
                  PreCache(Expense.account))
```

Making Joins a Little Friendlier

If you would prefer to keep your queries type safe but you want a little more convenience in your joins between entities, you can define helper methods on your entities. One example would be finding all of the tags for a given Expense, as shown in Listing 6-28. Using this method in our example has an advantage over using HasManyThrough in that an explicit join method will pull from the database each time instead of just once at query.

Listing 6-28. Join Convenience Method

```
def tags = ExpenseTag.findAll(
  By(ExpenseTag.expense, this.id)).map(_.tag.obj.open_!)
```

Using Utility Functionality

In addition to the first-class persistence support in Mapper and Record, the frameworks provide additional functionality to make writing data-driven applications much simpler. This includes things like automatic representation of objects and support for generating everything from simple forms for an entity up to a full-fledged CRUD implementation for your entities.

Generating a Display

If you want to display a Mapper instance as XHTML, simply call the asHtml method (toXHtml in Record) on your instance. The default implementation turns each field's value into a Text node via the toString method and concatenates the results, separated by new lines. If you want to change this behavior, override the asHtml on your field definitions. For example, if we wanted to control formatting on our dateOf field, we could modify the field as shown in Listing 6-29.

Listing 6-29. Custom Field Display

```
import _root_.java.text.DateFormat
...
object dateOf extends MappedDateTime(this) {
      DateFormat.getDateInstance(DateFormat.SHORT)
  override def asHtml =
   Text(dateFormat.format(is))
}
```

Note that in Record, dateOf contains a java.util.Calendar instance and not a java.util.Date, so we would need to use the getTime method on the value. Two similar methods, asJSON and asJs, will return the JSON and JavaScript object representation of the instance, respectively.

Generating Forms

One of the biggest pieces of functionality in the Mapper framework is the ability to generate entry forms for a given record. The toForm method on Mapper is overloaded so that you can control how your form is created. All three toForm methods on Mapper take a Box[String] as their first parameter to control the submit button. If the Box is Empty, no submit button is generated; otherwise, the String contents of the Box are used as the button label. If you opt to skip the submit button, you'll need to provide it yourself via binding or some other mechanism, or you can rely on implicit form submission (when the user hits enter in a text field, for instance). The first toForm method simply takes a function to process the submitted form and returns the XHTML as shown in Listing 6-30.

Listing 6-30. Default toForm Method

```
myEntry.toForm(Full("Save"), { _.save })
```

As you can see, this makes it very easy to generate a form for editing an entity. The second toForm method allows you to provide a URL, which the Mapper will redirect to if validation succeeds on form submission (this is not provided in Record). This can be used for something like a login form, as shown in Listing 6-31.

Listing 6-31. Custom Submit Button

```
myEntry.toForm (Full("Login"), "/member/profile")
```

The third form of the toForm method is similar to the first form, with the addition of a redoSnippet parameter. This allows you to keep the current state of the snippet when validation fails so that the user doesn't have to re-enter all of the data in the form.

The Record framework allows for a little more flexibility in controlling form output. The MetaRecord object allows you to change the default templateOverride form template that the form uses by setting the formTemplate var. The template may contain any XHTML you want, but specifically, the toForm method will do special handling for the following tags:

- <lift:field_label name="..." />: The label for the field with the given name will be rendered here.
- <lift:field name="..." />: The field itself (specified by the given name) will be rendered here. Typically, this will be an input field, although it can be anything type appropriate. For example, a BooleanField would render a check box.

- `<lift:field_msg name="..." />`: Any messages, such as from validation, for the field with the given name will be rendered here.

As an example, if we wanted to use tables to lay out the form for our expense entry, the row for the description field could look like Listing 6-32.

Listing 6-32. Custom Form Template

```
<tr>
  <th><lift:field_label name="description" /></th>
  <td><lift:field name="description" />
      <lift:field_msg name="description" /></td>
</tr>
```

Technically, the `field_msg` binding looks up Lift messages (see Appendix B) based on the field's `uniqueId`, so you can set your own messages outside of validation using the `S.{error,notice,warning}` methods, as shown in Listing 6-33.

Listing 6-33. Setting Messages via S

```
S.warning(myEntry.amount.uniqueFieldId,
          "You have entered a negative amount!")
S.warning("amount_id", "This is brittle")
```

For most purposes, though, using the validation mechanism discussed in the next section would be the appropriate way to handle error checking and reporting.

Validating Forms

Validation is the process of checking a field during form processing to make sure that the submitted value meets requirements. This can be as simple as ensuring that a value was submitted or as complex as comparing multiple field values together.

Validation is achieved via a `List` of functions on a field that take the field value as input and return a `List[FieldError]` (or `Box[Node]` in Record). To indicate that validation succeeded, simply return an empty `List`. Otherwise, the list of `FieldErrors` you return are used as the failure messages to be presented to the user. A `FieldError` is simply a case class that associates an error message with a particular field.

As an example, let's say we don't want someone to be able to add an `Expense` entry in the future. First, we need to define a function for our `dateOf` field that takes a `Date` as an input (for Record, `java.util.Calendar` and not `Date` is the actual value type of `DateTimeField`) and returns the proper `List`. We show a simple function in Listing 6-34. In the method, we simply check to see if the millisecond count is greater than the current time and return an error message if so.

Listing 6-34. Date Validation

```
import _root_.java.util.Date
...
def noFutureDates (time : Date) = {
  if (time.getTime > System.currentTimeMillis) {
    List(FieldError(this,
        Text("You cannot make future expense entries")))
  } else {
    List[FieldError]()
  }
}
```

The next step is to tie the validation into the field itself. We do this by slightly modifying our field definition for date to set our list of validators, as shown in Listing 6-35.

Listing 6-35. Setting Validators

```
object dateOf extends MappedDateTime(this) {
  override def validations = noFutureDates _ :: Nil
}
```

Note that we need to add the underscore for each validation function to be partially applied on the submitted value. When our form is submitted, all of the validators for each field are run, and if all of them return Empty, validation succeeds. If any validators return Full(...), the contents of the Box are displayed as error messages to the user.

Supporting CRUD Operations

Adding CRUD support to your Mapper classes is very simple. We just mix in the CRUDify trait to our class, and it provides a full set of add, edit, list, delete, and view pages automatically. Listing 6-36 shows our Expense class with CRUDify mixed in.

Listing 6-36. Mixing in CRUDify

```
class Expense extends LongKeyedMapper[Expense]
  with CRUDify[Long,Expense] {
  ... normal def here ...
  // disable delete functionality
  override def deleteMenuLoc = Empty
}
```

The CRUDify behavior is very flexible. There are plenty of defs, you can override to control the templates for pages or whether pages are shown at all (as we do in our example). As an added bonus, CRUDify automatically creates a set of menus for SiteMap (see Chapter 5) that we can use by appending them onto the rest of our menus as shown in Listing 6-37.

Listing 6-37. Using CRUDify Menus

```
class Boot {
  def boot {
    val menus = ... Menu(Loc(...)) :: Expense.menus
    LiftRules.setSiteMap(SiteMap(menus : _*))
  }
}
```

Using Life Cycle Callbacks

Mapper and Record provide for a set of callbacks that allow you to perform actions at various points during the life cycle of a given instance. If you want to define your own handling for one of the life cycle events, all you need to do is override and define the callback, since `MetaMapper` already extends the `LifecycleCallbacks` trait. Note that there is a separate `LifecycleCallbacks` trait in each of the Record and Mapper packages, so make sure that you import the correct one. For example, if we wanted to notify a comet actor whenever a new `Expense` entry is saved, we could change our `Expense` class as shown in Listing 6-38.

Listing 38. Life Cycle Callbacks

```
object Expense extends LongKeyedMapper[Expense]
  ...
  override def afterSave { myCometActor ! this }
}
```

The life cycle hooks are executed at the main operations in an instance life cycle:

- `Create`: When a new instance is created
- `Delete`: When an instance is deleted
- `Save`: When a fresh instance is first saved (corresponding to a table insert)
- `Update`: When an instance that already exists in the database is updated (corresponding to a table update)
- `Validation`: When form validation occurs

For each of these points, you can execute your code before or after the operation is run.

Knowing the Base Field Types

The Record and Mapper frameworks define several basic field types. Table 6-1 shows the corresponding types between Mapper and Record, as well as a brief description of each type.

Table 6-1. The Mapper and Record Field Types.

MAPPER	RECORD	NOTES
`MappedBinary`	`BinaryField`	Represents a byte array. You must provide your own overrides for `toForm` and `asXHtml/asHtml` for input and display.
`MappedBirthYear`	Not applicable	Holds an `Int` that represents a birth year. The constructor takes a `minAge` parameter that is used for validation.
`MappedBoolean`	`BooleanField`	Represents a `Boolean` value. The default form representation is a check box.
`MappedCountry`	`CountryField`	Represents a choice from an enumeration of country phone codes as provided by the `net.liftweb.mapper.Countries.I18NCountry` class. The default form representation is a select.
`MappedDateTime`	`DateTimeField`	Represents a timestamp (`java.util.Calender` for Record, `java.util.Date` for Mapper). The default form representation is a text input.
`MappedDouble`	`DoubleField`	Represents a `Double`.
`MappedEmail`	`EmailField`	Represents an e-mail address with a maximum length.
`MappedEnum`	`EnumField`	Represents a choice from a given `scala.Enumeration`. The default form representation is a select.
`MappedEnumList`	Not applicable	Represents a choice of multiple enumerations. The default form representation is a set of check boxes, one for each `enum` value.
`MappedFakeClob`	Not applicable	Fakes a character large object (CLOB) value (really stores `String` bytes to a `BINARY` column).

Table 6-1 (Continued)

MAPPER	RECORD	NOTES
`MappedGender`	Not applicable	Represents a `Gender` enumeration. Display values are localized via the `I18NGenders` object. Internationalization is covered in Appendix D.
`MappedInt`	`IntField`	Represents an `Int` value.
`MappedIntIndex`	Not applicable	Represents an indexed `Int` field (typically a primary key). In Record, this is achieved with the `KeyField` trait.
`MappedLocale`	`LocaleField`	Represents a locale as selected from the `java.util.Locale.getAvailableLocales` method. The default form representation is a select.
`MappedLong`	`LongField`	Represents a `Long` value.
`MappedLongForeignKey`	Not applicable	Represents a mapping to another entity via the other entities `Long` primary key. This functionality is not yet supported in Record.
`MappedLongIndex`	Not applicable	Represents an indexed `Long` field (typically a primary key). In Record, this is achieved with the `KeyField` trait.
`MappedPassword`	`PasswordField`	Represents a password string. The default form representation is password input (obscured) text.
`MappedPoliteString`	Not applicable	Just like `MappedString`, but the default value is an empty string, and the input is automatically truncated to fit the database column size.
`MappedPostalCode`	`PostalCodeField`	Represents a validated postal code string. The field takes a reference to a `MappedCountry` (`CountryField` in Record) at definition and validates the input string against the selected country's postal code format.

Table 6-1 (Continued)

MAPPER	RECORD	NOTES
`MappedString`	`StringField`	Represents a string value with a maximum length and optional default value.
`MappedStringForeignKey`	Not applicable	Represents a mapping to another entity via the other entity's `String` primary key. This functionality is not yet supported in Record.
`MappedStringIndex`	Not applicable	Represents an indexed `String` field (typically a primary key). In Record, this is achieved with the `KeyField` trait.
`MappedText`	Not applicable	Represents a `String` field that stores to a CLOB column in the database. This can be used for large volumes of text.
`MappedTextArea`	`TextAreaField`	Represents a `String` field that will use an HTML text area element for its form display. When you define the field, you can override the `textareaCols` and `textareaRows` `defs` to control the dimensions of the text area.
`MappedTimeZone`	`TimeZoneField`	Represents a time zone selected from `java.util.TimeZone.getAvailableIDs`. The default form representation is a select.
`MappedUniqueId`	Not applicable	Represents a unique string of a specified length that is randomly generated. The implementation doesn't allow the user to write new values to the field. This can be thought of as a globally unique ID (GUID).

Defining Custom Field Types

The basic `MappedField` types cover a wide range of needs, but sometimes, you may find yourself wanting to cover a specific type. In our example, we would like a decimal value for our expense amount. Using a `double` would be inappropriate due to imprecision and rounding errors, so instead, we base it on `scala.BigDecimal`.

Note For more information on why not to use doubles for monetary calculations, please see http://stephan.reposita.org/archives/2008/01/11/once-and-for-all-do-not-use-double-for-money/.

Our first task is to specify the class signature and constructors, as shown in Listing 6-39. Note that the BigDecimal we're using here is scala.BigDecimal, not java.math.BigDecimal. We'll cover how we make this work with JDBC (which doesn't support scala.BigDecimal) in a moment.

Listing 6-39. MappedDecimal Constructors

```
import _root_.java.math.{MathContext, RoundingMode}

class MappedDecimal[T <: Mapper[T]] (val fieldOwner : T,
                                     val context : MathContext,
                                     val scale : Int) extends
 MappedField[BigDecimal,T] {
  // ... constructor taking initial value ...
  def this(fieldOwner : T,
     value : BigDecimal, context: MathContext) = {

    this(fieldOwner, context, value.scale)
    setAll(value) // we'll cover this later in this section
  }

  def this(fieldOwner : T, value : BigDecimal) = {
    this(fieldOwner, MathContext.UNLIMITED, value.scale)
    setAll(value)
  }
}
```

The first part of the class definition is the type signature; basically, the type [T <: MappedField[T]] indicates that whatever type "owns" this field must be a Mapper subclass. The <: syntax specifies an upper type bound and is explained in more detail at http://www.scala-lang.org/node/136. With our primary constructor, we specify the owner Mapper as well as the MathContext (this controls rounding and precision, or the total number of digits) and scale of the decimal value. The scale in BigDecimal essentially represents the number of digits to the right of the decimal point. In addition, we specify ancillary constructors to take an initial value with or without an explicit MathContext.

Now that we have the constructors in place, we need to define several abstract methods on MappedField. The first of these is a method to provide a default value. The default value is used for uninitialized fields or if validation fails. We also need to specify the class for our value type by implementing the dbFieldClass method.

Listing 6-40 shows both of these methods. In our case, we default to a zero value, with the scale set as specified in the constructor. Note that BigDecimal instances are generally immutable, so the setScale method returns a new instance. We also provide the vars and methods that handle the before and after values of the field. These values are used to handle persistence state; if you change the value of the field, the original value is held until the instance is saved to the database. The st method is used internally to set the value of the field when instances are rehydrated from the database.

Listing 6-40. Setting a Default Value

```
private val zero = BigDecimal("0")

def defaultValue = zero.setScale(scale)

def dbFieldClass = classOf[BigDecimal]

private var data : BigDecimal = defaultValue

private var orgData : BigDecimal = defaultValue

private def st (in : BigDecimal) {
  data = in
  orgData = in
}

protected def i_is_! = data

protected def i_was_! = orgData

override def doneWithSave() {
  orgData = data
}
```

The next set of methods we need to provide deal with when and how we can access the data. Listing 6-41 shows the overrides that set the read and write permissions to `true` (the default is `false` for both) as well as the `i_obscure_!` and `real_i_set_!` methods. The `i_obscure_!` method returns the a value that is used then the user doesn't have read permissions. The `real_i_set_!` method is what actually stores the internal value and sets the `dirty` flag when the field is updated.

Listing 6-41. Access Control

```
override def readPermission_? = true

override def writePermission_? = true

protected def i_obscure_!(in : BigDecimal) = defaultValue

protected def real_i_set_!(value : BigDecimal): BigDecimal = {
  if (value != data) {
    data = value
    dirty_?(true)
  }
  data
}
```

The next two methods that we need to provide deal with actually setting the value of the field. The first is `setFromAny`, which takes an `Any` parameter and must convert it into a `BigDecimal`. The second, `setFromString`, is a subset of `setFromAny` in that it takes a `String` parameter and must return a `BigDecimal`. Our implementation of these two methods is shown in Listing 6-42. We've also added a `setAll` method so that we have a common place to properly set scale and rounding modes on the value of the field.

Listing 6-42. setFrom. . . Methods

```
def setFromAny (in : Any) : BigDecimal =

  in match {
    case n :: _ => setFromString(n.toString)
    case Some(n) => setFromString(n.toString)
    case Full(n) => setFromString(n.toString)
    case None | Empty | Failure(_, _, _) | null =>
      setFromString("0")
    case n => setFromString(n.toString)
  }

def setFromString (in : String) : BigDecimal = {
  this.setAll(BigDecimal(in))
```

```
    data
  }

  protected def setAll (in : BigDecimal) = this.set(coerce(in))

  protected coerce (in : BigDecimal) =

  new BigDecimal(in.bigDecimal.setScale(scale,
    context.getRoundingMode))
```

Our implementations are relatively straightforward. The only special handling we need for setFromAny is to properly deal with Lists, Boxes, Options, and the null value. The BigDecimal constructor takes Strings, so the setFromString method is easy. The only addition we make over the BigDecimal constructor is to properly set the scale and rounding on the returned value.

Our final step is to define the database-specific methods for our field, as shown in Listing 6-43. The first method we implement is targetSQLType. This method tells Mapper what the corresponding SQL type is for our database column. The jdbcFriendly method returns a value that can be used in a JDBC statement; here's where we need to use the bigDecimal value on our scala.BigDecimal to obtain the real java.math.BigDecimal instance from whatever our current value is.

Similarly, the real_convertToJDBCFriendly method needs to return a java BigDecimal for a given scala BigDecimal input. The buildSet... methods return functions that can be used to set the value of our field based on different input types. These are essentially conversion functions. Finally, the fieldCreatorString specifics what we would need in a CREATE TABLE statement to define this column. In our case, we need to take into account the precision and scale of decimal; we use default precision if we're set to unlimited, but it's important to understand that actual precision for the default DECIMAL type varies between database vendors.

Listing 6-43. Database-Specific Methods

```
def targetSQLType = Types.DECIMAL

def jdbcFriendly(field : String) = i_is_!.bigDecimal

def real_convertToJDBCFriendly(value: BigDecimal): Object =
  value.bigDecimal

def buildSetBooleanValue(accessor : Method, columnName : String):
  (T, Boolean, Boolean) => Unit = null

def buildSetDateValue(accessor : Method, columnName : String) :
  (T, Date) => Unit =(inst, v) =>
    doField(inst, accessor, {case f: MappedDecimal[T] =>
      f.st(if (v == null) defaultValue else
```

```
        coerce(BigDecimal(v.getTime)))})

def buildSetStringValue(accessor: Method, columnName: String):
(T, String) => Unit = (inst, v) =>
  doField(inst, accessor, {case f: MappedDecimal[T] =>
    f.st(coerce(BigDecimal(v)))})

def buildSetLongValue(accessor: Method, columnName : String) :
(T, Long, Boolean) => Unit = (inst, v, isNull) =>
   doField(inst, accessor, {case f: MappedDecimal[T] =>
      f.st(if (isNull) defaultValue else coerce(BigDecimal(v)))})

def buildSetActualValue(accessor: Method,
                        data: AnyRef,
                        columnName: String) : (T, AnyRef) =>
  Unit = (inst, v) => doField(inst, accessor, {case f:
    MappedDecimal[T] => f.st(coerce(BigDecimal(v.toString)))})

def fieldCreatorString(dbType: DriverType, colName: String):
String = {
  val suffix = if (context.getPrecision == 0) ""
    else {
     "(" + context.getPrecision + "," + scale + ")"
              }
  colName + " DECIMAL" + suffix
}
```

Working with ProtoUser and MegaProtoUser

In addition to all of the database-related features, Mapper contains an extra goody to help you quickly set up small sites. The `ProtoUser` and `MegaProtoUser` traits are two built-in traits that define a simple user account. The `ProtoUser` trait defines some basic fields for a user: `email`, `firstName`, `lastName`, `password`, and `superUser` (a Boolean to provide basic permissions). There are also a number of `def`s used to format the fields for display or to provide form labels. Listing 6-44 shows an example of a `ProtoUser`-based Mapper class that overrides some of the formatting `def`s.

Listing 6-44. A Simple ProtoUser

```
class User extends ProtoUser[User] {

  override def shortName = firstName.is

  override lastNameDisplayName = "surname"

}
```

The MegaProtoUser trait, as its name implies, extends the ProtoUser trait with a whole suite of functionality. The main thrust of MegaProtoUser (and its associated metaobject, MetaMegaProtoUser) is to automatically handle all of the scaffolding for a complete user management system, with:

- A user registration page with configurable validation via e-mail
- A login page that automatically handles authentication
- A lost password page that does reset via e-mail
- A change password page
- A user edit page
- A simple method to generate SiteMap menus for all of these pages

Of course, you can customize any of these by overriding the associated methods on the MetaMegaProtoUser object. Listing 2-1 in Chapter 2 shows an example of sprucing up the signup and login pages by overriding the loginXHtml and signupXHtml methods. Listing 6-45 shows how easy it is to then hook the MetaMegaProtoUser menus into SiteMap.

Code Listing 6-45. Hooking MetaMegaProtoUser into Boot

```
class Boot {
  def boot {
    ...
    LiftRules.setSiteMap(
      SiteMap(List(..., User.sitemap) :_*))
    ...
  }
}
```

Using Advanced Mapper Features

In this section, we'll cover some of the advanced features of Mapper.

Using Multiple Databases

It's common for an application to need to access data in more than one database. Lift supports this feature through the use of overrides on your MetaMapper classes. First, we need to define the identifiers for the various databases using the ConnectionIdentifier trait and overriding the jndiName def. Lift comes with one premade: DefaultConnectionIdentifier. Its jndiName is set to lift, so it's recommended that you use something else. Let's say we have two databases: sales and employees. Listing 6-46 shows how we would define the ConnectionIdentifier objects for these.

Listing 6-46. Defining Connection Identifiers

```
object SalesDB extends ConnectionIdentifier {

  def jndiName = "sales"

}

object EmployeeDB extends ConnectionIdentifier {

  def jndiName = "employees"

}
```

Simple enough. Now, we need to create connection managers for each one, or we can combine the functionality into a single manager. To keep things clean, we'll use a single manager, as shown in Listing 6-47. Scala's match operator allows us to easily return the correct connection.

Listing 6-47. A Multidatabase Connection Manager

```
... standard Lift and Mapper imports ...
import _root_.java.sql._

object DBVendor extends ConnectionManager {

  Class.forName("org.postgresql.Driver")

   def newConnection(name : ConnectionIdentifier) = {
    try {
      name match {
        case SalesDB =>
          Full(DriverManager.getConnection(
            "jdbc:postgresql://localhost/sales",
            "root", "secret"))
        case EmployeeDB =>
          Full(DriverManager.getConnection(

            "jdbc:postgresql://server/employees",
            "root", "hidden"))
    } catch {
      case e : Exception => e.printStackTrace; Empty
    }
  }
  def releaseConnection (conn : Connection) { conn.close }
}
```

A special case of using multiple databases is sharding (for more information on sharding, see `http://highscalability.com/unorthodox-approach-database-design-coming-shard`). Sharding is a means to scale your database capacity by associating entities with one database instance out of a federation of servers based on some property of the entity. For instance, we could distribute user across three database servers by using the first character of the last name: A–H goes to server one; I–P goes to server two, and Q–Z goes to server three. As simple as this sounds, there are some important factors to remember:

- Sharding increases the complexity of your code.
- To get the most benefit out of sharding, you need to carefully choose and tune your selector. If you're not careful, you can get an uneven distribution where some servers handle significantly more load than others, defeating the purpose of sharding. The example we've given here of using the last name is, in practice, a very poor choice. We recommend reading `http://startuplessonslearned.blogspot.com/2009/01/sharding-for-startups.html` for a good overview of the pros and cons of various selector strategies.
- When you use sharding, you can't just use normal joins anymore, since the data isn't all within one instance. This means more work on your part to properly retrieve and associate data.

Mapper provides a handy feature for sharding that allows you to choose which database connection you want to use for a specific entity. There are two methods we can use to control the behavior: `dbSelectDBConnectionForFind` and `dbCalculateConnectionIdentifier`. `dbSelectDBConnectionForFind` is used in a find by primary key and takes a partial function (typically a match clause) to determine which connection to use. `dbCalculateConnectionIdentifier` is used when a new instance is created to decide where to store the new instance. As an example, say we've defined two database connections, `SalesA` and `SalesB`. We want to place new instances in `SalesA` if the amount is less than $100 and `SalesB` otherwise. Listing 6-48 shows our method in action.

Listing 6-48. Sharding in Action

```
class  extends LongKeyedMapper[] {

  ... fields, etc ...

  override def dbCalculateConnectionIdentifier = {
    case n if n.amount.is > 100 => SalesA
    case _ => SalesB
  }

}
```

Performing SQL-Based Queries

If, despite all that Mapper covers, you find yourself still wanting more control over the query, two more options are available to you: `findAllByPreparedStatement` and `findAllByInsecureSql`. The `findAllByPreparedStatement` method allows you to, in essence, construct your query completely by hand. The added benefit of using a `PreparedStatement` (see `http://java.sun.com/javase/6/docs/api/java/sql/PreparedStatement.html` for more details) means that you can easily include user-defined data in your queries. The `findAllByPreparedStatement` method takes a single function parameter; this function needs to take a `SuperConnection` (essentially a thin wrapper on `java.sql.Connection`) and return a `PreparedStatement` instance. Listing 6-49 shows our previous example of looking up all `Tags` for recent `Expense` entries using `findAllByPreparedStatement` instead. The query that you provide must at least return the fields that are mapped by your entity, but you can return other columns as well (they'll just be ignored) in case you just want to do a `select *`.

Listing 6-49. Using findAllByPreparedStatement

```
def recent = Tag.findAllByPreparedStatement(
{ superconn =>
  superconn.connection.prepareStatement(
    "select distinct Expense.id, Tag.tag" +
    "from Tag" +
    "join ExpenseTag et on Tag.id = et.tag " +
    "join Expense ex on ex.id = et.expense " +
    "where ex.dateOf > (CURRENT_DATE - interval '30 days')")
})
```

The `findAllByInsecureSql` method goes even further, executing the string you submit directly as a statement without any checks. The same general rules apply as for `findAllByPreparedStatement`, although you need to add the `IHaveValidatedThisSQL` parameter as a code audit check. In either case, the ability to use full SQL queries can allow you to do some very powerful things, but it comes at the cost of losing type safety and possibly making your application nonportable.

As a last resort, Mapper provides support for nonentity SQL queries through a few methods on the database object. The first method we'll look at is `DB.runQuery`. This method allows you to provide a full SQL query string and is overloaded to take a parameterized query if you desire. It returns a `Pair[List[String],List[List[String]]`, with the first `List[String]` containing all of the column names and the second `List` corresponding to each row in the result set. For example, let's say we wanted to compute the sums of each tag for a given account. Listing 6-50 shows how we could accomplish this using a parameterized query against the database.

Listing 6-50. Using DB.runQuery

```
DB.runQuery(
"select Tag.name, sum(amount) from Expense ex " +
"join ExpenseTag et on et.expense = ex.id " +
"join Tag on et.tag = Tag.id " +
"join Account on Account.id = ex.account " +
"where Account.id = ? group by Tag.name order by Tag.name",
myAccount.id)

// might return:

(List("tag", "sum"]),

 List(List("food","42.00"),

 List("home","75.49"),

 List("work","2.00")))
```

If you need full control over the query and full access to the result set, DB provides some low-level utility methods. The most basic is DB.use, which takes a connection identifier as well as a function that takes a SuperConnection (a thin wrapper on JDBC's connection). This forms a loan pattern that lets Mapper deal with all of the connection open and release details (for more on the loan pattern, see http://scala.sygneca.com/patterns/loan). The DB.exec method takes a provided connection, executes an arbitrary SQL statement on it, and then applies a provided function to the result set. Similarly, the DB.prepareStatement method allows you to create a prepared statement and apply a function to it. You can combine these methods to run any arbitrary SQL, as shown in Listing 6-51.

Listing 6-51. Using DB.use

```
// recompute an account balance from all of the expenses

DB.use(DefaultConnectionIdentifier) { conn =>

  val balance =

    // Should us a prepared statement here. This is for
    // example only

    DB.exec(conn,
      "select sum(ex.amount) from Expense ex where ex.account = " +
      myAccount.id) {

      rs => if (!rs.next) BigDecimal(0)
```

```
        else
          (new BigDecimal(rs.getBigDecimal(1)))
      }

    DB.prepareStatement("update account set balance = ? " +
      "where account.id = ?", conn) { stmt =>

      stmt.setBigDecimal(1, balance.bigDecimal)

      stmt.setLong(2, resetAccount.id)

      stmt.executeUpdate()

    }

  }
```

Conclusion

In this chapter, we discussed the two major ORMs included in Lift: Mapper and Record. We've shown how you can define entities using the Mapper field types and how to coordinate between the entity and its `Meta` object. We've shown how you can customize the display and schema of your behavior with custom form control, CRUD support and indexing, as well as how to query for entities using Mapper's type-safe query support. Finally, we showed you in-depth customization of Mapper behavior, made possible by writing your own field types, using multiple databases, and using raw SQL queries.

Chapter 7: Advanced Lift Architecture

Congratulations! You've either made it through the introduction to Lift, or maybe you've just skipped the basics and jumped right to the advanced material; either way, the next group of chapters will be exciting. In this chapter, we're going to dive into some of the advanced mechanisms that Lift uses for rendering and processing so that you have a thorough understanding of what's going on before we explore further.

Understanding Lift Architecture

Before we jump into the specific details of the architecture, let's refresh your memory about the basics. Figure 7-1 highlights the main Lift components and where they live in the ecosystem. Scala compiles down to Java bytecode, so Lift actually runs on top of the JVM. Lift applications are typically run in a Java EE web container, such as Jetty or Tomcat. As we explained in Chapter 1, Lift is set up to act as a `Filter` that serves as the entry point (for more on filters, see `http://java.sun.com/j2ee/1.4/docs/api/javax/servlet/Filter.html`). The way you use the rest of the framework varies from application to application, depending on how simple or complex you make it.

Figure 7-1. Lift Architecture

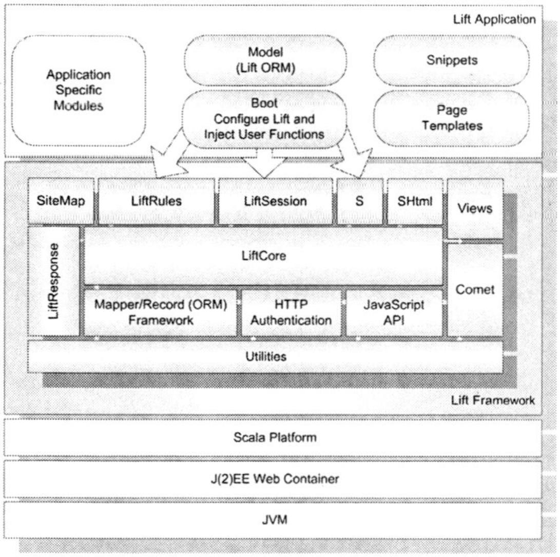

The major components outlined in the diagram follow:

- `LiftCore` is the engine of the framework responsible for the request/response life cycle, the rendering pipeline, invoking users' functions, and so on. We don't directly cover the core in this book, since essentially, all of the functionality that we do cover sits on top of the core.
- `SiteMap` contains the web pages for a Lift application (see Chapter 5).
- `LiftRules` allows you to configure Lift. We cover this in various sections throughout the book.
- `LiftSession` is the session state representation (see the "Managing Sessions" section).
- `S` is the stateful object impersonating the state context for a given request/response life cycle (see the "Working with Advanced S Object Features" section).
- `SHtml` contains helper functions for XHTML artifacts (see Chapters 4 and 9).
- Views are the `LiftView` objects representing views as XML content. Thus pages can be composed from other sources and not only from HTML files (see Chapter 3).
- `LiftResponse` represents the abstraction of a response that will be propagated to the client. (see the "Exploring LiftResponse in Detail" section).
- Comet represents the Comet actors layer, which allows the sending of asynchronous content to the browser (see Chapter 9).
- The Mapper or Record (ORM) framework is the lightweight ORM library provided by Lift. The Mapper framework is the proposed ORM framework for Lift 1.0, and the Record framework will be out for next releases (see Chapter 6).
- You can use either basic or digest HTTP authentication in your Lift application; both provide you more control than using a web container's HTTP authentication model (see the "Obtaining HTTP Authentication" section).
- JS API, the JavaScript abstraction layer, contains Scala classes and objects that abstract JavaScript artifacts. Such objects can be combined to build JavaScript code (see Chapter 8).
- Utilities contain a number of helper functions that Lift uses internally and are available to your application.
- The term "J(2)EE" was chosen on purpose to emphasize the compatibility with J2EE specifications (versions 1.3 and 1.4) as well as Java EE 5 specifications.

Understanding the Request/Response Life Cycle

We briefly discussed the request/response life cycle in Chapter 3, and now, we're going to cover it in depth. This will serve not only to familiarize you with the full processing power of Lift but to introduce some of the other advanced topics we'll be discussing in this and later chapters.

One important thing we'd like to mention is that most of the configurable properties are in LiftRules, and are of type RulesSeq, which allows you to specify a list of functions or values that are applied in order. The RulesSeq class defines prepend and append methods that allow you to add new configuration items at the beginning or end of the configuration, so you can prioritize things like partial functions and compose various methods together to control Lift's behavior. You can think of a RulesSeq as a Seq on steroids, tweaked for Lift's usage.

Transforming a Request into a Response

This section outlines the process of transforming a request into a response. We provide references to the sections of this book where we discuss each step in case you want to go there for more information.

Begin by executing early functions. These functions represent a mechanism that allows a user function to be called on the HttpServletRequest before it enters the normal processing chain. This can be used for, for example, to set the XHTML output to UTF-8. This is controlled through LiftRules.early.

Next, perform the URL rewriting. We already covered rewriting URLs in detail in Chapter 5. Controlled via LiftRules.rewrite, this functionality is useful for creating user-friendly URLs, among other things. The result of the transformation will be checked for possible rewrites until there are no more matches or until the transformation is explicitly stopped by setting the stopRewriting val in ReqwriteResponse to true. It is relevant to know that you can have rewriter functions for each session, hence you can have different rewriter in different contexts. These session rewriters are prepended to the LiftRules rewriters before their application.

Once your URLs are written, call the LiftRules.onBeginServicing hooks. These hooks act as a mechanism that allows you to add your own hook functions to be called when Lift is starting to process the request. You could set up logging here, for instance.

After that, check for user-defined stateless dispatch in LiftRules.statelessDispatchTable. If the partial functions defined in this table match the request, they are used to create a LiftResponse that is sent to the user, bypassing any further processing. These are very useful for building things like REST APIs. The term "stateless" refers to the fact that, at the time the dispatch function is called, the stateful object (called S) is not available and the LiftSession is not created yet. Custom dispatch is covered in the "Setting Session DispatchPF Functions" section.

Create a LiftSession if there was no stateless dispatch defined. The LiftSession holds various bits of state for the request and is covered in more detail in the "Managing Sessions"section.

Next, call LiftSession.onSetupSession. This is a mechanism for adding hook functions that will be called when the LiftSession is created. We'll get into more details when we discuss Lift's session management in the "Managing Sessions" section.

Initialize the S object. The S object represents the current state of the request and response (see the "Working with Advanced S Object Features" section).

After your S object is successfully initialized, call any LoanWrapper instances that you've added through S.addAround. A LoanWrapper is a way to insert your own processing into the render pipeline, similar to how Filter works in the Servlet API. This means that when your LoanWrapper implementation is called, Lift passes you a function allowing you to chain the processing of the request. With this functionality, you can execute your own pre- and post-condition code. A simple example of this would be if you need to make sure that something is configured at the start of processing and cleanly shut down when processing terminates. LoanWrappers are covered in the "Wrapping Lift's Processing Logic" section.

After that, you'll need to process the stateful request, as outlined in the next section.

Next, you'll call LiftRules.onEndServicing hooks, which are the stateless end-servicing hooks, called after the S object context is destroyed. And you'll call any functions defined in LiftRules.beforeSend. This is the last place where you can modify the response before it's sent to the user.

Now, you're ready to convert the LiftResponse to a raw byte stream and send it to client as an HTTP response. Finally, call any functions defined in LiftRules.afterSend. Typically, these would be used for cleanup.

Now that you understand the complete process for changing a request to a response, let's take a more in-depth look at what happens when a stateful request is processed, before moving on to discuss function mapping.

Processing a Stateful Request

To begin processing a stateful request, check the stateful dispatch functions defined in LiftRules.dispatch. This mechanism for dispatch is similar to the stateless dispatch configuration in LiftRules.statelessDispatchTable that we discussed, except that these functions are executed in the context of a LiftSession and an S object (see the "Working with Advanced S Object Features" section). The first matching partial function is used to generate a LiftResponse that is returned to the client. If none of the dispatch functions match, processing continues. Dispatch functions are covered in the "Setting Session DispatchPF Functions" section. This flow is wrapped by LiftSession.onBeginServicing/onEndServicing calls.

If this is a Comet request, you're ready to process it and return the response. Comet is a method for performing asynchronous updates of the user's page without a reload, and we cover Comet techniques in Chapter 9.

If this is an Ajax request, you'll need to execute the user's callback function; the specific function is mapped via a request parameter (essentially a token). The result of the callback is returned as the response to the user. The response can be a JavaScript snippet, an XML construct, or virtually any `LiftResponse`. For an overview of `LiftResponse`, please see the "Exploring LiftResponse in Detail" section. This flow is wrapped by `LiftSession.onBeginServicing/onEndServicing` calls.

If this is a regular HTTP request, you should follow these steps:

1. Call the `LiftSession.onBeginServicing` hooks. Mostly, `onBegin` and `onEnd` functions are used for logging. Note that `LiftRules` also have `onBeginServicing` and `onEndServicing` functions, but these are wrapping more Lift processing, not only stateful processing.

2. Check the user-defined dispatch functions that are set for each session (see `S.addHighLevelSessionDispatcher` in the "Setting Per-Session DispatchPF Functions" section). This is similar to `LiftRules.dispatch` except that you can have different functions set up for a different session depending on your application logic. If there is a function applicable, execute it, and return its response. If there is no per-session dispatch function, process the request by executing the Scala function that user set up for specific events (such as when clicking a link, clicking the submit button, or executing a function that when a form field is set). Please see the SHtml object discussion in Chapter 4 for details on form event functions.

3. Check the `SiteMap` and `Loc` functions. We cover SiteMap extensively in Chapter 5.

4. Look up the template based on the request path. Lift will locate the templates. To do so, first, check the partial functions defined in `LiftRules.viewDispatch`:

   - If a function is defined for this path, invoke it, and return `Either[()=> Can[NodeSeq],LiftView]`. This allows you to return the function for handling the view directly or delegate to a `LiftView` subclass (`LiftView` is covered in Chapter 3).

   - If no `viewDispatch` functions match, look for the template using the `ServletContext`'s `getResourceAsStream`.

   - If the template is still not found for classes in view folder from the paths declared in boot through `LiftRules.addToPackages`, Lift will look for classes that extend `InsecureLiftView` and invoke the corresponding function or classes that extend `LiftView` and invoke the dispatch function.

5. Process the templates by executing snippets, combining templates, and so forth:

   - Merge <head /> elements, as described in Chapter 3.

   - Update the internal functions map. Basically, this associates the user's Scala functions with tokens that are passed around in subsequent requests using HTTP query parameters. We cover this mechanism in detail in the "Maping Lift Functions" section.

- Clean up notices (see Appendix B) since they were already rendered they are no longer needed. Notices are covered in the "Notice/Warning/Error messages" section from Chapter 3.
- Call LiftRules.convertResponse. Basically, this glues together different pieces if information such as the actual markup, the response headers, cookies, and so on into a LiftResponse instance.
- Check to see if Lift needs to send an HTTP redirect. For an overview of Lift's redirect handling, please see Chapter 3.

6. Call the `LiftSession.onEndServicing` hooks, the counterparts to `LiftSession.onBeginServicing`.
7. Call `LiftRules.performTransform`, which is actually configured via the `LiftRules.responseTransformers` `RulesSeq`. This is a list of functions on `LiftResponse => LiftResponse` that allows the user to modify the response before it's sent to the client.

We realize that this is a lot of information to digest in one pass, so as we continue to cover the specific details of the rendering pipeline, you may want to keep a bookmark here so that you can come back and process the new information in the greater context of how Lift is working.

Mapping Lift Functions

As we mentioned in Chapter 4, Lift utilizes Scala closures and functions for almost all processing of client data. Because of this, Lift's ability to associate functions with specific form elements, AJAX calls, and so forth is critical to its operation. This association of functions, commonly known as mapping, is handled through a combination of request parameters, Scala closures, and session data. We feel that understanding how mapping works is important if you want to work on advanced topics.

At its most basic, mapping of functions is just that—a map of the user's currently defined functions. To simplify things, Lift actually uses one of four subclasses of `net.liftweb.http.S.AFuncHolder`:

- `BinFuncHolder` is used for binding functions for file uploading. It will hold a `FileParamHolder=> Any` function, which is used to process the file data after upload (see Chapter 4 for details).
- `SFuncHolder` is used for binding `String=> Any` functions. This function corresponds to a single HTTP query parameter, except that the parameter name is unique to this request (we'll cover naming shortly).
- `LFuncHolder` is used for binding `List[String]=> Any` functions. This is essentially the same as `SFuncHolder` but for multiple values.

- NFuncHolder used for binding ()=> Any functions. Typically, these are used for event callbacks (such as form submission).

Wherever Lift takes a function callback, that callback is converted to one of these types behind the scenes. Also, on the backend, each function is assigned a token ID (generated by Helpers.nextFuncName), which is then added to the session, typically via S.addFunctionMap or S.mapFunc. The token is generally used as the form element name so that the tokens for a given form are passed back to Lift when the form is submitted. In AJAX, the token is used as an HTTP query parameter of the AJAX callback from the client JavaScript code. In either case, Lift processes the query parameters within LiftSession.runParams and executes each associated function in the function mapping.

As a concrete example, let's look at a simple binding in a form. Listing 7-1 shows a small example snippet that will request a person's name and print it out when the person clicks the submit button.

Listing 7-1. Function-Binding Snippet

```
... standard Lift imports ...
import _root_.scala.xml.NodeSeq

class HelloWorld {
  def greet (xhtml : NodeSeq) : NodeSeq = {

    var name = ""

    def process() = {
      Log.info(name)
    }

    bind("form", xhtml,
         "name" -> SHtml.text(name, name = _),
         "greet" -> SHtml.submit("Greet", process))

  }
}
```

Listing 7-2 shows the corresponding template using our sample snippet.

Listing 7-2. Function-Binding Template

```
<lift:surround with="default" at="content">
  <lift:Test.greet form="GET">
    <form:name /> <form:greet />
  </lift:Test.greet>
</lift:surround>
```

Finally, Listing 7-3 shows an example of the resulting HTML that's generated when a user views the template. As you can see, each of the elements with callbacks has a corresponding form element with a token ID for the name value. Since we've used the GET CGI method here (we usually recommend using POST in the real world), when we submit the form our URL would look like /greet.html?F541542594358JE2=...&F541542594359PM4=Greet.

For SFuncHolder mappings, the value of the request parameter is passed directly. For NFuncHolders, the presence of the token in the query parameter list is enough to fire the function. For BinFuncHolder and LFuncHolder mappings some additional processing is performed to coerce the submitted values into proper values for the functions to handle.

Listing 7-3. Function-Binding Result

```
...
<form method="get" action="/greet.html">
  <input name="F541542594358JE2" type="text" value=""/>
  <input name="F541542594359PM4" type="submit" value="Greet"/>
</form>
... 119
```

Normally, you do not have to directly deal with the function holder classes, since the generator functions in SHtml handle that internally. However, if you're in a situation when you need to bind functions by yourself (such as building your own widget where SHtml doesn't provided needed elements), you can use the previously mentioned S.addFunctionMap or S.mapFunc to do the registration for you.

Exploring LiftResponse in Detail

In some cases, particularly when using dispatch functions (see the "Setting Session DispatchPF Functions" section), you may want explicit control over what Lift returns to the user. The LiftResponse trait is the base of a complete hierarchy of response classes that cover a wide variety of functionality, from simply returning an HTTP status code to returning a byte stream or your own XML fragments. In this section, we'll cover some of the more common classes.

Basic HTTP Equivalent Responses

LiftResponse has several subclasses that correspond to well-known HTTP response codes as defined in RFC2616 (see http://www.w3.org/Protocols/rfc2616/rfc2616-sec10.html for more details on what the codes represent). These can be used when you want to send a standard response to the client. The standard responses are:

- `OkResponse`: Represents a 200 (OK) response without a body (Normally, any properly processed Lift response will use the 200 code but will include the processed template or view content as the body.)
- `CreatedResponse`: Represents a 201 response
- `AcceptedResponse`: Represents a 202 response
- `NoContentResponse`: Represents a 204 response
- `ResetContentRespons`: Represents a 205 response
- `PermRedirectResponse`: Represents a 301 response
- `TemporaryRedirectResponse`: Represents a 307 response
- `BadResponse`: Represents a 400 response
- `UnauthorizedResponse`: Represents a 403 response using basic authentication (See the "Obtaining HTTP Authentication" section for more details.)
- `UnauthorizedDigestResponse`: Represents a 403 response using digest authentication (See the "Obtaining HTTP Authentication" section for more details.)
- `NotFoundResponse`: Represents a 404 response
- `MethodNotAllowedResponse`: Represents a 405 response
- `NotAcceptableResponse`: Represents a 406 response
- `GoneResponse`: Represents a 410 response
- `UnsupportedMediaTypeResponse`: Represents a 415 response
- `InternalServerErrorResponse`: Represents a 500 response
- `NotImplementedResponse`: Represents a 501 response
- `BadGatewayResponse`: Represents a 502 response
- `ServiceUnavailableResponse`: Represents a 503 response

Redirecting the Client

Redirection to a different page can be handled via the `RedirectResponse` or the `RedirectWithState` `LiftResponse`. The `RedirectWithState` response can be used to pass notices or functions to be executed on the redirect as shown in Listing 7-5.

Listing 7-5. RedirectWithState

```
// In boot function

import net.liftweb.http._
import MessageState._

...
class Boot {
  def boot = {
    LiftRules.dispatch.prepend {
      case Req("redirect1" :: _, _, _) => () =>
        Full(RedirectWithState("/page1",
          "My error" -> NoticeType.Error))

      case Req("redirect2" :: _, _, _) => () =>
        Full(RedirectWithState("/page2",
          RedirectState(() =>
            println("Called on redirect!"),
            "My error" -> NoticeType.Error)))
  }
}
```

First, we added a `DispatchPF` function that pattern matches for paths starting with `redirect1` and `redirect2`. Let's see what happens in each case:

- `redirect1`: We are returning a `RedirectWithState` response. It will do HTTP redirect towards `/page1`, and the state is impersonated by the tuple `"MyError" -> Error`. Because the `MessageState` object holds an implicit conversion function from `Tuple2` to `MessageState`, it suffices to just provide the tuple here. Essentially, we are saying that when the browser sends the redirect request to server, we already have an error notice set up and the `<lift:msgs>` tag from your `/page1` will show this `"My error"` error message.
- `redirect2`: Similarly, it does an HTTP redirect to browser toward your `/page2`, but now we are passing a `RedirectState` object. This object holds a `() => Unit` function that will be executed when the browser sends the redirect request and the `Notice-s` represented by a repeated parameter `(String, NoticeType.Value)*`. In fact, the mapping between the actual message and its type: `Notice`, `Warning`, or `Error`.

Sending Content to the Client

Now that we've covered basic responses, let's look at some ways that you can use `LiftResponse` subclasses to send data back to the user. The first subclass we're interested in is the `BasicResponse` class. This class represents a response with content and is itself subclassed by the `InMemoryResponse` and `StreamingResponse` classes. All of the other responses that are used to send data back to the client are based on `InMemoryResponse` or `StreamingResponse`, so we'll cover them now.

InMemoryResponse

The `InMemoryResponse` class allows you to return an array of bytes directly to the user along with a set of HTTP headers and cookies and a response code. An example of using `InMemoryResponse` was given in the "Setting Session DispatchPF Functions" section, showing how we can directly generate a chart PNG in memory and send it to the user. This is generally useful as long as the data you need to generate and send is relatively small; when you start getting into larger buffers, you can run into memory constraints as well as garbage collection pressure if you're serving a large number of requests.

StreamingResponse

The `StreamingResponse` class is similar to the `InMemoryResponse`, except that instead of reading from a buffer, it reads from an input object. The input object is not required to be a subclass of `java.io.InputStream`; rather, it is only required to implement the method `def read(buf: Array[Byte]): Int`.

Note Type matching against a method signature is done with Scala's structural typing, which we don't cover in this book. For more info, see `http://scala.sygneca.com/patterns/duck-typing-done-right`, or the *Scala Language Specification*, section 3.2.7

This very generalized type requirement allows you to essentially send back anything that can provide an input stream. Additionally, you can provide a `()=>` unit function (cleanup, if you will) that is called when the input stream is exhausted.

As an example, let's define a snippet to use piped streams to send an image to a user. Listing 7-4 shows how we can use `PipedInputStream` and `PipedOutputStream` from `java.io` to send the data back to the user.

Listing 7-4. Streaming File Method

```
... standard Lift imports ...
object Image {
  def sendFile (filename : String) : Box[LiftResponse] = {
  // Get file handle
  val file : File = ...
  val length = file.length
    val fileInput = new java.io.FileInputStream(file)
  Full(StreamingResponse(fileInput,
    () => { fileInput.close },
    length,
    ("Content-Type" -> "image/png") :: Nil,
    Nil,
    200))
}
```

Note that we use the cleanup function to close the file once we're finished so that we make sure to release resources.

Returning Text to the Client

The first response class that we'll look at that builds on `InMemoryResponse` is `PlainTextResponse`. It can be used to send `String` data with a `Content-Type` of `text/plain` back to the client along with headers and an arbitrary response code. Listing 7-6 shows an example of how we can match the /ping URL to reply with the word `"pong"`.

Similarly, there is a `CSSResponse` that is essentially the same but sets the `Content-Type` header to `text/css`.

Returning XML to the Client

There is often a desire to return XML to the client to support a number of API methodologies (REST, XML-RPC, Atom, etc.). The `NodeResponse` base class has a number of subclasses that can be used to transform a `scala.xml.NodeSeq` into an appropriate response for the client.

As an example, let's say that you would like to handle a URL ending in `/rest` by returning an XML response. The content type, and everything else, is taken care of by `XmlResponse`, as shown in Listing 7-6. The `XmlResponse` sends the data with a `Content-Type` of `text/xml`. If you would like this to be different, you can use the `XmlMimeResponse`.

Going one step further, the `XhtmlResponse` class can be used to send your XML as XHTML, providing additional support for HTTP headers, cookies, and an optional `DocType` header.

Finally, there are a handful of specialized XML response classes specifically for the Atom syndication format:

- AtomResponse
- AtomCategoryResponse
- AtomCreatedResponse
- AtomServiceResponse

We won't be covering Atom here, but see http://en.wikipedia.org/wiki/Atom_(standard) for more details.

Listing 7-6. Various ContentResponses

```
// In your bootstrap
class Boot {
  def boot = {
    ...
    LiftRules.dispatch.prepend {
      case Req("ping" :: Nil, _, _) => () => Full(PlainTextResponse("pong"))
      case Req("rest" :: Nil, _, _) => () => Full(XmlResponse(
        <persons>
          <name>John</name>
          <name>Jane</name>
        </persons>
      ))
    }
    ...
  }
}
```

Managing Sessions

Lift is a stateful framework, and naturally, this state needs to be managed. You may already be familiar with HttpSession and how a Java EE web container identifies an HttpSession: either by a JSESSIONID cookie or by a JSESSIONID URI sequence (in case of URL rewriting). Similarly, Lift uses a LiftSession reference, which is not actually persisted in HttpSession. As a matter of fact, Lift does not really use the HttpSession provided by the web container to maintain conversational state, but rather uses a bridge between the HttpSession and the LiftSession. This bridge is represented by SessionToServletBridge class, which implements both javax.servlet.http.HttpSessionBindingListener and javax.servlet.http.HttpSessionActivationListener and works like this:

1. When receiving an HTTP request without a stateless dispatch function to execute, Lift does the stateful processing. Before doing that, it checks to see if there is a `LiftSession` associated with this HTTP session ID. This mapping is kept on a `SessionMaster` Scala actor.
2. If there is no associated `LiftSession` in the SessionMaster actor, create it, and add a `SessionToServletBridge` attribute on HttpSession. This will make Lift aware of the session when the container terminates the HttpSession or when the HTTP session is about to be made passive or activated.
3. When the container terminates the HTTP session, `SessionToServletBridge` sends a message to the `SessionMaster` actor to terminate the `LiftSession`, which includes the following steps:
   - Call any defined LiftSession.onAboutToShutdownSession hooks.
   - Send a ShutDown message to all Comet actors pertaining to this session.
   - Clean up any internal LiftSession state.
   - Call LiftSession.onShutdownSession hooks.

The `SessionMaster` actor is also protected by another watcher actor. This watcher Actor receives the `Exit` messages of the watched actors. When it receives an `Exit` message, it will call the users' failure functions and restart the watched actor (see the `ActorWatcher.failureFuncs` function documentation for more details).

Even while Lift is handling session management, you still have the ability to manually add attributes to the `HttpSession` object. We do not recommend this unless you really must. A simpler way to keep your own session variables is to use `SessionVars`. For more details about `SessionVar`, please see Chapter 3.

Using Sticky Sessions

You are probably asking, "So we have internal session management, how do we cope with that in a clustered environment? And how are sessions replicated?" The answer is, "They aren't."

There is no intention to use the web container's session replication, as these technologies appear to be inferior to other solutions on the market. Relying on Java serialization brings a lot of performance concerns, and alternative technologies have been investigated, and they are still under investigation.

Until there is a standard session replication technology, you can still cluster you application using a sticky session. This means that all requests pertaining to a HTTP session must be processed by the same cluster node. This processing can be done by software or hardware load balancers, as they would dispatch the requests based on `JSESSIONID` cookie. Another approach is to do the dispatching based on a URI or on query parameters. For example, a query parameter like `serverid=1` is configured in the load balancer to always be dispatched to the node 1 of the cluster, and so on.

The sticky session approach does have some drawbacks. For instance, assumed you are logged into the application, and you do your stuff. Suddenly, the node designated to your session crashes. At this moment, you lost your session. The next request would be automatically dispatched by the load balancer to another cluster node, and depending how your application is built, this may mean that you need to log in again. Then again, if part of the state was persisted in the database, you may resume your work from some point and avoid logging in. But whether you need to log in again is determined by application-specific behavior that is beyond the scope of this discussion.

The advantages of sticky sessions are related to application performance, since in this model, the state does not need to be replicated in all cluster nodes which for significant state information can be quite time/resources consuming.

Using Lift's Garbage Collection

As you have seen, Lift tailors Scala functions with client-side artifacts (XHTML input elements, AJAX requests, etc.). Naturally, these functions are kept into the session state. Also, for every rendered page, a page ID is generated, and functions bound for these pages are associated with this page ID. To prevent accumulation of such mappings, Lift has a mechanism of purging unused functions. Basically the idea is as follows:

- On the client side, a script periodically sends to the server an AJAX request impersonating a lift garbage collection request.
- On the server side, Lift updates the timestamps of the functions associated with this page ID. The functions older than `LiftRules.unusedFunctionsLifeTime` (default value is 10 minutes) become eligible for garbage collection as they are dereferenced from the current session. The frequency of such AJAX requests is given by `LiftRules.liftGCPollingInterval`, which by default is set to 75 seconds.
- Each AJAX request includes the page ID, as new functions may be bound as a result of processing the AJAX request, depending on the application code. Such functions that are dynamically bound are automatically associated with the same page ID.

You can, of course, turn off this garbage collection mechanism by setting `LiftRules.enableLiftGC = false` typically in your `Boot`. You can also fine-tune the garbage collection mechanisms to fit your application needs, by changing the default `LiftRules` variables, shown in Listing 7-7.

Listing 7-7. LiftRules Garbage Collection Variables

```
/**
 * By default lift uses a garbage-collection mechanism of
 * removing unused bound functions from LiftSesssion
 * Setting this to false will disable this mechanims and
 * there will be no Ajax polling request attempted.
 */
var enableLiftGC = true;


/**
 * If Lift garbage collection is enabled, functions that
 * are not seen in the page for this period of time
 * (given in milliseonds) will be discarded, hence
 * eligible for garbage collection.
 * The default value is 10 minutes.
 */
var unusedFunctionsLifeTime: Long = 10 minutes


/**
 * The polling interval for background Ajax requests to
 * prevent functions of being garbage collected.
 * Default value is set to 75 seconds.
 */
var liftGCPollingInterval: Long = 75 seconds

/**
 * The polling interval for background Ajax requests to
 * prevent functions of being garbage collected.
 * This will be applied if the Ajax request will fail.
 * Default value is set to 15 seconds.
 */
var liftGCFailureRetryTimeout: Long = 15 seconds
```

Wrapping Lift's Processing Logic

Lift provides the ability to allow user functions to be part of processing life cycle. In these cases, Lift allows you to provide your own functions, and the actual Lift's processing function is passed to your function—your own function is responsible for calling the Lift processing logic. Let's look at how exactly you can do this in Listing 7-8.

Listing 7-8. LoanWrapper Example

```
... standard Lift imports...
class Boot {

  def boot {
    ...
    S.addAround(new LoanWrapper { // Y
      def apply[T](f: => T): T = {
        println("Y -> hello to the request!")
   // Let Lift do normal request processing.
        val result = f
     println("Y -> goodbye!")
        result
      }
    })

    S.addAround(new LoanWrapper { // X
      def apply[T](f: => T): T = {
        println("X -> hello to the request!")
   // Let Lift do normal request processing.
        val result = f
        println("X -> goodbye!")
        result
      }
    })
 }
```

The code is pretty straightforward in the sense that we add two `LoanWrapper` instances to the `S` object. (Note that we're using the `S` object, not `LiftRules`, meaning that `LoanWrappers` are applicable only for stateful processing. See the "Understanding the Request/Response Life Cycle" section for when, exactly, `LoanWrappers` are invoked.)

Now, let's see what happens when the preceding code processes a request from a client. You can think of the invocation sequence as `X(Y(f))`, where `f` is the Lift function that impersonates the core processing. Therefore, you'll see the following output in the console:

```
X -> hello to the request!
Y -> hello to the request!
<Lift's logic ... whatever is printed here>
Y -> goodbye!
X -> goodbye!
```

This feature allows you use a resource before Lift does and release them after Lift has finished processing the stateful request and before the `LiftResponse` object is constructed.

Using Additional Snippet Features

By now, you should have a fairly good idea of how snippets work and how you can use them. There are a few things that we haven't covered yet, including how to access query parameters directly, and how to use snippets to calculate attribute values.

Passing Parameters to Snippets

For example, let's say we wanted to control the number of `Expense` entries shown in our Account detail page. We would add a `count` attribute to the tag, as shown in Listing 7-9.

Listing 7-9. Snippet Markup Attributes

```
<lift:Accounts.detail count="10">

  ...
</lift:Accounts.detail>
```

But how do we read the *default* attribute from the snippet code? Actually, it's as simple as calling the `S.attr` function, as shown in Listing 7-10.

Listing 7-10. Snippet Code Attributes

```
class Accounts {
  ...
  def detail (xhtml : NodeSeq ) : NodeSeq = {

    val count =
      S.attr("default").map(_.toInt) openOr Integer.MAX_VALUE
    ...
    entries = Expense.findAll(...).take(count)
    ...
  }
}
```

Using Snippets for Tag Attributes

You can use snippets to calculate the attributes for a given tag, just like you can use them to calculate tag contents. An example is shown in Listing 7-11.

Listing 7-11. Snippet Tag Attributes

```
// In your page you can have
<div lift:snippet="MyDivThing:calcDir"> ... </div>
...
// Your snippet
class MyDivThing {
  def calcDir = new UnprefixedAttribute("dir",
    "rtl", Null)
}
```

The utility of this support is quite obvious in many situations. For instance, when supporting right-to-left languages, you can set the direction of the page to be `rtl` quite easily.

You have seen how we can pass XML parameters to snippets, but what if we want to pass parameters to the nodes that will be bound? For instance, in our expense entry table (`/src/main/webapp/templates-hidden/entry_table.html`), we might want to pass an `ampm` attribute like this:

```
<entry:date ampm="true"/>
```

where the time will be displayed in 12-hour format, as opposed to 24-hour format. But how can we access the `ampm` parameter? Listing 7-12 shows how.

Listing 7-12. Snippet Content Attributes

```
class Account {
  val ampmFormat : DateFormat = ...
  val 24hFormat : DateFormat = ...
  ...
  def expenseTable (...) : NodeSeq = {
    ...
    bind ("entry", chooseTemplate(...), ...,
          "date" -> {node: NodeSeq =>

// Select the formatter based on the attr presence
            val dateFormatter =
              BindHelpers.attr("ampm").map(ignore =>
                ampmFormat).get(24hFormat)
            Text(dateFormatter.format(entry.dateOf.is))}
  }
}
```

The key aspect here is the `BindHelpers` object. You can use it for obtaining information about node attributes. This context is maintained internally using `ThreadLocals` and closures. Note that the context is cleared after the `bind` method is executed. In our example, for the time node, we are actually binding a function that takes the child nodes of the `<ledger:time>` node. When our function is called by Lift, we can access the `BindHelpers`, such as the attributes of the current node. The sequence `<string> -> <right-hand-side-expression>` is turned into a `BindParam` object using implicit conversions. It is important to note that `BindParam.calcValue` function is called in the correct context so that `BindHelpers` can be safely used.

It is sometimes more convenient to just put node attributes in the markup and not worry about them in the Scala code. Consider the example in Listing 7-13, from our `index.html` page, where we set attributes for our date entry form field.

Listing 7-13. Snippet Mix-in Attributes

```
<lift:surround with="default" at="content">
...
<tr>
  <td><e:account /></td>
  <td><e:dateOf e:id="entrydate" e:maxlength="10"/></td>
...
</lift:surround>
```

In this example, we prefix the `id` attribute for the `dateOf` node. Lift will automatically add the attributes prefixed with the same node prefix (e, in this case) to the resulting bind element for `dateOf`. Therefore, the resulting node will be something like the following:

```
<input ... id="entrydate" maxlength="10" />
```

Working with Advanced S Object Features

The `S`, or stateful, object is a very important part of Lift. The `S` context is created when a client request is received that needs to be handled as a stateful request. Please see the "Understanding the Request/Response Life Cycle" section for more details on the state creation and handling. The actual state information is kept inside the `S` object using `java.lang.ThreadLocal` variables, since `S` is a singleton. This means that if you have any code that is executed in the stateful context, you can safely use any `S` object goodies, which include cookies, localized text, time and locale information, dispatch functions, HTTP request headers, response document type, and others.

Managing Cookies

You can retrieve cookies from the request or set cookies to be sent in the response. Cookies are covered in Chapter 3.

Localization (also called L10N) and internationalization (also called I18N) are very important aspects of many web applications that deal with different languages. These topics are covered in Appendix D.

Managing the Time Zone

The S.timeZone function returns the current time zone as computed by the LiftRules.timeZoneCalculator function. By default, the LiftRules method simply executes TimeZone.getDefault, but you can provide your own Box[HttpServletRequest]=> TimeZone partial function to define your own behavior. Examples would include allowing users to choose their own time zones or to use geographic lookup of the user's IP address.

Setting Session DispatchPF Functions

You can set DispatchPF functions that operate in the context of a current session. Essentially, you can bind DispatchPF functions with a given name. Relevant functions follow:

- S.highLevelSessionDispatcher returns a List[LiftRules.DispatchPF].
- S.highLevelSessionDispatchList returns a List[DispatchHolder].
- S.addHighLevelSessionDispatcher maps a name with a given DispatchPF.
- S.removeHighLevelSessionDispatcher removes the DispatchPF given its name.
- S.clearHighLevelSessionDispatcher removes all DispatchPF associations.

Rewriting Sessions

Session rewriters allow you to modify an HTTP request (URI, query parameters, etc.) before the request is actually processed. This is similar with LiftRules.rewrite variable, but here, you can apply rewriters for a given session. Hence, you can have different rewrites in different contexts. The relevant functions follow:

- S.sessionRewriter returns a List[RewriteHolder].
- S.addSessionRewriter maps a LiftRules.RewritePF with a given name.
- S.removeSessionRewriter removes a rewriter by a name.
- S.clearSessionRewriter removes all session rewriters.

Accessing HTTP Headers

Accessing HTTP header parameters from the request and adding HTTP header parameters to the HTTP response are very common operations. You can easily perform these operations using the following functions:

- S.getHeaders returns a List[(String, String)] containing all HTTP headers grouped by name and value pair.

- `S.setHeader` sets a HTTP header parameter by specifying the name and value pair.

Managing the Document Type

You can also read and write the XML document type set for the current response. You can use the following functions:

- `S.getDocType` returns the document type that was set for the current response.
- `S.setDocType` sets a document type for the current response object.

Performing Other Functions

Besides the aspects we've just mentioned, `S` allows you to do the following, though we won't cover this functionality in detail here:

- Access the raw `HttpServletRequest` and `HttpSession` if you really need them.
- Manage the function map. The function map generates an association between a string and a function. This string represents a query parameter that will cause Lift to execute your function, if it's received with a HTTP request. Normally, function names are automatically generated by Lift, but you can also provide you own. Please see the "Mapping Lift Functions" section for more details.
- Manage wrappers as explained in the "Wrapping Lift's Processing Logic" section.
- Manage notices as explained in Appendix B.
- Manage HTTP redirects, as explained in the `S.redirectTo` functions and the "Exploring LiftResponse in Detail" section in Chapter 3.
- Use the XML attributes of a snippet, as explained in the "Using Additional Snippet Features" section.

Managing Resources with ResourceServer

`ResourceServer` is a Lift component that manages resources like JavaScript and CSS. Although the web container can manage file resources, it does not serve these resources if they are inside JAR files. The default URI path for serving such resources is given by the `LiftRules.resourceServerPath` variable, which, by default, is set to `classpath`. The resource's folder location inside JAR files is given by the `ResourceServer.baseResourceLocation` variable, which, by default, is set to `toserve`. Let's assume the following folder structure inside you Lift project:

```
lift-proj/src/main/resources/toserve/css/mystyle.css
```

Maven will create the toserve folder in the WAR file generated. Then, in your web page, you add something like this:

```
<link rel="stylesheet" href="/classpath/css/mystyle.css"
type="text/css"/>
```

Because the first URI part matches with LiftRules.resourceServerPath, Lift will tell ResouceServer to load this resource from toserve folder. But it will fail, because there is one thing left to do. We need to tell ResourceServer to allow the loading of mystyle.css resource. We can do this from Boot by calling the following:

```
ResourceServer.allow {
  case "css" :: _ => true
}
```

We're basically telling Lift to allow any resource found in css folder under toserve. Note that toserve comes from ResourceServer.baseResourceLocation, which can be changed.

Obtaining HTTP Authentication

HTTP authentication is described by RFC-2617 (see http://www.isi.edu/in-notes/rfc2617.txt for the exact specification), which outlines the means of protecting server resources and allowing access only to authorized entities. As you may know, any Java EE web container provides HTTP authentication support mostly using the Java Authentication and Authorization Service (JAAS). You can read more about JAAS at http://java.sun.com/javase/6/docs/technotes/guides/security/jaas/JAASRefGuide.html. But this approach is not without caveats. For instance, if you provide a LoginModule or CallbackHandler implementation, it will not be loaded by the web application class loader but instead by the container class loader (at least in Tomcat). In this case, if your code has other dependencies, you cannot use these dependencies from your web application, since the web application sits below container's class loader in the delegation chain. Therefore using Scala's power, the developer experience of protecting server resources using HTTP authentication can be simplified a lot compared with having to manage the requisite HTTP headers and responses yourself. Lift supports both basic and digest authentication.

Using Basic HTTP Authentication

One of the simplest forms of HTTP authentication is basic authentication. With this mechanism, a simple username and password in the HTTP request for pages that indicate that they require authentication. Listing 7-14 demonstrates a simple authentication setup.

Listing 7-14. Authentication Example

```
import auth._
class Boot {
  def boot = {
    ...
    LiftRules. httpAuthProtectedResource.append {
      case (ParsePath("users" :: _, _, _, _)) =>
           Full(AuthRole("admin"))
    }
    LiftRules.authentication =
 HttpBasicAuthentication("lift") {

      case ("John", "12test34", req) =>
        println("John is authenticated!")
        userRoles(AuthRole("admin"))
        true
    }
   ...
  }
```

We just told Lift that the /users path is a protected resource and is accessible only by users that have the role admin. Here, we have both authentication and authorization. If this function returns an empty box, this resource is not bound to any role and only authentication, not authorization, will be performed.

Second, using LiftRules.authentication, we told Lift that we want BasicAuthentication, and of course, we are passing the function that actually does the authentication. This function is actually PartialFunction[(String, String, Req), Boolean]. The members of the tuple are the username, password, and the Req object. In Listing 7-14, we're basically saying that if user is authenticating himself as "John" and password is "12test34", the access to the protected resource will be granted (since our function returns true). But in our authentication function, we also specify the role for user "John" as being admin. userRole is a RequestVar that will be used later on by Lift.

At runtime, when the user tries to access /users, Lift knows that this is a protected resource and only an admin can access it. Therefore, Lift sends the client a 401 HTTP status (Unauthorized Response). The user will enter the credentials, and if they match with username "John" and password "12test34", we got a successful authentication, and because the role we set is admin, which matches with the role assigned to the protected resource, the /users resource is served to client.

A role is an n-ary tree structure, so when we assign a role to an httpAuthProtectedResource, we can actually provide an entire tree such as the one shown in Figure 7-2.

Figure 7-2. Roles Hierarchy Example

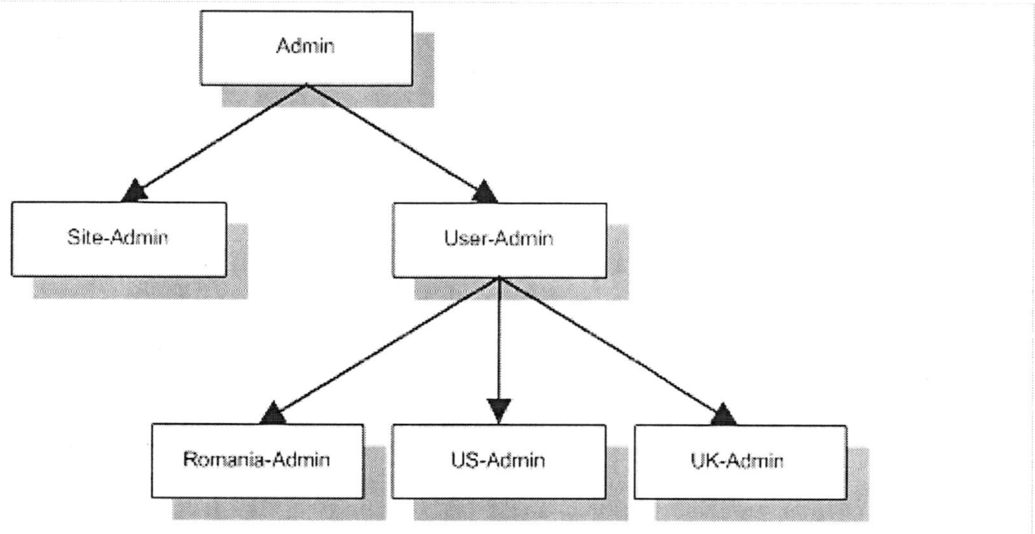

Assume that your application uses a roles structure like the one shown in Figure 7-2. The `Admin` is the all-mighty role for administrators: `Admin` can do what any subrole can do and more. Next, we have the `Site-Admin` to monitor the application and the `User-Admin` to manage user. After that, the `Romania-Admin` can manage users from Romania, `US-Admin` can manage users from the United States, and `UK-Admin` can manage users from the United Kingdom.

Now, a `User-Admin` can manage users from anywhere, but a `Site-Admin` cannot manage any users. A `Romania-Admin` has neither the privileges of `User-Admin` nor `Admin`, nor can it manage the United States or United Kingdom users. You got the picture here—the lower a role is in the hierarchy, the less privileged it is. Listing 7-15 shows the code based on Figure 7-2.

Listing 7-15. Authentication Example with Multiple Roles

```
import auth._

class Boot {

  def boot = {

    ...

val roles = AuthRole("Admin",
                                    AuthRole("Site-Admin"),
                                        AuthRole("User-Admin",
                                           AuthRole("Romania-Admin"),
                                           AuthRole("US-Admin"),
```

```
                                    AuthRole("UK-Admin")
                                  )
                                )

      LiftRules.protectedResource.append {
        case (ParsePath("users" :: _, _, _, _)) =>
               roles.getRoleByName("Romania-Admin")
      }

      LiftRules.authentication =
        HttpBasicAuthentication("lift") {
        // Normally you fetch the user's information form a data-base system.
        case ("John", "12test34", req) =>
   println("John is authenticated !")
                                   userRoles(AuthRole("User-Admin"))
                             true
      }
     ...
    }
  }
```

In this case, if a user is authenticated, authorization will also succeed, because the user's role is `User-Admin`, which is a parent of `Romania-Admin`. If the `/users` resource had been assigned with the `User-Admin` role and user John had the `Romania-Admin` role, even if credentials are correct, the authorization fails, and a 401 HTTP status is sent to client.

In conclusion, you have a simple authentication and authorization mechanism in Listing 7-15, and of course, the authentication function would typically validate the credentials against a database and fetch the roles from there. In Listing 7-15, we did not actually fetch the user information from the database to keep the example simple.

Using HTTP Digest Authentication

So far, we talked about basic authentication and authorization. Lift also support HTTP digest authentication, in which the password information that user enters in the browser is never propagated on the server. Listing 7-16 shows how we use it.

Listing 7-16. Digest Authentication with Multiple Roles

```
import auth._

class Boot {

  def boot = {
    ...

    val roles = AuthRole("Admin",
                         AuthRole("Site-Admin"),
                           AuthRole("User-Admin",
                              AuthRole("Romania-Admin"),
                              AuthRole("US-Admin"),
                              AuthRole("UK-Admin")
                           )
                         )

    LiftRules.protectedResource.append {
      case (ParsePath("users" :: _, _, _, _)) =>
             roles.getRoleByName("Romania-Admin")
    }

    LiftRules.authentication =
      HttpDigestAuthentication("lift") {

      case ("John", req, func) => if (func("12test34")) {
        println("John is authenticated !")
        userRoles(AuthRole("useradmin"))
        true
      } else {
        println("Not verified")
        false
      }
    }
   ...
  }
}
```

Everything we talked about concerning roles is still valid. However, we're now using digest authentication. Note that, in this case, the client did no provide the actual password, but our function is provided with the user name, the Req object, and a callback function. Because digest authentication implies check sum calculations, there is no need to burden the user with such things. However, our code calls this callback function by providing the password (which can be retrieved from database, because we know the user name). If this function returns true, the digest that client sent and the one that Lift calculated match, and we have a successful authentication.

It is also important to know that the digest authentication mechanism uses a nonce sequence. This sequence is generated by the server when sending the client the authentication challenge (401 HTTP status). To avoid replay attacks, this nonce is valid only for a period of time, by default, 30 seconds. You can change this default by overriding the following:

```
override def HttpDigestAuthentication.nonceValidityPeriod =
  <a value in milliseconds>
```

If you use Lift's TimeHelpers to override, you do so as follows:

```
override def HttpDigestAuthentication.nonceValidityPeriod = 50 seconds
// where seconds is a function and there are implicit conversion functions
// from "primitives" to TimeSpans type.
```

If this period expires, even if the authentication and authorization succeed, Lift will challenge the authentication again by returning 401 HTTP status and a new nonce and will not serve the resource until authentication is accomplished.

It is important to know that a user can be assigned multiple roles, not just one. This can be done by calling

```
userRoles(AuthRole("US-Admin", "Site-Admin"))
// AuthRole overloaded apply function takes a repeated
// parameter.
```

This is pretty much it as far as HTTP authentication and authorization go, but one more thing is worth mentioning. If your application does not persist the user's password and instead persists only an internally calculated digest, you should not use HTTP digest authentication. The reason is that in order to match the client's digest, the server needs to calculate it, and for that calculation, it needs the password. However, because the application stores a digest, the user's password cannot be recovered, and the HTTP digest cannot be calculated. This is a mismatch between the two concepts: HTTP digest authentication given by RFC-2617 and the unrecoverable password storage.

Conclusion

We hope that, by reading this chapter, you've gained insight into some of the advanced functionality of Lift, particularly the low-level hooks that you can use to fine-tune Lift's behavior when servicing requests. We've shown how you can further customize your templates using snippet-calculated attributes as well as prefixed attributes that reduce or eliminate the need to put markup in your code. Finally, we've shown how you can serve up your own internal resources and protect your application with standard authentication techniques.

Chapter 8: Lift and JavaScript

In this chapter, we'll be discussing some of the techniques that Lift provides for simplifying and abstracting access to JavaScript on the client side. Using these facilities follows Lift's model of separating code from presentation by allowing you to essentially write JavaScript code in Scala. Lift also provides a layer that allows you to use advanced JavaScript functionality via either the jQuery (`http://jquery.com/`) or YUI (`http://developer.yahoo.com/yui/`) user interface libraries.

Using High-Level JavaScript Abstractions

You may have noticed that Lift already comes with rich client side functionality in the form of AJAX and COMET support (see Chapter 9). Whenever you use this support, Lift automatically generates the proper `<script>` elements in the returned page so that the libraries are included. Lift goes one step further, however, by providing a class hierarchy representing JavaScript expressions. For example, with an AJAX form element in Lift, the callback method must return JavaScript code to update the client side. Instead of just returning a raw JavaScript string to be interpreted by the client, you return an instance of the `net.liftweb.http.js.JsCmd` trait (either directly or via implicit conversion) that is transformed into the proper JavaScript for the client.

`JsCmd` represents a JavaScript command that can be executed on the client. There is an additional base trait called `JsExp` that represents a JavaScript expression. The differences between them are not usually important to the developer, since a `JsExp` instance is implicitly converted to a `JsCmd` one. Also note that, while Lift's JavaScript classes attempt to keep things type-safe, there are some limitations; in particular, Lift can't check semantic things like whether the variable you're trying to access from a given `JsCmd` actually exists. Besides the obvious use in techniques like AJAX and COMET, Lift also makes it simple to attach JavaScript to regular Scala XML objects, such as form fields.

As a simple example, let's look at how we might add a simple alert to a form if it doesn't validate. In this example, we'll assume we have a `name` form field that shouldn't be blank. Listing 8-1 shows a possible binding from our form snippet.

Let's break this down a bit. First, when you reference form elements (or any elements for that matter) from JavaScript, each of those elements needs to have an `id` attribute. We add the `id` attribute to our text field by passing a `Pair[String,String]`. Next, we need to define our actual validation. We do this by adding some JavaScript code to the `onclick` attribute of our submit button. The `onclick` attribute evaluates whatever JavaScript code is assigned when the button is clicked; if the JavaScript code evaluates to `true`, submission continues. If it evaluates to `false`, submission is aborted. In our case, we use the `JsIf` case class to check to see if the value of our `myName` field is equal to an empty string. In this case the `JE` object holds an implicit conversion from a Scala String to a Str (JavaScript string) instance. The second argument to JsIf is the body to be executed if the condition is true. In our case, we want an alert to pop up for the user and stop form submission. The JsCmd trait (which Alert mixes in) provides a & operator, which allows you to chain multiple commands together. Here, we follow the Alert with JsReturn, which returns the specified value; again, there's an implicit conversion from Boolean to JsExp, so we can simply provide the false value.

Listing 8-1. Simple Form Validation

```
import JsCmds._

import JE._

var myName = ""

bind(...

  "name" -> SHtml.text(myName, myName = _, "id" -> "myName"
  "submit" -> SHtml.submit("Save", ..., "onclick" ->

    JsIf(JsEq(ValById("myName"), ""),

      Alert("You must provide a name") &
      JsReturn(false))

    )

)
```

Understanding JsCmd and JsExp

If you peruse the Lift API documentation, you'll find a large number of traits and classes under the JsCmds and JE objects; these provide the vast majority of the functionality you would need to write simple JavaScript code directly in Lift. Having said that, however, it's important to realize that the Lift classes are intended to be used for small code fragments. If you need to write large portions of JavaScript code for your pages, we recommend writing that code in pure JavaScript in an external file and including that file in your pages. In particular, if you write your code as JavaScript functions, you can use the JE.Call class to execute those functions from your Lift code. Table 8-1 gives a brief overview of the available JsCmds, while Table 8-2 shows the JE expression abstractions.

Table 8-1. Basic JsCmd Commands

COMMAND	DESCRIPTION
`After`	Executes the given `JsCmd` fragment after a given amount of time
`Alert`	Corresponds directly to the JavaScript `alert` function
`CmdPair`	Executes two `JsCmd` fragments in order
`FocusOnLoad`	Forces focus on the given XML element when the document loads
`Function`	Defines a JavaScript function with name, parameter list, and `JsCmd` body
`JsBreak`, `JsContinue`, and `JsReturn`	Corresponds directly to the JavaScript `break`, `continue`, and `return` keywords
`JsFor`, `JsForIn`, `JsDoWhile`, and `JsWhile`	These define loop constructs in JavaScript with conditions and execution bodies
`JsHideId` and `JsShowId`	Hides or shows the HTML element with the given `id` and is actually handled via the `LiftArtifacts`' hide and show methods
`JsIf`	Corresponds to the JavaScript `if` statement, with a condition, body to execute if the condition is true, and optional `else` body statement
`JsTry`	Defines a `try/catch` block that can optionally alert if an exception is caught
`JsWith`	Defines a `with` statement to reduce object references
`OnLoad`	Defines a JavaScript statement that is executed on page load
`Noop`	Defines an empty JavaScript statement
`RedirectTo`	Uses `window.location` to redirect to a new page
`ReplaceOptions`	Replaces options on a form `Select` with a new list of options

Table 8-1 (Continued)

COMMAND	DESCRIPTION
`Run`	Executes the given string as raw JavaScript code
`Script`	Defines a `<script>` element with proper CDATA escaping to conform to XHTML JavaScript support
`SetElemById`	Assigns a value returned by the given expression to a given element by `id` and specifies properties on the element using optional parameters
`SetExp`	Defines an assignment to an arbitrary JavaScript expression from another JavaScript expression
`SetHtml`	Sets the contents of a given HTML node by `id` to a given `NodeSeq` and is especially useful in AJAX calls that update parts of the page
`SetValById`	Defines an assignment to a given element's `value` property

Table 8-2. Basic JE Abstractions

EXPRESSION	DESCRIPTION
`AnonFunc`	Defines an anonymous JavaScript function
`Call`	Calls a JavaScript function by name, with parameters
`ElemById`	Obtains a DOM element by its `id`, with optional property access
`FormToJson`	Converts a given form (by `id`) into a JSON representation
`Id`, `Style`, and `Value`	Represents the `id`, `style`, and `value` element attributes
`JsArray`	Constructs a JavaScript array from a given set of JavaScript expressions

Table 8-2 (Continued)

Expression	Description
JsEq, JsNotEq, JsGt, JsGtEq, JsLt, and JsLtEq	Comparison tests two JavaScript expressions (JsExp instances also have a === operator which is equivalent to JsEq.)
JsTrue, JsFalse, and JsNull	Represents the true, false, and null values
JsFunc	Similar to Call and executes a JavaScript function
JsObj	Represents a JavaScript object with a Map for properties
JsRaw	Represents a raw JavaScript fragment and can be used if Lift doesn't provide functionality via abstractions
JsVal	Represents an abritrary JavaScript value
JsVar	Represents a JavaScript variable, with optional property access
Num	Represents a JavaScript number; JE object contains implicit conversions from Scala numeric types to Num
Str	Represents a Javascript String; JE object contains implicit conversions from a Scala String to Str
Stringify	Calls JSON.stringify to convert a JavaScript object into a JSON string representation
ValById	Represents the value property of a given element by id

Exploring JavaScript Abstraction Examples

As you can see, Lift provides a large coverage of JavaScript functionality through its abstraction layer. Even if you've written a lot of JavaScript code, the abstractions don't always map one-to-one, and it can take some effort to wrap your head around this situation. We're going to provide a few examples to help you understand how it works. We'll start off with a simple example of an AJAX callback (AJAX is covered in Chapter 9). Listing 8-2 shows how we can update an HTML element with new content via the AJAX call. In this case, we're changing a chart image based on some passed parameters. Our HTML needs to contain an element with an id of expense_graph; this element will have its children replaced with whatever NodeSeq we pass as the second argument.

Listing 8-2. Using SetHtml

```
def updateGraph() = {
  // vals acctName and graphType are named elsewhere.
  val dateClause : String = ...

  val url = "/graph/" + acctName + "/" + graphType + dateClause

  JsCmds.SetHtml("expense_graph", <img src={url} />)

}
```

As a more complex example, we could add some JavaScript behavior combining AJAX with some client-side state, as shown in Listing 8-3.

Listing 8-3. Client-Side Comparisons

```
import js.JE._ // for implicit conversions

def moreComplexCallback(value : String) = {

  JsIf(ValById("username") === value.toLowerCase, {

    JsFunc("logAccess", "Self-share attempted").cmd &
    Alert("You can't share with yourself!")

  })

}
```

Using jQuery and Other JavaScript Frameworks

We mentioned earlier that Lift uses the jQuery JavaScript framework by default. Lift wouldn't be Lift, however, if it didn't provide a mechanism for using other frameworks. The way that lift determines which JavaScript framework to use is via thenet.liftweb.http.js.JSArtifacts trait along with the LiftRules.jsArtifacts var. Lift comes with two default implementations of JSArtifacts: net.liftweb.http.js.jquery.JQueryArtifacts and net.liftweb.http.js.yui.YUIArtifacts.

If you want to use a different framework, you must provide a concrete implementation of the JSArtifacts trait specific to that framework. The jQuery support in Lift extends beyond just the JSArtifacts support; there are also a number of JSExp and JsCmd traits and classes in the net.liftweb.http.js.jquery package that provide jQuery-specific implementations for standard expressions and commands.

Changing one implementation or another can be done from LiftRules.jsArtifacts variable, which by default points to JQueryArtifacts. Typically, this is done in Boot, as shown in Listing 8-4.

Listing 8-4. Configuring Lift YUI

```
import net.liftweb.http.js.yui.YUIArtifacts


class Boot {

  def boot = {
    ...
    LiftRules.jsArtifacts = YUIArtifacts
    ...
  }
 }
```

In addition to changing LiftRules, you also need to take into account that other frameworks have their own scripts and dependencies that you'll need to include in your pages. For YUI, you would need to include (at minimum) the scripts in Listing 8-5.

Listing 8-5. Lift YUI Scripts

```
<script src="/classpath/yui/yahoo.js"
  type="text/javascript"/>

<script src="/classpath/yui/event.js"
  type="text/javascript"/>

<script src="/classpath/yui/dom.js"
  type="text/javascript"/>

<script src="/classpath/yui/connection.js"
  type="text/javascript"/>

<script src="/classpath/yui/json.js"
  type="text/javascript"/>

<script src="/classpath/liftYUI.js"
  type="text/javascript"/>
```

Of course, to keep things simple, you could either place all of these items in a template that you could embed, or you could combine the files into a single JavaScript source file.

We have some simple recommendations on using different JavaScript frameworks from within Lift:

- If you don't necessarily need YUI widgets or if you can find similar functionality in jQuery plug-ins, we recommend using the jQuery framework and its plug-ins. Lift provides much better support out of the box for jQuery, as there are plenty of helper objects and functions around jQuery functionality.
- Do not mix jQuery and YUI unless you really know what you are doing, as getting both of them together leads to a number of collisions.

Using XML and JavaScript

What we've covered so far is pretty much standard JavaScript behind some Lift facades. There are situations, however, when you want to do things that are complicated or outside the scope of typical JavaScript functionality. For example, you might need to build dynamic DOM elements from JavaScript code, say to build an HTML list. Lift has a very nice way of dealing with such situation in just a few lines of code. The main functionality for this is provided via the `Jx*` classes, like `net.liftweb.http.js.Jx`, which you can use to transform a `scala.xml.NodeSeq` into JavaScript code that generates the corresponding nodes on the client side. Listing 8-6 shows a simple example of emitting a `<div>` on a page via JavaScript.

Listing 8-6. A Trivial Jx Example

```
import net.liftweb.http.js._

import JE._


val div = Jx(<div>Hi there</div>)
```

This code generates the JavaScript code shown in Listing 8-7.

Listing 8-7. Emitted Jx Code

```
function(it) {

  var df = document.createDocumentFragment();

  var vINIJ1YTZG5 = document.createElement('div');

  df.appendChild(vINIJ1YTZG5);
```

```
    vINIJ1YTZG5.appendChild( document.createTextNode('Hi there'));

    return df;

}
```

As you can see, Lift took our XML code and transformed it into a JavaScript function that dynamically creates a document fragment containing the given `NodeSeq`. The `it` parameter can be any JavaScript object; we'll cover how you use it in a moment. The name of the `var` is automatically and randomly generated to ensure uniqueness.

Of course, if that was all Lift was doing that's not much help. At this point, we've only generated a function that generates XML. Let's take a look on a more complex example that shows the real power of the `Jx` classes. Assume we have a JavaScript Object Notation (JSON) structure that contains an array of objects containing `firstName` and `lastName` properties. This JSON structure could look something like Listing 8-8.

Listing 8-8. Sample JSON Structure

```
var  list = {

    persons: [

      {name: "Thor", race: "Asgard"},

      {name: "Todd", race: "Wraith"},

      {name: "Rodney", race: "Human"}

    ]

}


// Guess what I've been watching lately ?
```

Now we can use a combination of `Jx` classes to render this content as an HTML dynamic list, as shown in Listing 8-9.

Listing 8-9. Rendering a JSON List via Jx

```
def renderPerson =
   Jx(<li class="item_header"> {JsVar("it", "name")}  is {JsVar("it",
"race")}</li>)

  Jx(<ul>{JxMap(JsVar("it.persons"), renderPerson)}</ul>)
```

This code does the following:

1. Construct an `<ul>` list that contains a collection of elements.

2. `JxMap` takes a JavaScript object, in this case `it.persons` (remember `it` is the parameter of the generated function), iterates for each element of the array, and applies the `renderPerson` function. Of course, each element of the array will be a JSON object containing name and race properties.

3. The `renderPerson` function generates a JavaScript function as we've already shown and renders the JavaScript code that generates the `<li>` elements containing the name value followed by `is` followed by the race value.

4. If we send this generated JavaScript function to client and call it by passing the list variable from step 3, the function will create the following document fragment:

```
<ul>
 <li class="item_header">Thor is Asgard</li>
 <li class="item_header">Todd is Wraith</li>
 <li class="item_header">Rodney is Human</li>
</ul>
```

With a couple of lines of code, we've managed to generate the JavaScript code that creates document fragments dynamically.

Table 8-3 describes `Jx` classes that you may find interesting.

Table 8-3. Jx-Related Classes

CLASS	DESCRIPTION
`JxBase`	The parent trait for all other `Jx` classes
`JxMap`	Iterates over a JavaScript array and applies a function on each element
`JxMatch`	Match a `JsExp` against a sequence of `JsCase`
`JxCase`	Contains a `JsExp` for matching purposes and the `NodeSeq` to be applied in case the matching succeeds
`JxIf`	Contains a `JsExp` and a `NodeSeq` to be applied only if `JsExp` is evaluated to `true`
`JxIfElse`	Similar with `JxIf` but it contains the `else` branch
`Jx`	The basic application of the transformation from a `NodeSeq` to the JavaScript code

Using JSON

JSON (`http://www.json.org`) is a way of structuring information in JavaScript code. One of its most common uses is to represent structured information on the wire, for example, a JavaScript AJAX API where the server response is in fact a JSON construct. Let's look at an example in Listing 8-10.

Listing 8-10. An AJAX JSON Response

```
class SimpleSnippet {

  def ajaxFunc() : JsCmd = {

   JsCrVar("myObject", JsObj(("persons", JsArray(
                JsObj(("name", "Thor"), ("race", "Asgard")),
                JsObj(("name", "Todd"), ("race", "Wraith")),
                JsObj(("name", "Rodney"), ("race", "Human"))
)))) & JsRaw("alert(myObject.persons[0].name)")

  }
```

```
  def renderAjaxButton(xhtml: NodeSeq): NodeSeq = {

    bind("ex", xhtml,
      "button" ->
        SHtml.ajaxButton(Text("Press me"), ajaxFunc _))
  }
}
```

Your template would look like Listing 8-11.

Listing 8-11. AJAX Template

```
    ...


<lift:SimpleSnippet.renderAjaxButton>

         <ex:button/>

</lift:SimpleSnippet.renderAjaxButton>


...
```

First, we have a simple snippet function called `renderAjaxButton`, where we're binding the `<ex:button/>` tag and rendering a XHTML button tag that, when clicked, will send an AJAX request to server. When this request is received, the `ajaxFunc` is executed, and the `JsCmd` response is turned into a JavaScript content type response. In `ajaxFunc`, we construct a JSON object (the same one we used previously for the persons object). We assign the JSON structure to the JavaScript variable `myObject` and call `alert` on the first element on the `persons` object. The rendered JavaScript code that will be sent down the wire is shown in Listing 8-12.

Listing 8-12. Generated JavaScript

```
var myObject =
  {'persons': [{'name': 'Thor', 'race': 'Asgard'},
  {'name': 'Todd', 'race': 'Wraith'} ,
  {'name': 'Rodney', 'race': 'Human'}]};

alert(myObject.persons[0].name);
```

In your page, when you click the button, you'll get an alert dialog saying "Thor". Here, we used the `JsRaw` class, which basically renders the exact thing you passed to it: raw JavaScript code.

Now that we've covered sending JSON from the server to the client, let's look at going in the opposite direction. Lift provides a mechanism for sending form data to the server encapsulated in a JSON object. In and of itself, sending the data in JSON format is relatively simple; where Lift really adds value is via the `net.liftweb.http.JsonHandler` class. This class provides a framework for simplifying processing of submitted JSON data. To start, let's look at the example template code for a JSON form shown in Listing 8-13.

Listing 8-13. A Simple JSON Form

```
<lift:surround with="default" at="content">
<lift:JSONForm.head />

<lift:JSONForm.show>

  <input type="text" name="name" />
  <br />
  <input type="text" name="value" />
  <br />
  <input type="radio" name="vehicle" value="Bike" />
  <input type="radio" name="vehicle" value="Car" />
  <input type="radio" name="vehicle" value="Airplane"/>
  <br />

  <select name="cars">
    <option value="volvo">Volvo</option>
    <option value="saab">Saab</option>
    <option value="opel">Opel</option>
    <option value="audi">Audi</option>
  </select>

  <button type="submit">Submit</button>

</lift:JSONForm.show>

<div id="json_result"></div>

</lift:surround>
```

As you can see, the XHTML template is relatively straightforward. The snippet code shown in Listing 8-14 is where things really get interesting.

Listing 8-14. JSON Form Snippet Code

```
class JSONForm {

def head = <head>{Script(json.jsCmd)}</head>

def show(html: NodeSeq): NodeSeq =  SHtml.jsonForm(json, html)

import JsCmds._


object json extends JsonHandler {

  def apply(in: Any): JsCmd = SetHtml("json_result",
    in match {

case j @ JsonCmd("processForm", _, p: Map[String, _], _) => {
  // process the form or whatever
  Log.info("Cars = " + urlDecode(p("cars")))
  Log.info("Name = " + urlDecode(p("name")))
  <b>{p}</b>
}

case x =>
   <b>Problem... didn't handle JSON message {x}</b>
})
}
}
```

The first thing we define is the head function. Its purpose is simply to generate the JavaScript functions that set up the form handling on the client side. That means that, when the submit button is clicked, the contents of the form are turned into JSON and submitted via an AJAX call to the server. The `show` function defines the connection between the concrete `JsonHandler` instance that will process the form and the template HTML that contains the form. We perform this binding with the `SHtml.jsonForm` method. This wraps the HTML with a `<form>` tag and sets the `onsubmit` event to do JSON bundling.

The key part of the equation is our `JsonHandler` object. The `apply` method will be called when the JSON object is submitted to the server. If the JSON is properly parsed, you'll get a `JsonCmd` instance that you can use Scala's matching to pick apart. The `apply` function needs to return a `JsCmd` (JavaScript code), which, in this case, sets the HTML content of the `json_result` `div` element. When the form is stringified into its JSON representation, Lift uses a `command` property indicating the action that needs to be done on server and the actual JSON data. In the case of JSON forms, the command is always `processForm`, as this is important for pattern matching as shown in Listing 8-14. The actual form content is a Map object that can be easily used to obtain the values for each form field.

Using JqSHtml Object

SHtml-generated code is independent of the JavaScript framework used. However, net.liftweb.http.jquery.JsSHtml object contains artifacts that are bound with jQuery framework. For instance, it contains the autocomplete function that renders an input type text element, but when you start typing, it will suggest words starting with what you typed already. Please see http://www.pengoworks.com/workshop/jquery/autocomplete.htm for examples.

Creating a More Complex Lift and JavaScript Example

We've seen so far how we can abstract JavaScript code at Scala level using Lift's Js abstraction. You can model endless cases by using these abstractions. But let's take a look at an example that's a bit more complex. We'll create a fast search; it will return a list of items that contain a sequence typed into a text box once you press Enter. The list of items will be rendered in a <div>.

Listing 8-15. Example Template

```
<lift:surround with="default" at="content">
  <lift:Hello.ajaxian>
    <text:show/>
  </lift:Hello.ajaxian>

  <div id="items_list">

  </div>

</lift:surround>
```

So we just have a really simple snippet and the <div> placeholder in the markup enlisted. Next, let's see how the Lift snippet for this markup looks like.

Listing 8-16. Example Snippet

```
import JE._

import _root_.net.liftweb.http.js.jquery.JqJE._
import _root_.net.liftweb.http.SHtml._
import _root_.scala.xml.NodeSeq
import _root_.net.liftweb.util.Helpers._

import JsCmds._
```

```
val  names = "marius" :: "tyler" :: "derek" :: "dave" :: "jorge":: "viktor" ::
Nil

def ajaxian(html: NodeSeq) : NodeSeq = {

  bind("text", html,

      "show"  -> ajaxText("Type something", {value => {

         val matches = names.filter(e =>  e.indexOf(value) > -1)

         SetHtml("items_list", NodeSeq.Empty) &

           JsCrVar("items",  JsArray(matches.map(Str(_)):_*))  &
             JsCrVar("func", Jx(<ul>{
               JxMap(JsVar("it"),
               Jx(<li><a href="">{JsVar("it")}</a> </li>))
             }</ul>).toJs) &
            (ElemById("items_list") ~> JsFunc("appendChild",  Call("func",
JsVar("items"))))

        }})
    )
}
```

Listing 8-16 is probably already familiar to you. We are calling the `ajaxText` function, which renders an input text element. When you press Enter, an AJAX request will be sent and the anonymous function that we bound here will be executed. Here is what happens:

1. First, filter out the names that contain the provided value in the input text, meaning that we'll obtain all elements that contain the provided sequence.
2. Then, return the `JsExp` instance that we are building:
    - `SetHtml` is clearing out the `<div>` element that we're using as a real estate for our search results list.
    - Then, we declare a JavaScript variable that is an array containing the resulting items that matched the search criteria.
    - Next, we declare the `func` variable, which obviously is a function. You've seen in Listings 8-6 and 8-9 how to use the `Jx` artifacts. Now, we are building an HTML list (`<ul>`) that for each element from the `it` variable will build the `<li>` sequences. The `it` variable is actually the parameter that this function takes which is the items array that we defined as `JsCrVar("items",  JsArray(matches.map(Str(_)):_*))`.

- After that, we obtain the HTML node denominated by items_list id and call the appendChild function of the Node object. The ~> function is use to call functions of objects. Of course, to the appendChild function, we need to provide a parameter. This parameter is the document fragment returned by the func function. When calling the func function, we are passing items variable defined by JsCrVar("items", JsArray(matches.map(Str(_)):_*)).

As you undoubtedly noticed, in this section, we composed a small JavaScript code example by chaining multiple JavaScript expressions and commands using the & function.

Conclusion

In this chapter, you've learned a few things about Lift's support for building JavaScript expressions inside server side code. These objects and classes provided by Lift can be combined in many ways to express the behavior of the client side (the browser) and actually propagate the generated JavaScript to the browser to be executed. Of course Lift itself handles the propagation of the JavaScript code and all you have to do is to construct the JsExp and JsCmd constructs.

Chapter 9: Lift with AJAX and Comet

In this chapter, we're going to discuss using Lift with AJAX and Comet, two approaches to improving the user experience through dynamic web pages. While a full treatment of the techniques and technologies behind these approaches is beyond the scope of this book, we are going to cover the basics of how AJAX and Comet work. In particular, we're going to look at how Lift handles them behind the scenes to simplify your work.

Understanding the Basics of Asynchronous Requests

AJAX and Comet are variations on the traditional model of the web application request/response life cycle. In the traditional model, the user starts by making a request for a page. The server receives this request, performs processing, and sends a response back to the user. The response is then rendered by the user's browser. At this point, there are no further interactions between the user and the server until the user clicks a link or performs some other action that starts a completely new request/response life cycle. AJAX and Comet extend this model to allow for asynchronous updates from either the user to the server (AJAX) or from the server back to the user (Comet).

If we take the example of adding a comment to a blog post, the traditional model has the user fill in a form, click the submit button, and send the request to the server. The server processes and adds the comment and then sends the updated blog post back to the user with the newly added comment. If other people are viewing the blog at the same time, they won't see the new comment until they reload the page.

In the AJAX model of this session, the display of the new comment is not tied to the response from the server. When the user clicks the submit button, the request to add the comment is sent to the server in the background. While it's being processed by the server, a JavaScript fragment (the "J" in AJAX) updates the user's page via the Document Object Model, or DOM (more information on the DOM can be found at `http://www.w3.org/DOM/`) and adds the comment without the need for a full page reload. Comet changes the traditional model by using a long-polling HTTP request in the background that allows the server to push data to the browser without requiring additional requests. Essentially, this is like AJAX, except in the opposite direction.

While the AJAX model increases the richness of the user experience for a single client at a time, Comet can do the same for multiple users. Going back to our example of a blog post, Comet would enable the server to notify everyone viewing the current blog post to automatically have their pages updated when the new comment is added.

Figures 9-1, 9-2, and 9-3 show a graphical representation of how the models differ in terms of timeline and server interaction.

Figure 9-1. Traditional Application Model

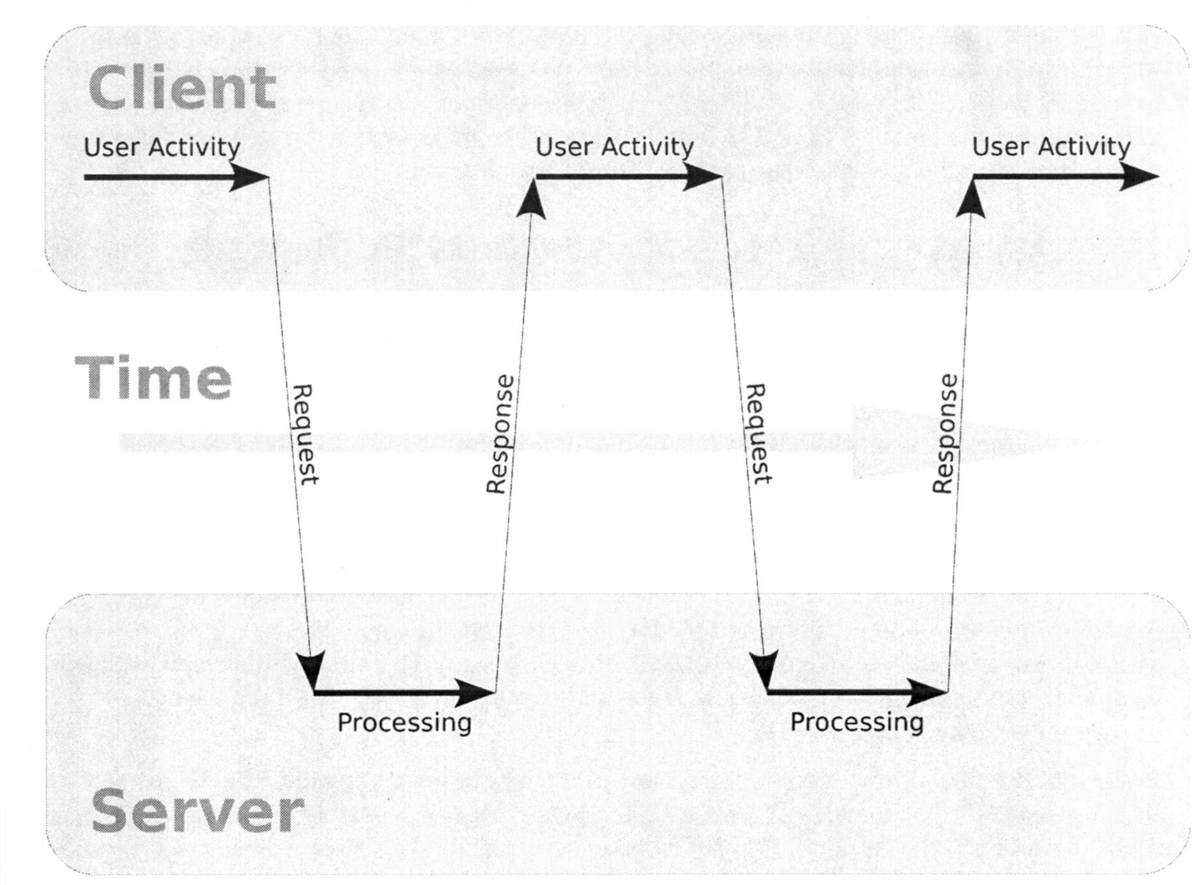

Figure 9-2. The AJAX Application Model

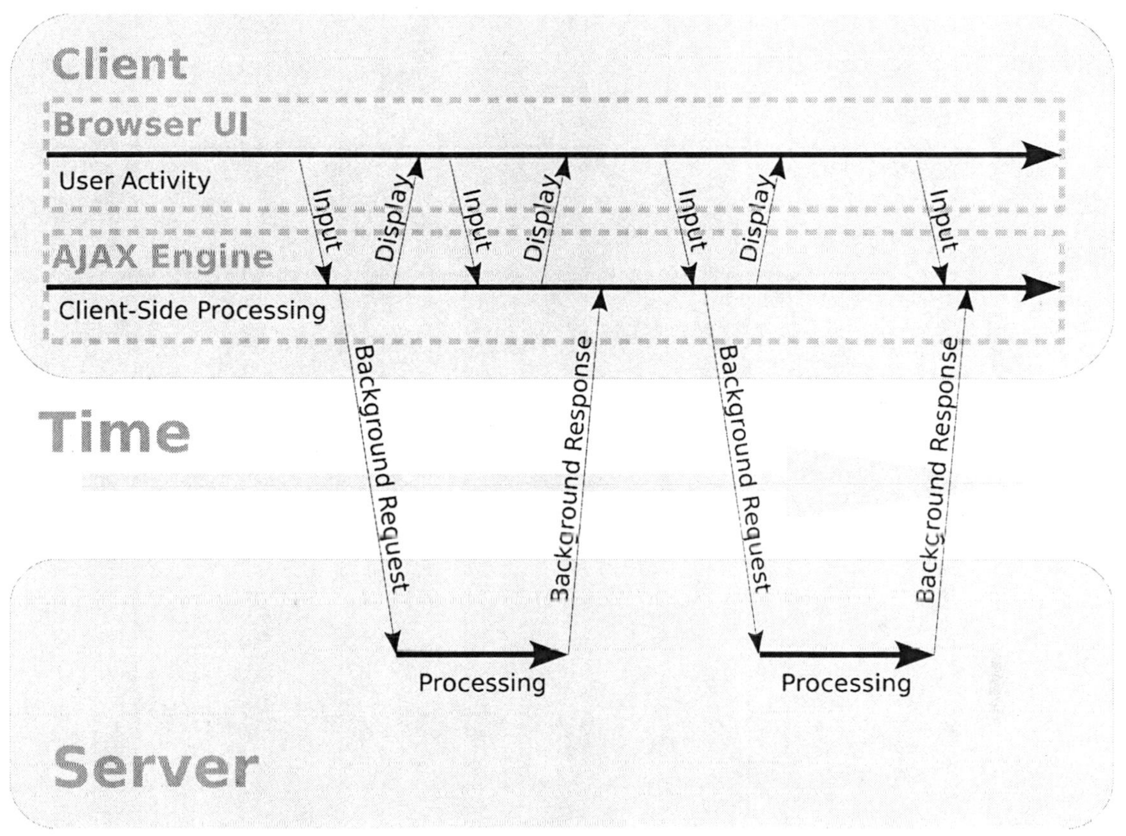

Figure 9-3. Comet Application Model

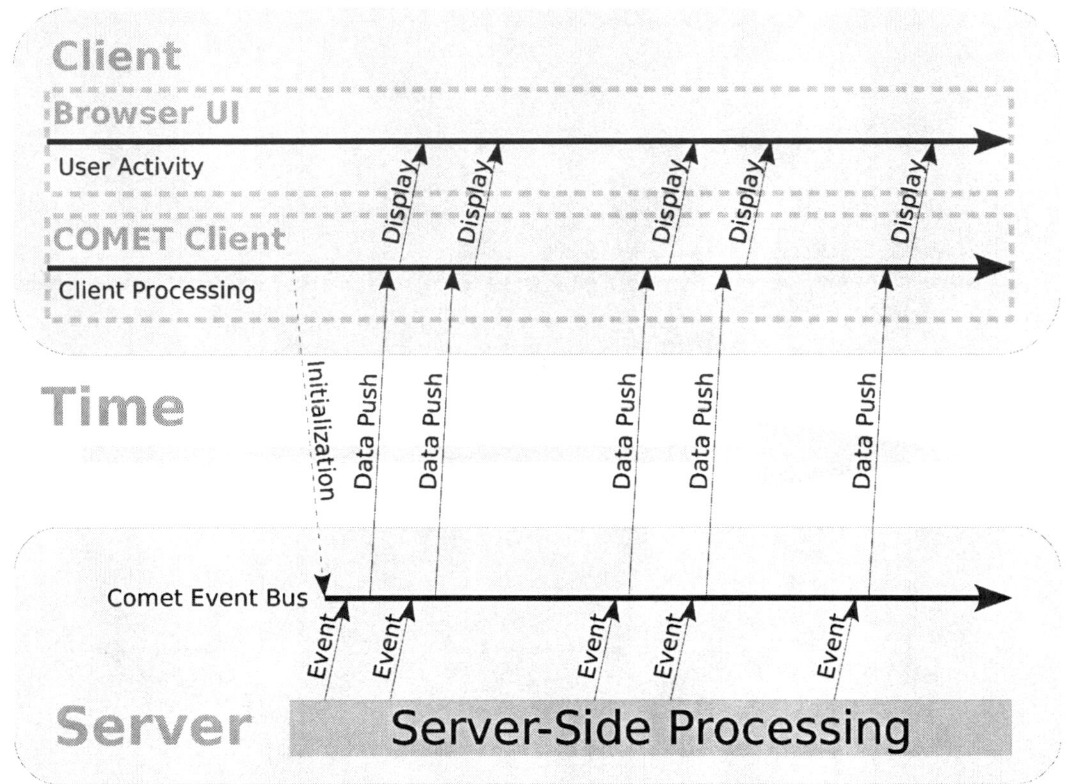

Using AJAX in Lift

In previous chapters, we've shown how to synchronously process forms (Chapter 4) and use JavaScript to perform client-side behavior (Chapter 8). AJAX blends these Lift techniques to give you powerful support for asynchronous client-server interaction. As with standard form and link elements, Lift uses methods on the `SHtml` object to generate AJAX components in a concise manner. We'll cover each of the AJAX-specific `SHtml` methods in a later section, but for now, we want to cover the high-level aspects of using AJAX in Lift.

The first thing we want to point out is that AJAX generators take callback methods just like regular element generators. The major difference is that while standard `SHtml` generator callbacks return `Any`, AJAX callbacks must return `JsCmd`. The reason is that the return from the callback is itself a client-side callback that can be used to update the client content. An example is shown in Listing 9-1. In this example, we generate a button, that when clicked, will print out a message on our console and then the contents of the `<div>` named `my-div` to a `Text` element. As you can see, adding client-side content changes is trivial.

Listing 9-1. A Simple AJAX Example

```
import _root_.net.liftweb.http.SHtml._
import _root_.net.liftweb.http.js.JE._
import _root_.net.liftweb.http.js.JsCmds._
def myFunc(html: NodeSeq) : NodeSeq = {
  bind("hello", html, "button" ->
  ajaxButton(Text("Press me"),
  {() =>
    println("Got an Ajax call")
    SetHtml("my-div", Text("That's it")) })
}
```

The second important aspect of Lift's AJAX support is that, behind the scenes, Lift provides a robust mechanism for AJAX submission. For example, Lift provides its own JavaScript that handles retrying when the submission times out. You can control the timeout duration and retry count through `LiftRules`'s `ajaxPostTimeout` (in milliseconds) and `ajaxRetryCount` variables, respectively.

The third aspect of Lift's AJAX support is that it's so easy to enable. Lift automatically takes care of adding the proper JavaScript libraries to your templates when they're rendered and sets up the proper callback dispatch for you. By default, dispatch is done relative to the `/ajax_request` path in your web context, but Lift allows you change this via `LiftRules.ajaxPath`.

The final aspect is the flexibility the library provides. Besides standard form elements and links that can be AJAXified, Lift also provides the `SHtml.ajaxCall` method, which constructs a `JsExp` that you can use directly on any element. In addition, it allows you to construct a `String` argument to your callback function via JavaScript so that you have full access to client-side data.

Considering a More Complex AJAX Example

Let's take a look at a comparison example. You've seen how to use `SHtml.ajaxButton`, and in Listing 9-2, you'll see how can we achieve the same effect using `SHtml.ajaxCall` and `SHtml.ajaxInvoke`.

Listing 9-2. AJAX Comparison Example

```
class SimpleSnippet {
  def ajaxFunc1() : JsCmd =
  JsRaw("alert('Button1 clicked')")
  def ajaxFunc2(str: String) : JsCmd = {
  Log.info("Received " + str)
  JsRaw("alert('Button2 clicked')")
  }
  def ajaxFunc3() : JsCmd =
  JsRaw("alert('Button3 clicked')")

 def renderAjaxButtons(xhtml: NodeSeq): NodeSeq = {
    bind("ex", xhtml,
      "button1" -> SHtml.ajaxButton("Press Me", ajaxFunc1 _),
      "button2" -> <button>Press Me 2</button> %
        ("onclick" -> SHtml.ajaxCall(Str("Button-2"), ajaxFunc2 _)._2),
      "button3" -> <button>Press me 3</button> %
        ("onclick" -> SHtml.ajaxInvoke(ajaxFunc3 _)._2)
      )
  }
}
```

Basically, in Listing 9-2, we created three AJAX buttons using three different `SHtml` functions. The difference between `ajaxCall` and `ajaxInvoke` is that, for `ajaxCall`, you can specify a parameter that will be sent to the server. This parameter is the result of the `JsExp` computation. For an overview of `SHtml` functions, please see Chapter 4.

Exploring AJAX Generators in Detail

Table 9-1 provides a brief synopsis of the AJAX generators on `SHtml`.

Table 9-1. AJAX Generators on SHtml

FUNCTION	DESCRIPTION
`ajaxButton`	Renders a button that will submit an AJAX request to server
`a`	Renders an anchor tag that, when clicked, will submit an AJAX request
`makeAjaxCall`	Renders the JavaScript code that will submit an AJAX request
`span`	Renders a span element that, when clicked, will execute a `JsCmd`
`ajaxCall`	Renders the JavaScript code that will submit an AJAX request and send the value returned by the `JsExp` provided
`ajaxInvoke`	Similar to `ajaxCall` but there is no value to be sent to the server
`toggleKids`	Provides the toggle effect on an element and sends an AJAX call when clicked
`ajaxText`	Renders an input text element that will send an AJAX request on blur
`jsonText`	Renders an input type text element the will send a JSON request on blur
`ajaxCheckbox`	Renders a check box element that, when clicked, will send an AJAX call
`ajaxSelect`	Renders a select element that sends an AJAX request providing the selected value when the selection changes
`ajaxForm`	Wraps a `NodeSeq` that represents the form's content and makes an AJAX call when the form is submitted
`jsonForm`	Similar to `ajaxForm`, but on the client side, the form is JSONified and the JSON content sent to the server and processed by `JsonHandler`
`swappable`	Renders a span that contains one visible element and the other hidden (When the visible element is clicked, it will be hidden, and the other one will be shown.)

Using Comet in Lift

Figure 9-3 diagrams the interaction between client and server for the Comet model. There are several resources on the Web that explain the history of Comet (`http://en.wikipedia.org/wiki/Comet_(programming)` is a good overview), so we won't cover that here. In essence, Comet is not a technology but a technique that allows a web application to push messages from server to client. Think about a web chat application when you are chatting with your friends and you see message. Let's take a glance at how messaging works:

1. The client sends an AJAX request to server. The server does not respond immediately but waits until a message needs to be sent for that client.
2. When a message is available, the server actually responds to the initial request from the client.
3. The client receives the response, processes it, and issues another AJAX request, and the process continues.

Of course, things are more complicated than that. For instance, when the client is sending the request to the server, the response may not actually be provided immediately. During this delay, the connection could be dropped for whatever reason, and the client should be smart enough to reestablish the connection automatically.

But there is another problem—scalability. If we have these long-term connections, the server would typically put the processing threads into a waiting state until messages are available to actually respond to client. Having waiting threads is a scalability killer, because numerous threads from the web container's thread pool will lie in the wait state doing nothing until, before you know it, your entire thread pool is empty. The immediate consequence is that your server can't handle any other request processing. Because of this, such an approach is totally unacceptable.

The key to scalability is nonblocking I/O. Most operating systems support nonblocking I/O, which actually means that, when you read from or write to an I/O source (say, the streams from a socket), there is no blocking operation. So if you read from a stream, your read function would immediately return regardless of whether data is available or not. In Java, nonblocking I/O can be used by the means of the Java New I/O (NIO) library using `Selectors` and the Reactor pattern. If you're not familiar with NIO, there's a nice overview available at `http://gee.cs.oswego.edu/dl/cpjslides/nio.pdf`. Non-blocking I/O has a major positive impact on scalability, because the threads are returned to the thread pool very quickly and can be reused for processing other requests. In this model, the threads are allocated to connections only when data is available for processing, which inherently leads to a better thread-management system.

Having nonblocking I/O enabled by the web container also has a major impact on application scalability with regard to long-lived connections from client to server. In addition, the Lift framework has support for Jetty `Continuations`, which work like this:

1. You application receives a request and wants to wait to respond, as there is no message yet.
2. You call suspend on the Jetty `Continuation` object. Here, Jetty will throw a special exception that will be caught in the container. The current thread is immediately returned to the thread pool, so it can process other requests.
3. Assume that, after a while, you have a message for that particular client. You call resume on the same `Continuation` object. This time, Jetty will actually replay the initial HTTP request, and your servlet behaves like that request was just received from the client and, of course, returns the appropriate response.

More details on Jetty's Continuations are available on the web site at `http://docs.codehaus.org/display/JETTY/Continuations`. If you run your Lift application in a Jetty container, Lift will automatically detect that and utilize the `Continuation` mechanism. Currently, on other containers, Comet in Lift will still work but won't scale as well because `Continuations` aren't supported. However, the Servlet 3.0 specification contains a more generic facility called Suspended Requests, which will make this feature usable across a variety of containers.

Understanding Actors in Scala

You need to understand that Comet support in Lift is primarily driven via Scala actors. Scala actors are based on the concepts of the Erlang (`http://erlang.org/`) Actors model, where an actor is an asynchronous component that receives and sends or replies to messages. In Erlang, processes communicate via a very simple and effective messaging system built into the virtual machine.

Note We won't go into too much detail regarding Scala actors, as you can find very detailed information in the paper by Philipp Haller located here: Philipp Haller and Martin Odersky, "Scala Actors: Unifying Thread-Based and Event-Based Programming," *Theoretical Computer Science* 410 (2009): 202–20.

In Scala, however, actors are supported at the library level and not at the language level. While less well integrated, this approach does provide greater flexibility, as the Actor library evolution does not impact the language itself. Since Scala typically sits on top of the JVM, Scala actors are not bound to processes but rather to JVM threads. The key of understanding the scalability of Scala actors is that knowing that no one-to-one relationship exists between actors and threads. For instance, when an actor is waiting for a message, we don't end up having a thread waiting for a lock. Instead, the actor body is impersonated by a closure that captures the rest of the computation. This closure is cached internally until a message is designated for this actor to consume. In particular, Scala's Actor library leverages the `match` construct to allow very fine-grained selection of messages for processing. Another interesting note is that the actor body (the part inside of the `react` function) never returns normally; in fact, the return type of the react function is `Nothing`.

Let's take a look at a simple example in Listing 9-3.

Listing 9-3. Ping-Pong Example

```
import scala.actors._
import scala.actors.Actor._
object PingPong extends Application {
  var count = 0;
  val pong = actor {
  loop {
   react {
    case Ping => println("Actor Pong Received Ping")
    sender ! Pong
    case Stop => println("Stopping Pong"); exit()
   }
  }
  }
  val ping = actor {
  pong ! Ping
  loop {
   react {
    case Pong => println("Actor Ping Received Pong")
     count = count + 1;
    if (count < 3) {
     sender ! Ping
    } else {
     sender ! Stop
     println("Stopping Ping")
     exit()
    }
   }
  }
 }
```

```
}
case object Ping
case object Pong
case object Stop
```

In this trivial example, we have two actors exchanging Ping, Pong, and Stop messages (note that the messages are case objects for pattern-matching purposes). Also note that we did not explicitly use threads anywhere. We also did not use any thread blocking techniques, such as synchronized blocks. We didn't because we don't have to. Actors' message-passing mechanism is generally thread safe (although deadlock is still possible due to dependent actors; see http://ruben.savanne.be/articles/concurrency-in-erlang-scala for more details). Note that threads are used internally, and in this specific example, the execution may even occur on the same thread. The reason is that internally the Actor library uses a thread pool, and when an actor receives a message, the execution occurs in a thread from the thread pool. Using a small pool of worker threads is also a key to actors' scalability: they allow threads to be used very efficiently and returned to the pool as soon as the actor consumes the message.

Getting deeper into the details of actions is beyond the scope of this book, but we recommend that you read other materials in order to fully understand Scala actors. In particular, Philipp Haller has a nice page summarizing papers and tutorials on actors at http://lamp.epfl.ch/~phaller/actors.html.

Building a Comet-Enabled Application

As you have seen, Comet support in Lift is provided by Scala actors. Lift greatly simplifies the use of actors by providing the CometActor trait; you simply extend the trait and provide some functionality to do your Comet work. Note that your CometActor subclass needs to exist in a comet subpackage that you configured via LiftRules.addToPackages. For example, if you call LiftRules.addToPackages("com.myapp") in your Boot class, your Comet actors must exist in the com.myapp.comet package.

Let's take a look at a simple example. Let's say that we want to build a Clock example where the server sends the current time to the client every 10 seconds. First, we need a template like the one in Listing 9-4.

Listing 9-4. Comet Clock Markup Example

```
<lift:surround with="default" at="content">
  <lift:comet type="Clock" name="Other">
    Current Time: <clk:time>Missing Clock</clk:time>
  </lift:comet>
</lift:surround>
```

In our template, we use the <lift:comet> tag to bind the CometActor to the portion of the template where it will render content, and the body of the <lift:comet> tag is quite similar to the body of a snippet. The <clk:time> tag will be bound by the Clock actor. The type attribute tells Lift which CometActor to call, and the name attribute is the name of this CometActor. Name is a discriminator that allows you to have more then one CometActor of the same type. Next, we need to define our actor as shown in Listing 9-5.

Listing 9-5. Clock Comet Actor Example

```
class Clock extends CometActor {
  override def defaultPrefix = Full("clk")
  def render = bind("time" -> timeSpan)
  def timeSpan = (<span id="time">{timeNow}</span>)
  // schedule a ping every 10 seconds so we redraw
  ActorPing.schedule(this, Tick, 10000L)
  override def lowPriority :
   PartialFunction[Any, Unit] = {
    case Tick => {
      println("Got tick " + new Date());
      partialUpdate(SetHtml("time",
                            Text(timeNow.toString)))
      // schedule an update in 10 seconds
      ActorPing.schedule(this, Tick, 10000L)
    }
  }
}
case object Tick
```

First, our actor defines the default prefix, which should be used for all nodes that will be bound inside <lift:comet> tag. In our case, we're using the <clk:time> tag.

Next, we have the render function where we do the binding between the <clk:time> node and the result of the timespan function. Basically, the <clk:time> node will be replaced by the span element returned by the timespan function. It is important to note that Comet content rendered by the <lift:comet> tag is a <span> tag by default. This default can be changed by overriding the parentTag function in your comet actor.

timeNow is a function from the TimeHelpers trait that returns the current system time. We use the net.liftweb.util.ActorPing.schedule method to send a Tick message back to our actor after 10 seconds. This method will be called when the Clock class is instantiated.

Finally, we have the lowPriority function that returns a PartialFunction. To process messages in your CometActor, you can override the functions highPriority, mediumPriority, and lowPriority to process your application-specific messages. This multiplicity of functions is just a way of prioritizing application messages. The only thing that we do here is to pattern match the messages. In this simple example, we have only the Tick object. When a Tick is sent by the ActorPing, our code gets executed and the following actions occur:

1. We print the current time at the console (just for fun).
2. We call the partialUpdate function. With a partial update, we can update specific fragments on the client side and not actually re-render the entire content that the CometActor may produce. This optimization allows us to send something very specific to be updated on the client side. If we call reRender(true) instead, the entire real estate on the client side will be re-rendered. Getting back to our partialUpdate call, we are basically saying that we want to set the XHTML content for the element that has the id "time". This is the span element returned by timeSpan function.
3. We tell ActorPing to send another Tick message after 10 seconds.

As you have seen, with just a few lines of code, we were able to create a Clock application in which the server updates the client every 10 seconds. Of course, this is just a trivial example, but now, you should have a clear picture of how CometActor works, so you can build more complex cases for your Lift application.

Accessing Comet Actors from Other Code

So far, our example has only shown a self-contained CometActor for the clock. But what if we want to have interaction between different clients? Scala's actors are still the answer, but with a twist—we can use a singleton actor object that coordinates with the CometActor objects so that it can send messages to all of them. First, we define our singleton actor, as shown in Listing 9-6.

Listing 9-6. Singleton Actor

```
case class SubscribeClock(clock : Clock)
case class UnsubClock(clock : Clock)
object ClockMaster extends Actor {
  private var clocks : List[Clock] = Nil
  def act = loop {
    react {
      case SubscribeClock(clk) =>
        clocks ::= clk
      case UnsubClock(clk) =>
        clocks -= clk
      case Tick =>
        clocks.foreach(_ ! Tick)
    }
  }
}
```

We've defined two case classes representing messages for subscribing and unsubscribing to the ClockMaster actor. The ClockMaster itself is a simple Actor (not a CometActor) that defines a simple message loop. It can either subscribe a new clock, unsubscribe to an existing clock, or distribute a `Tick` to all subscribed clocks. The other half of this equation slightly modifies our `Clock` class (as shown in Listing 9-7) so that it subscribes and unsubscribes to the `ClockMaster` at initialization and shutdown, respectively.

Listing 9-7. Modified Clock Class

```
...
def localSetup {
  ClockMaster ! SubscribeClock(this)
. super.localSetup()
}
def localShutdown {
  ClockMaster ! UnsubClock(this)
  super.localShutdown()
}
```

Now, we can add an AJAX button (to an administration page, of course) that would allow the administrator to update everyone's clocks at once. Listing 9-8 shows how we would bind in the button.

Listing 9-8. The Admin Tick

```
bind("admin", xhtml, "tick" ->
     SHtml.ajaxButton("Tock!", {
       () => ClockMaster ! Tick
     }))
```

Here's what's happening behind the scenes in our modified Clock application. Lift first identifies a Comet request by matching against the path given by the `LiftRules.cometPath` variable. Essentially the flow is as follows:

1. Lift gets a Comet request. Lift checks the `CometActors` to see if there are any messages. If there are no messages to be sent to this client, and the application is running in a Jetty container, the Jetty continuation is suspended, but no response is actually sent to client.
2. Later, when your Comet actor is asked to render or partially update, the response is calculated, and the Jetty continuation is resumed.
3. When Lift gets the resumed request from the container it returns the response calculated by the `CometActor` to the client.

Note that `CometActors` work even if you are not using Jetty container; the only issue is that you won't benefit from the improved scalability of the suspend/resume mechanism offered by the Jetty container.

Conclusion

In this chapter, we explored how easily you can create AJAX and Comet interfaces in Lift. We discussed the underlying techniques used for AJAX and Comet, as well as how Lift provides support functions and classes to simplify writing apps that utilize these techniques. We showed examples of how to use the `SHtml` object to create AJAX-enabled form elements and how to customize things like the AJAX request path in Lift. We reviewed Scala actors and how the `CometActor` trait is used to make a Comet event handler. We also discussed how Lift works to alleviate scalability issues with Comet on supported containers. Finally, we wrote a simple Clock application and showed how you can mix AJAX and Comet in the same application.

Chapter 10: JPA Integration

The Java Persistence API (JPA) is the evolution of a number of frameworks in Java to provide a simple database access layer for plain Java objects (and, transitively, Scala objects). JPA was developed as part of the Enterprise Java Beans 3 (EJB3) specification, with the goal of simplifying the persistence model. You can read more about the standard at `http://java.sun.com/javaee/overview/faq/persistence.jsp`. Prior versions of Enterprise Java had used the Container Managed Persistence (CMP) framework, which required many boilerplate artifacts in the form of interfaces and XML descriptors. As part of the overarching theme of EJB3 to simplify and use convention over configuration, JPA uses sensible defaults and annotations heavily, while allowing for targeted overrides of behavior via XML descriptors. JPA also does away with many of the interfaces used in CMP and provides a single `javax.persistence.EntityManager` (EM) class for all persistence operations. An additional benefit is that JPA was designed so that it could be used both inside and outside of the enterprise container, and several projects (Hibernate, TopLink, JPOX, etc.) provide stand-alone implementations of `EntityManager`.

As you saw in Chapter 6, Lift already comes with a very capable database abstraction layer, so why would we want to use something else?

- JPA is easily accessible from both Java and Scala. If you are using Lift to complement part of a project that also contains Java components, JPA allows you to use a common database layer between both and avoid duplication of effort. It also means that if you have an existing project based on JPA, you can easily integrate it into Lift.
- JPA gives you more flexibility with complex and/or large schemas. While Lift's Mapper provides most of the functionality you would need, JPA provides additional life cycle methods and mapping controls when you have complex needs. Additionally, JPA has better support for joins and relationships between entities.

JPA can provide additional performance improvements via second-level object caching. It's possible to roll your own in Lift, but JPA allows you to cache frequently accessed objects in memory so that you avoid hitting the database entirely.

Introducing JPA

To provide a concrete example to build on while learning how to integrate JPA, we'll be building a small Lift application to manage a library of books. The completed example is available under the Lift git repository in the `sites` directory and is called `JPADemo`.

Basic coverage of the JPA operations is in the "Operating on Entities" section. If you want more detail on JPA, particularly with advanced topics like locking and hinting, several very good tutorials can be found online at http://java.sun.com/developer/technicalArticles/J2EE/jpa/ and http://www.jpox.org/docs/1_2/tutorials/jpa_tutorial.html.

Our first step is to set up a master project for Maven. This project will have two modules under it, one for the JPA library and one for the Lift application. In a working directory of your choosing, issue the following command:

```
mvn archetype:generate \
  -DarchetypeRepository=http://scala-tools.org/repo-snapshots \
  -DarchetypeGroupId=net.liftweb \
  -DarchetypeArtifactId=lift-archetype-jpa-basic \
  -DarchetypeVersion=1.1-SNAPSHOT \
  -DgroupId=com.foo.jpaweb \
  -DartifactId=JPADemo \
  -Dversion=1.0-SNAPSHOT
```

This will use the basic JPA archetype to create a new project for you with modules for the persistence and web portions of the project.

Note We have split the module out into two projects because it aids deployment on Java EE servers to have the Persistence module be an independent JAR file. If you don't need that, you can simply merge the contents of the two modules into a single project, and it will work on its own. Note that you'll need to merge the pom.xml file's dependencies and plug-in configurations from all three POMs. Lift comes with an archetype that handles this already, albeit without the demonstration code we show here. Simply use the lift-archetype-jpa-blank-single archetype, and you'll get a blank project (with minimal files for JPA and Lift) that you can use for your application. There's also a blank archetype that uses two modules if you want that; it's called lift-archetype-jpa-blank.

You will get a prompt asking you to confirm the settings we've chosen; just press Enter. At the time of this writing, we have to use the snapshot version of the archetype, because it didn't make the Lift 1.0 deadline, but otherwise, it's a stable archetype. You will also see some Velocity warnings about invalid references; these can be safely ignored and will hopefully be fixed by version 1.1. After the archetype is generated, you should have the following tree structure:

```
JPADemo
|-- README
|-- pom.xml
|-- spa
|  |-- pom.xml
|  `-- src ...
`-- web
   |-- pom.xml
   `-- src ...
```

If you look at the src directories, you'll see that our code is already in place! If you're making your own application, you can either use the previously mentioned blank archetypes to start from scratch or use the basic archetype and modify the POMs, Scala code, and templates to match your needs. For now, let's go over the contents of the project.

Using Entity Classes in Scala

The main components of a JPA library are the entity classes that compose your data model. For our example application, we need two primary entities: Author and Book.

Let's take a look at the Author class first, shown in Listing G-1. The listing shows our import of the entire javax.persistence package as well as several annotations on a basic class. If you're coming from the Java world in JPA, the annotations should look very familiar. The major differences between Java and Scala annotations are that the parameter list is enclosed in curly braces ({}) in Scala, and each parameter in a Scala annotation is considered a val, which explains the presence of the val keyword within the annotations.

You may also note that we must specify the target entity class; although Scala uses generics, the generic types aren't visible from Java with the 2.7.3 version of the Scala compiler (current at the time of this writing), so the Java JPA libraries can't deduce the correct type (it appears that this will be fixed in the 2.8 release; see http://lampsvn.epfl.ch/trac/scala/ticket/1847 for more deatils).

We also need to use the Java Collections classes for Set, List, and so on, since those are what JPA is based on. With a little bit of implicit conversion magic (to be shown later), this has very little impact on our code. One final item to note is that the Scala compiler does not support nested annotations as of version 2.7.3 (see https://lampsvn.epfl.ch/trac/scala/ticket/294 for details), so where we would normally use them (join tables, named queries, etc.), we will have to use the orm.xml descriptor, which we cover next.

Using the orm.xml Descriptor

As we stated in the last section, in some instances, the Scala compiler doesn't fully cover the JPA annotations (nested annotations in particular). Some would also argue that queries and other ancillary data (table names, column names, etc.) should be separate from code. Because of that, JPA allows you to specify an external mapping descriptor to define and/or override the mappings for your entity classes. The basic `orm.xml` file starts with the DTD type declaration, as shown in Listing G-2. Following the preamble, we can define a package that will apply to all subsequent entries so that we don't need to use the fully qualified name for each class. In our example, we would like to define some named queries for each class. Putting them in the `orm.xml` allows us to modify them without requiring a recompile. The complete XML Schema Definition (XSD) can be found at `http://java.sun.com/xml/ns/persistence/orm_1_0.xsd`.

In this case, we have used the `orm.xml` file to augment our entity classes. If, however, we would like to override the configuration, we may use that as well on a case-by-case basis. Suppose we wished to change the column name for the Author's `name` property. We can add (per the XSD) a section to the `Author` entity element as shown in Listing 10-1. The `attribute-override` element lets us change anything that we would normally specify on the `@Column` annotation and gives us an extremely powerful method for controlling our schema mapping outside of the source code. We can also add named queries in the `orm.xml` so that we have a central location for defining or altering the queries.

Listing 10-1. Author Override in orm.xml

```
...
<entity class="Author">
  <named-query name="findAllAuthors">
    <query><![CDATA[from Author a order by
      a.name]]></query>
  </named-query>
  <attribute-override name="name">
    <column name="author_name" length="30" />
  </attribute-override>
</entity>
...
```

Working with Attached and Detached Objects

JPA operates with entities in one of two modes: attached and detached. An attached object is one that is under the direct control of a live JPA session. That means that the JPA provider monitors the state of the object and writes it to the database at the appropriate time. Objects can be attached either explicitly via the persist and merge methods (see the "Persisting, Merging, and Removing Entities" section, or implicitly via query results, the `getReference` method, or the `find` method.

As soon as the session ends, any formerly attached objects are now considered detached. You can still operate on them as normal objects, but any changes are not directly applied to the database. If you have a detached object, you can reattach it to your current session with the merge method; any changes since the object was detached, as well as any subsequent changes to the attached object, will be applied to the database at the appropriate time. The concept of object attachment is particularly useful in Lift, because it allows us to generate or query for an object in one request cycle and then make modifications and merge in a different cycle.

As an example, our library application provides a summary listing of authors on one page (`src/main/webapp/authors/list.html`) and allows editing of those entities on another (`src/main/webapp/authors/add.html`). We can use the `SHtml.link` generator on our list page, combined with a `RequestVar`, to pass the instance (detached once we return from the list snippet) to our edit snippet. Listing 10-2 shows excerpts from our library application snippets demonstrating how we hand off the instance and do a merge within our edit snippets submission-processing function (`doAdd`).

Listing 10-2. Passing Detached Instances Around an Application

```
// in src/main/scala/net/liftweb/jpademo/snippets/Author.scala
... package and imports ...
class AuthorOps {
  def list (xhtml : NodeSeq) : NodeSeq = {
    val authors = ...
    authors.flatMap(author => bind("author", xhtml, ...
        // use the link closure to capture the current
        // instance for edit insertion
        "edit" -> SHtml.link("add.html",
          () => authorVar(author), Text(?("Edit")))))
  }
  ...
  // Set up a requestVar to track the author object for edits and adds
  object authorVar extends RequestVar(new Author())
  // helper def
  def author = authorVar.is
  def add (xhtml : NodeSeq) : NodeSeq = {
    def doAdd () = {
      ...
      // merge and save the detached instance
      Model.mergeAndFlush(author)
      ...
    }
    // Hold a val here so that the closure grabs it instead of the def
    val current = author
    // Use a hidden element to reinsert the instance on form submission
    bind("author", xhtml,
      "id" -> SHtml.hidden(() => authorVar(current)), ...,
      "submit" -> SHtml.submit(?("Save"), doAdd))
  }
}
```

Obtaining a Per-Session EntityManager

Ideally, we would like our JPA access to be as seamless as possible, particularly when it comes to the object life cycle. In JPA, objects can be attached to a current persistence session, or they can be detached from a JPA session. This gives us a lot of flexibility (which we'll use later) in dealing with the objects themselves, but it also means that we need to be careful when we're accessing object properties. JPA can use lazy retrieval for instance properties; in particular, this is the default behavior for collection-based properties. What this means is that if we're working on a detached object and we attempt to access a collection contained in the instance, we're going to get an exception that the session that the object was loaded in is no longer live. What we'd really like to do is have some hooks into Lift's request cycle that allows us to set up a session when the request starts and properly close it down when the request ends. We still have to be careful with objects that have been passed into our request (from form callbacks, for instance), but in general, we'll be guaranteed that, once we've loaded an object in our snippet code, we have full access to all properties at any point within our snippets.

Fortunately for us, Lift provides just such a mechanism. In fact, Lift supports several related mechanisms for life cycle management (notably, `S.addAround` with the `LoanWrapper`), but for now, we're going to focus on just one: `RequestVar`. `RequestVar` represents a variable associated with the lifetime of the request. This is in contrast to `SessionVar`, which defines a variable for the lifetime of the user's session. `RequestVar` gives us several niceties over handling request parameters ourselves, including type safety and a default value. We go into more detail on `RequestVar` and `SessionVar` in Chapter 3.

In addition to the Lift facilities, we also use the ScalaJPA project (`http://scala-tools.org/mvnsites-snapshots/scalajpa/`) to handle some of the boilerplate of utilizing JPA. ScalaJPA provides some nice traits that Scalafy the JPA `EntityManager` (EM) and `Query` interfaces, as well as accessors that make retrieving an EM simple. To use ScalaJPA, we simply add the following dependency to our POM; see Listing 10-3.

Listing 10-3. Using ScalaJPA

```
<dependency>
  <groupId>org.scala-tools</groupId>
  <artifactId>scalajpa</artifactId>
  <version>1.1-SNAPSHOT</version>
</dependency>
```

Note that at the time of this writing, the library is at `1.1-SNAPSHOT`, but should be promoted to 1.1 soon.

We leverage ScalaJPA's `LocalEMF` and `RequestVarEM` traits to provide a simple `RequestVar` interface to obtain the EM via local lookup (via the `javax.persistence.Persistence` class), as shown in Listing 10-4. It's trivial to use Java Naming (JNDI) to retrieve an EM instead by substituting the JndiEMF trait for the LocalEMF trait. JNDI is typically used with Java EE containers such as JBoss or GlassFish to provide loose coupling and container management of resources, although it's possible to set up JNDI in Servlet containers like Tomcat or Jetty. The details of setting up JNDI, as well as JNDI configuration of the persistence module are beyond the scope of this book.

Listing 10-4. Setting up an EntityManager via RequestVar

```
import _root_.org.scala_libs.jpa._
object Model extends LocalEMF("jpaweb") with
  RequestVarEM
```

Once we have this object set up, we can access all of the ScalaEntityManager methods directly on Model.

Handling Transactions

We're not going to go into too much detail here; there are better documents available if you want to go into depth on how the Java Transaction API (JTA) or general transactions work. In particular, the Enterprise Java Tech Tip at http://java.sun.com/developer/EJTechTips/2005/tt0125.html provides a nice overview of transactions in Java. Essentially, a transaction is a set of operations that are performed atomically; that is, they either all complete successfully or none of them do. The classic example is transferring funds between two bank accounts: you subtract the amount from one account and add it to the other. If the addition fails and you're not operating in the context of a transaction, the client has lost money!

In JPA, transactions are required. If you don't perform your operations within the scope of a transaction, you will either get an exception (if you're using JTA), or you will spend many hours trying to figure out why nothing is being saved to the database. There are two ways of handling transactions under JPA: resource-local and JTA. Resource-local transactions are what you use if you are managing the EM factory yourself (corresponding to the LocalEMF trait). Similarly, JTA is what you use when you obtain your EM via JNDI. Technically, it's also possible to use JTA with a locally managed EM, but that configuration is beyond the scope of this book.

Generally, we would recommend using JTA where it's free (i.e., when deploying to a Java EE container) and using resource-local when you're using a servlet container such as Jetty or Tomcat. If you will be accessing multiple databases or involving resources like EJBs, it is much safer to use JTA so that you can utilize distributed transactions. Choosing between the two is as simple as setting a property in your persistence.xml file (and changing the code to open and close the EM). Listing 10-5 shows examples of setting the transaction-type attribute to RESOURCE_LOCAL and to JTA. If you want to use JTA, you can also omit the transaction-type attribute since JTA is the default.

Listing 10-5. Setting the Transaction Type

```
<persistence-unit name="jpaweb"
    transaction-type="RESOURCE_LOCAL">
  <non-jta-datasource>myDS</non-jta-datasource>
...or ...
<persistence-unit name="jpaweb" transaction-type="JTA">
  <jta-datasource>myDS</jta-datasource>
```

You must make sure that your EM setup code matches what you have in your `persistence.xml`. Additionally, the database connection must match; with JTA, you must use a `jta-data-source` (obtained via JNDI) for your database connection. For resource-local transactions, you can either use a `non-jta-datasource` element, or you can set the provider properties, as shown in Listing 10-6. In this particular example, we're setting the properties for Hibernate, but similar properties exist for JPOX (`http://www.jpox.org/docs/1_2/persistence_unit.html`), TopLink (`http://www.oracle.com/technology/products/ias/toplink/JPA/essentials/toplink-jpa-extensions.html`), and others.

If you'll be deploying into a Java EE container, such as JBoss or GlassFish, then you get JTA support almost for free since JTA is part of the Java EE specification. If you want to deploy your application on a lightweight container like Jetty or Tomcat, we would recommend that you look into using an external JTA coordinator such as JOTM, Atomikos, or JBoss Transaction Manager, since embedding a JTA provider in your container is a nontrivial task.

Listing 10-6. Setting Resource-Local Properties for Hibernate

```
<persistence>
 <persistence-unit name="jpaweb"
    transaction-type="RESOURCE_LOCAL">
  <properties>
   <property name="hibernate.dialect"
     value="org.hibernate.dialect.PostgreSQLDialect"/>
   <property name="hibernate.connection.driver_class"
     value="org.postgresql.Driver"/>
   <property name="hibernate.connection.username"
     value="somUser"/>
   <property name="hibernate.connection.password"
     value="somePass"/>
   <property name="hibernate.connection.url"
     value="jdbc:postgresql:jpaweb"/>
  </properties>
 </persistence-unit>
</persistence>
```

One final note in regard to transactions is how they're affected by `Exceptions`. Per the specification, any exceptions thrown during the scope of a transaction, other than javax.persistence.NoResultException or javax.persistence.NonUniqueResultException, will cause the transaction to be marked for rollback.

Using ScalaEntityManager and ScalaQuery

Now that we've gone through setting up our EntityManager, let's look at how we actually use them in an application. As a convenience, ScalaJPA defines two thin wrappers on the existing javax.persistence.EntityManager and javax.persistence.Query interfaces to provide more Scala-friendly methods. This means that we get Scala's collection types (i.e., List instead of java.util.List) and generic signatures so that we can avoid explicit casting. The ScalaEntityManager trait provides a wrapper on the EntityManager class and is included as part of the RequestVarEM trait that we've mixed into our Model object. The API for ScalaEntityManager can be found at http://scala-tools.org/mvnsites/scalajpa/scaladocs/org/scala_libs/jpa/ScalaEntityManager.html.

Next, we have the ScalaQuery trait, with API docs at http://scala-tools.org/mvnsites/scalajpa/scaladocs/org/scala_libs/jpa/ScalaQuery.html. Like ScalaEntityManager, this is a thin wrapper on the Query interface. In particular, methods that return entities are typed against the ScalaQuery itself, so you don't need to do any explicit casting in your client code. We also have some utility methods to simplify setting a parameter list as well as obtaining the result(s) of the query.

Operating on Entities

In this section we'll demonstrate how to work with entities and cover some important tips on using JPA effectively.

Persisting, Merging, and Removing Entities

The first step to working with any persistent entities is to actually persist them. If you have a brand new object, you can do this with the persist method:

```
val myNewAuthor = new Author; myNewAuthor.name = "Wilma"
Model.persist(myNewAuthor)
```

This attaches the myNewAuthor entity instance to the current persistence session. Once the object is attached, it should be visible in any subsequent queries, although it may not be written to the database just yet (see the "Understanding the Importance of the flush Methods and Exceptions" section). Note that the persist method is only intended for brand new objects. If you have a detached object and you try to use persist, you will most likely get an EntityExistsException, as the instance you're merging is technically conflicting with itself. Instead, you want to use the merge method to reattach detached objects:

```
val author = Model.merge(myOldAuthor)
```

An important thing to note is that the merge method doesn't actually attach the object passed to it; instead, it makes an attached copy of the passed object and returns the copy. If you mistakenly merge without using the returned value, as in the following lines, you'll find that subsequent changes to the object won't be written to the database:

```
Model.merge(myOldAuthor)
myOldAuthor.name = "Fred"
```

One nice aspect of the merge method is that it intelligently detects whether the entity you're merging is a new object or a detached object. That means that you can use merge everywhere and let it sort out the semantics. For example, in our library application, using merge allows us to combine the adding and editing functionality into a single snippet: If we want to edit an existing Author, we pass it into the method. Otherwise, we pass a brand new Author instance into the method, and the merge takes care of either case appropriately.

Removing an object is achieved by calling the remove method:

```
Model.remove(myAuthor)
```

The passed entity is detached from the session immediately and will be removed from the database at the appropriate time. If the entity has any associations on it (to collections or other entities), they will be cascaded as indicated by the entity mapping. An example of a cascade is shown in the Author listing (see Listing G-1). The books collection has the cascade set to REMOVE, which means that if an author is deleted, all of the books by that author will be removed as well. The default is to not cascade anything, so it's important that you properly set the cascade on collections to avoid constraint violations when you remove entities. It's also useful to point out that you don't actually need to have an entity loaded to remove it. You can use the getReference method to obtain a proxy that will cause the corresponding database entry to be removed:

```
Model.remove(Model.getReference(classOf[Author],
             someId))
```

Loading an Entity

There are actually three ways to load an entity object in your client code: using find, getReference, or a query.

The simplest way is to use the find method:

```
val myBook = Model.find(classOf[Book], someId)
```

The find method takes two parameters: the class that you're trying to load and the value of the ID field of the entity. In our example, the Book class uses the Long type for its ID, so we would put a Long value here. It returns either a Full Box if the entity is found in the database or Empty.

With find, the entity is loaded immediately from the database and can be used in both attached and detached states.

The next method you can use is the getReference method:

```
val myBook = Model.getReference(classOf[Book], someId)
```

This is very similar to the find method with a few key differences. First, the object that is returned is a lazy proxy for the entity. That means that no database load is required to occur when you execute the method, although providers may do at least a check on the existence of the ID. Because this is a lazy proxy, you usually don't want to use the returned object in a detached state unless you've accessed its fields while the session was open. The normal use of getReference is when you want to set up a relationship between two (or more) entities, since you don't need to query all of the fields just to set a foreign key, for example:

```
myBook.author =
  Model.getReference(classOf[Author], authorId)
```

When myBook is flushed to the database, the EM will correctly set up the relationship. The final difference is in how unknown entities are handled. Recall that the find method returns Empty if the entity cannot be found; with getReference, however, we don't query the database until the reference is used. Because of this, the javax.persistence.EntityNotFoundException is thrown when you try to access an undefined entity for the first time (this also marks the transaction for rollback).

The third method for loading an entity would be to use a query (named or otherwise) to fetch the entity. As an example, here's a query equivalent of the find method:

```
val myBook =
  Model.createQuery[Book](
   "from Book bk where bk.id = :id")
   .setParams("id" -> someId).findOne
```

The advantage here is that we have more control over what is selected by using the query language to specify other properties. One caveat is that, when you use the findOne method, you need to ensure that the query will actually result in a unique entity; otherwise, the EM will throw a NonUniqueResultException.

Loading Many Entities

Corresponding to the findOne method is the findAll method, which returns all entities based on a query. There are two ways to use findAll: using findAll and via a ScalaQuery instance.

The first is to use the convenience findAll method defined in the ScalaEntityManager class:

```
val myBooks =
  Model.findAll("booksByYear", "year" -> myYear)
```

This requires the use of a named query for the first arg, and subsequent args are of the form ("paramName" -> value). Named queries can be defined in your orm.xml, as shown in the "Using the orm.xml Descriptor" section. Named queries are highly recommended over ad-hoc queries, since they allow you to keep the queries in one location instead of being scattered all over your code. Named queries can also be precompiled by the JPA provider, which will catch errors at startup or in your unit tests (hint, hint) instead of when the query is run inside your code.

The second method is to create a ScalaQuery instance directly, set parameters, and execute it. In reality, this is exactly what the Model.findAll method is doing. The advantage in creating the instance yourself is that with the ScalaQuery instance, you can do things like set hinting, paging, and so on. For instance, if you wanted to do paging on the books query, you could do this:

```
val myBooks = Model.createNamedQuery("booksByYear")
       .setParams("year" -> myYear)
       .setMaxResults(20)
       .setFirstResult(pageOffset).findAll
```

Using Queries Wisely

In general, we recommend that you use named queries throughout your code. In our experience, the extra effort involved in adding a named query is more than offset by the time it saves you if you ever need to modify the query. Additionally, we recommend that you use named parameters in your queries. Named parameters are just that: parameters that are inserted into your query by name, in contrast to positional parameters.

As an example, Listing 10-7 shows a query using *named parameters*.

Listing 10-7. Using Named Parameters in a Query

```
select user from User where
  (user.name like :searchString or
   user.email like :searchString)
  and user.widgets > :widgetCount
```

And Listing 10-8 the same query using *positional parameters*.

Listing 10-8. Using Positional Parameters in a Query

```
select user from User where
  (user.name like ? or
   user.email like ?)
  and user.widgets > ?
```

This example shows several advantages of named parameters over positional ones:

- You can reuse the same named parameter within the same query, and you only set it once. In the example, we would set the same parameter twice using positional parameters.
- The parameters can have meaningful names.
- With positional parameters, you may have to edit your code if you need to alter your query to add or remove parameters.

In any case, you should generally use the parameterized query types, as opposed to hand-constructing your queries; using things like string concatenation opens your site to SQL injection attacks unless you're very careful. For more information on queries, there's an excellent reference for the EJBQL on the Hibernate web site at `http://www.hibernate.org/hib_docs/entitymanager/reference/en/html/queryhql.html`.

Converting Collection Properties

The `ScalaEntityManager` and `ScalaQuery` methods are already defined so that they return Scala-friendly collections such as `scala.collection.jcl.BufferWrapper` or `SetWrapper`. We have to use Java Collections (`http://java.sun.com/docs/books/tutorial/collections/index.html`) under the hood and then wrap them, because JPA doesn't understand Scala collections. For the same reason, collections in your entity classes must also use the Java Collections classes. Fortunately, Scala has a very nice framework for wrapping Java collections. In particular, the `scala.collection.jcl.Conversions` class contains a number of implicit conversions; all you have to do is import them at the top of your source file like so:

```
import scala.collection.jcl.Conversions._
```

Once you've done that, the methods are automatically in scope and you can use collections in your entities as if they were real Scala collections. For example, we may want to see if our `Author` has written any mysteries:

```
val suspenseful =
  author.books.exists(_.genre = Genre.Mystery)
```

Understanding the Importance of the flush Methods and Exceptions

It's important to understand that, in JPA, the provider isn't required to write to the database until the session closes or is flushed. That means that constraint violations aren't necessarily checked at the time that you persist, merge, or remove an object. Using the `flush` method forces the provider to write any pending changes to the database and immediately throw any exceptions resulting from any violations. As a convenience, we've written the `mergeAndFlush`, `persistAndFlush`, and `removeAndFlush` methods to do `persist`, `merge`, and `remove` with a subsequent flush, as shown in Code Listing 10-9, taken from the `Author` snippet code. You can also see that, because we flush at this point, we can catch any JPA-related exceptions and deal with them here. If we don't flush at this point, the exception would be thrown when the transaction commits, which is often very far (in the code) from where you would want to handle it.

Listing 10-9. Automatic Flush Methods

```
def doAdd () = {
  if (author.name.length == 0) {
    error("emptyAuthor",
          "The author's name cannot be blank")
  } else {
    try {
  Model.mergeAndFlush(author)
 redirectTo("list.html")
  } catch {
    case ee : EntityExistsException =>
      error("Author already exists")
    case pe : PersistenceException =>
       error("Error adding author")
       Log.error("Error adding author", pe)
    }
  }
}
```

Although the combination methods simplify things, we recommend that if you will be doing multiple operations in one session cycle that you use a single `flush` at the end, as shown in Listing 10-10.

Listing 10-10. Multiple JPA Operations

```
val container =
  Model.find(classOf[Container], containerId)
Model.remove(container.widget)
container.widget = new Widget("Foo!")
// next line only required if container.widget
// doesn't cascade PERSIST
Model.persist(container.widget)
Model.flush()
```

Validating Entities

Since we've already covered the Mapper framework and all of the extra functionality that it provides beyond being a simple ORM, we felt that we should discuss one of the more important aspects of data handling as it pertains to JPA: validation of data.

JPA currently doesn't come with a built-in validation framework, although the upcoming JPA 2.0 may use the JSR 303 (Bean Validation) framework as its default. Currently, Hibernate

Validator is one of the more popular libraries for validating JPA entities and can be used with any JPA provider. More information is available at the project home page at `http://www.hibernate.org/412.html`.

The validation of entities with Hibernate Validator is achieved, like the JPA mappings, with annotations. Listing 10-11 shows a modified `Author` class with validations for the name. In this case, we have added a `NotNull` validation as well as a `Length` check to ensure we are within limits.

Note Unfortunately, due to the way that the Validator framework extracts entity properties, we have to rework our entity to use a getter or setter for any properties that we want to validate; even the `scala.reflect.BeanProperty` annotation won't work.

Validation can be performed automatically via the `EntityListener` `org.hibernate.validator.event.JPAValidateListener` or programmatically via the `org.hibernate.validator.ClassValidator` utility class, as shown in Listing 10-11. Further usage and configuration is beyond the scope of this book.

Listing 10-11. The Author Class with Hibernate Validations

```
...
class Author {
  var name : String = ""

  @Column{val unique = true, val nullable = false}
  @NotNull
  @Length{val min = 2, val max = 100}
  def getName = name
  def setName(nm : String) { name = nm }
  ...
}
// In the snippet class
class AuthorOps {
  ...
  val authorValidator = new ClassValidator(classOf[Author])
  def add (xhtml : NodeSeq) : NodeSeq = {
    def doAdd () = {
      authorValidator.getInvalidValues(author) match {
        case Array() =>
          try {
        Model.mergeAndFlush(author)
            ...
```

```
            } catch {
              ...
            }
          case errors => {
        errors.foreach(err => S.error(err.toString))
      }
        }
  ...
    }
  }
```

Supporting User Types

JPA can handle all Java primitive types, their corresponding Object versions (java.lang.Long, java.lang.Integer, etc.), and any entity classes comprised of these types. Technically, JPA can handle more complex types; see the JPA specification, section 2.1.1, for details. Occasionally, though, you may have a requirement for a type that doesn't fit directly with those specifications. One example in particular would be Scala's enumerations. Unfortunately, the JPA specification currently doesn't have a means to handle this directly, although the various JPA providers such as TopLink and Hibernate provide mechanisms for resolving custom user types. JPA does provide direct support for Java enumerations, but that doesn't help us here, since Scala enumerations aren't an extension of Java enumerations. In this example, we'll be using Hibernate's org.hibernate.UserType (see the API documentation at http://www.hibernate.org/hib_docs/v3/api/org/hibernate/usertype/UserType.html) to support an enumeration for the Genre of a Book.

We begin by implementing a few helper classes besides the Genre enumeration itself. First, we define an Enumv trait, shown in Listing G-3. Its main purpose is to provide a valueOf method that we can use to resolve the enumerations database value to the actual enumeration.

We also add some extra methods so that we can encapsulate a description along with the database value. Scala enumerations can use either Ints or Strings for the identity of the enumeration value (unique to each val), and in this case, we've chosen Strings. By adding a map for the description (since Scala enumeration values must extend the Enumeration#Value class and therefore can't carry the additional string), we allow for the additional information. We could extend this concept to make the Map carry additional data, but for our purposes, this is sufficient.

To actually convert the Enumeration class into the proper database type (String, Int, etc.), we need to implement the Hibernate UserType interface, shown in the EnumvType listing, G-4. Line 18 of that listing shows that we will be using a varchar column for the enumeration value. Since this is based on the Scala Enumeration's Value method, we could technically use either Integer or character types here. We override the sqlTypes and returnedClass methods to match our preferred type and set the equals and hashCode methods accordingly.

Note that in Scala, the == operator on objects delegates to the equals method, so we're not testing reference equality here. The actual resolution of database column value to Enumeration is done in the nullSafeGet method; if we decided, for instance, that the null value should be returned as unknown, we could do this here with some minor modifications to the Enumv class (defining the unknown value, for one). The rest of the methods are set appropriately for an immutable object (Enumeration). The great thing about the EnumvType class, is that it can easily be used for a variety of types due to the et constructor argument; as long as we mix in the Enumv trait to our Enumeration objects, we get persistence essentially for free. If we determined instead that we want to use Integer enumeration IDs, we need to make only minor modifications to the EnumvType to make sure arguments match, and we're set.

Finally, the Genre object and the associated GenreType is shown in Listing 10-12. You can see that we create a singleton Genre object with specific member values for each enumeration value. The GenreType class is trivial now that we have the EnumvType class defined. To use the Genre type in our entity classes, we simply need to add the proper var and annotate it with the @Type annotation, as shown in Listing 10-13. We need to specify the type of the var because the actual enumeration values are of the type Enumeration.Val, which doesn't match our valueOf method in the Enumv trait. We also want to make sure we set the enumeration to some reasonable default; in our example, we have an unknown value to cover that case.

Listing 10-12. Genre and GenreType

```
package com.foo.jpaweb.model
object Genre extends Enumeration with Enumv {
  val Mystery = Value("Mystery", "Mystery")
  val Science = Value("Science", "Science")
  val Theater = Value("Theater", "Drama literature")
  // more values here...
}
class GenreType extends EnumvType(Genre) {}
```

Listing 10-13. Using the @Type annotation

```
@Type{val `type` = "com.foo.jpaweb.model.GenreType"}
var genre : Genre.Value = Genre.unknown
```

Running the Application

Now that we've gone over everything, it's time to run the application. Because we've split up the application into separate SPA and WEB modules, we need to first run mvn install from the SPA module directory to get the persistence module added to your maven repository. Once that is done, you can go to the WEB module directory and run mvn jetty:run to get it started.

Conclusion

In this chapter, we've shown that the Java Persistence API provides a robust, flexible framework for persisting data to your database and does so in a manner that integrates fairly well with Lift. We've demonstrated how you can easily write entities using a combination of annotations and the `orm.xml` descriptor, how to define your own custom user types to handle enumerations, the intricacies of working with transactions in various contexts, and leveraging the ScalaJPA framework to simplify your persistence setup.

Chapter 11: Third-Party Integrations

In this chapter, we'll explore how you can integrate Lift with some well-known third-party libraries and applications. These are often useful because they provide services and features that may be attractive to your users, or they may simplify your own development. First, we'll be looking at how you can utilize the OpenID framework to simplify your authentication handling and allow users to reduce the number of accounts they need to manage. Next, we'll look at how you can use the AMQP messaging protocol to enable asynchronous message passing for high performance and scalability. After that, we'll examine how you can sue PayPal services for commerce transactions from Lift. We'll follow that with an examination of the Facebook API for Lift, which you can use to write Facebook applications. Finally, we'll cover the API for the XMPP messaging protocol, with an example of how you can interface with Google Talk.

Integrating OpenID

The OpenID Foundation (`http://openid.net/`) is a group of technical and commerce businesses (including Google, PayPal, Yahoo, and Microsoft) that have come together to develop a system for distributing user authentication using standard and secure protocols and technologies. The basic goal is to allow users to utilize their existing accounts on web sites, blogs, and so on, across multiple sites. This simplifies account management from the user perspective and allows site builders to leverage existing infrastructure to hold user identity and authentication information. The number of sites accepting and providing OpenID service is growing and offers a very simple means to setting up user accounts for your site.

Lift provides OpenID support using OpenID4Java (`http://code.google.com/p/openid4java/`). It provides two fundamental traits, `net.liftweb.openid.OpenIdVendor` and `net.liftweb.openid.OpenIdConsumer`. To use these wrappers, you need to add the `lift-openid` module to your `pom.xml` file's dependencies.

`OpenIdVendor` contains variables that control behavior, such as these:

- `PathRoot`: This is the path sequence for processing OpenID requests, which defaults to `openid`.
- `LoginPath`: This variable contains the path sequence for processing login requests. The default value is `login`, and the login path will be `/openid/login`.
- `LogoutPath`: This one contains the path sequence for processing logout requests. The default value is `logout`, and the logout path will be `/openid/logout`.
- `ResponsePath`: This is the path sequence for processing login requests. The default value is `response`, and the response path will be `/openid/response`.

- `PostParamName`: This form parameter name contains the OpenID identity URL entered by the user.

Also the vendor trait contains the `loginForm` function that returns the login form containing an input text field for the OpenID identity and the submit button. The form will point to `/<PathRoot>/<LoginPath>`, where `PathRoot` and `LoginPath` are the variables described in the preceding list. You'll find an example in Listing 11-1.

Listing 11-1. Using OpenID

```
// Your template
<lift:OpenID.form>
  <openId:renderForm/>
</lift:OpenID.form>
// Your snippet
class OpenID {
  def renderForm(xhtml: NodeSeq) : NodeSeq = {
SimpleOpenIdVendor.loginForm
  }
}
class Boot {
  ...
  // This is needed in order to process the login
  // and logout requests, and also to process
  // the response comming from OpenID provider
  LiftRules.dispatch.append(
    SimpleOpenIdVendor.dispatchPF)
  ...
}
```

That is pretty much all you need to add into your Lift application. The authentication flow is as follows:

1. The user accesses your lift page containing the OpenID form.
2. The user enters an OpenID identity URL and submits the form. Note that you don't have to use the default login form; you can construct your own as long as the form is submitted to the correct path and contains the correct input text parameter name.
3. The `dispatchPF` function that we appended in Listing 11-1 will process the `/openid/login` request and send the authentication request to the identity provider site.
4. The identity provider will validate the user and redirect back to your Lift application's `/openid/response` path.
5. The response is validated using the OpenID4Java library.
6. The `OpenIdConsumer.postLogin` hook gets called.

Listing 11-2 shows what the `SimpleOpenIDVendor` trait looks like.

Listing 11-2. SimpleOpenIDVendor

```
trait SimpleOpenIdVendor extends OpenIdVendor {
 type UserType = Identifier
 type ConsumerType = OpenIdConsumer[UserType]
 def currentUser = OpenIdUser.is
 def postLogin(id: Box[Identifier],
              res: VerificationResult): Unit = {
   id match {
     case Full(id) => S.notice("Welcome "+id)
     case _ => S.error("Failed to authenticate")
   }
   OpenIdUser(id)
 }
 def logUserOut() {
   OpenIdUser.remove
 }
 def displayUser(in: UserType): NodeSeq =
   Text("Welcome "+in)
 def createAConsumer =
   new AnyRef with OpenIDConsumer[UserType]
}

object SimpleOpenIdVendor extends SimpleOpenIdVendor
```

Note the `postLogin` implementation. Of course, if you need a more complex post-login processing, you can extend `SimpleOpenIdVendor` by yourself. Besides the form processing, we just mentioned, the primary functionality of `SimpleOpenIdVendor` is the `currentUser` def, which will hold an `org.openid4java.discovery.Identifier` when the user is logged in and will be `Empty` otherwise.

Integrating AMQP

Advanced Message Queuing Protocol (AMQP) is an open Internet protocol for messaging. The official page for the AMQP protocol and working group is at `http://jira.amqp.org/confluence/display/AMQP/Advanced+Message+Queuing+Protocol`. Message-oriented middleware (MOM) is used to distribute portions of an application between different platforms and physical instances. This loose coupling allows for more flexibility to the developer in determining how to implement and deploy each component of an application. In a MOM system, different components communicate by passing messages, usually through a message routing broker (although some systems can use multicast or broadcast) to perform processing of the messages asynchronously.

There are several benefits to this arrangement:

- Asynchronous processing, combined with a persistent store on the broker, allows parts of the system to perform work when other parts may not be connected or may be degraded.
- The broker can perform content- or load-dependent routing of messages, giving more flexibility to the developer.
- The broker can perform transformations on the messages as they pass through the system. This allows the developer to modify behavior or content as needed without recoding components of the application.

Lift facilitates the work with AMQP using the RabbitMQ (`http://www.rabbitmq.com/`) Java implementation. To enable this API, you need to add the `lift-amqp` module to your `pom.xml` file's dependencies. There are two fundamental classes:

- `net.liftweb.amqp.AMQPSender`: Used for sending AMQP messages
- `net.liftweb.amqp.AMQPDispatcher`: Used for receiving AMQP messages

Listing 11-3 shows how we can use the existing `net.liftweb.amqp.StringAMQPSender` class to send `String` data.

Listing 11-3. Using AMQP to Send Messages

```
import net.liftweb.amqp._
import com.rabbitmq.client._
val params = new ConnectionParameters
// All of the params, exchanges, and queues are all
// just example data.
params.setUsername("guest")
params.setPassword("guest")
params.setVirtualHost("/")
params.setRequestedHeartbeat(0)
val factory = new ConnectionFactory(params)
val amqp =
  new StringAMQPSender(factory, "localhost", 5672,
                       "mult", "routeroute")
amqp.start
amqp ! AMQPMessage("hi")
```

As you can see, the `AMQSender` leverages Scala actors to send messages. This is done so that the `AMQSender` can hold a long-lived connection to the queue. Scala actors and AMQP messaging concepts play very well together, since both are based on the concept of message passing.

Listing 11-4 shows how the `net.liftweb.amqp.ExampleStringAMQPListener` is defined to receive and process the `String` AMQP messages that we send in our previous example.

Listing 11-4. Using AMQP to Receive Messages

```
package net.liftweb.amqp
import com.rabbitmq.client._

/**
 * Example class that accepts Strings coming in from the
 * ExampleSerializedAMQPDispatcher.
 */
class ExampleStringAMQPListener {
  val params = new ConnectionParameters
  params.setUsername("guest")
  params.setPassword("guest")
  params.setVirtualHost("/")
  params.setRequestedHeartbeat(0)

  val factory = new ConnectionFactory(params)
  // thor.local is a machine on your network with
  // rabbitmq listening on port 5672
  val amqp =
    new ExampleSerializedAMQPDispatcher[String](factory, "localhost", 5672)
  amqp.start

  // Example Listener that just prints the String it receives.
  class StringListener extends Actor {
    def act = {
      react {
case msg@AMQPMessage(contents: String) => println("received: " + msg); act
      }
    }
  }
  val stringListener = new StringListener()
  stringListener.start
  amqp ! AMQPAddListener(stringListener)
}
```

This code is taken directly from the GitHub source for the lift-amqp module. For most simple uses, you can simply modify the react loop (and possibly the type on the ExampleSerializedAMQPDispatcher if you're not using Strings). However, the point of showing this class is so you can understand how to use an AMQP consumer and how to configure it to match the client settings from Listing 11-3. The key here is to see how the actual messages are consumed. Note that the Listener actor is consuming the AMQPMessage, but the actor itself is provided to AMQPDispatcher. When a real AMQP message is received by AMQPDispatcher, it will just forward it to the user's Actor for actual processing. The SerializedConsumer class is actually doing the transformation of the raw data (an array of bytes) into AMQPMessage messages.

Integrating PayPal

PayPal (https://www.paypal.com) is a well-known service that allows you to make online payment transactions. Lift supports both the Payment Data Transfer (PDT) and Instant Payment Notification (IPN) APIs provided by PayPal. We won't be getting into the PayPal API details, as this information can be found on the PayPal site at https://www.paypal.com/pdt and https://www.paypal.com/ipn, respectively. However, we'll provide simple examples of how we'd use PDT in Listing 11-5 and IPN in Listing 11-6. To use these wrappers, you need to add the lift-paypal module to your pom.xml file's dependencies.

Listing 11-5. Using PDT

```
import net.liftweb.paypal._
object MyPayPalPDT extends PayPalPDT {
  // the path that paypal will redirect back to
  // upon transaction completion
  override def pdtPath = "paypal_complete"
  def paypalAuthToken =
    Props.get("paypal.authToken") openOr
      "cannot find auth token from props file"
  def pdtResponse:
    PartialFunction[(PayPalInfo, Req), LiftResponse] = {
      case (info, req) =>
        println("--- in pdtResponse");
        DoRedirectResponse("/account_admin/index");
    }
}
// in Boot
def boot(){
  ...
  LiftRules.statelessDispatchTable.append(MyPayPalPDT)
  ...
}
```

That is pretty much it. The pdtResponse function allows you to determine the behavior of you application once you receive the response from PayPal.

Listing 11-6. Using IPN

```
import net.liftweb.paypal._
object MyPayPalIPN extends PayPalIPN {
  def actions = {
    case (ClearedPayment, info, req) =>
      // do your processing here
    case (RefundedPayment, info, req) =>
      // do refund processing
```

```
    }
  }
  // in Boot
  def boot(){
    ...
    LiftRules.statelessDispatchTable.append(MyPayPalIPN)
    ...
  }
```

As you can see, everything is pretty straightforward. Just perform pattern matching on the `PaypalTransactionStatus`. It is worth to note that IPN is a machine-to-machine API, which happens in the background without end user interaction.

Integrating Facebook

Facebook (`http://www.facebook.com`) is a well-known site that allows people to easily interact, build social networks, share photos, and so on. Facebook also exposes HTTP APIs that allow other applications to interact with it (details are available at `http://wiki.developers.facebook.com/index.php/API`). The Lift framework allows your application to easily interact with Facebook by providing an abstraction layer over the Facebook API. Listing 11-7 shows how we can work with a given Facebook account to get a list of friends. To use this API, you'll need to add the `lift-facebook` module to your `pom.xml` file's dependencies.

Listing 11-7. Using The Facebook API

```
import net.liftweb.ext_api.facebook._
import net.liftweb.util.Props // for config stuff
FacebookRestApi.apiKey = Props.get("fbapikey")
FacebookRestApi.secret = Props.get("fbsecret")
// Invoke stateless calls
val respNode: Node = FacebookClient !? AuthCreateToken
val authToken = // extract authToken from respNode
// Obtain a stateful client based on the authToken
val faceBookClient =
  FacebookClient.fromAuthToken(authToken)
faceBookClient !? GetFriendLists
```

Once you have the `FacebookClient`, you can invoke numerous API methods described by `FacebookMethod` or `SessionlessFacebookMethod`. In Listing 11-7, we create the Facebook context by first obtaining an `authToken` and then obtaining a `faceBookClient` reference bound to the newly created session. After that, we're just obtaining the friends list.

Integrating XMPP

The Extensible Messaging and Presence Protocol, or XMPP (more details at `http://xmpp.org/`) is an XML-based protocol presence and real-time communication used for instant messaging, among other things, and has been developed by the Jabber open-source community (`http://xmpp.org/about/jabber.shtml`).

Lift provides an XMPP dispatcher implementation that your application can use to receive instant messages, manage rosters, and so on. This support relies on the Smack XMPP client library (`http://www.igniterealtime.org/downloads/index.jsp`) and Scala actors. To use this API, you'll need to add the `lift-xmpp` module to your `pom.xml` file's dependencies. Let's look at how we can write our own chat actor to sign in to a Google Talk account to receive messages and status changes and print them to the console. Listing 11-8 shows how we define the basic `ConsoleChatActor`.

Listing 11-8. Using XMPP

```
import _root_.net.liftweb.xmpp._

class ConsoleChatActor(val username: String,
      val password: String)
    extends Actor {
  def connf() =
    new ConnectionConfiguration("talk.google.com", 5222,
                                "gmail.com")
  def login(conn: XMPPConnection) =
    conn.login(username, password)
  val xmpp = new XMPPDispatcher(connf, login)
  xmpp.start
```

As you can see, we've defined a basic constructor with authentication information and set up the plumbing for our `net.liftweb.xmpp.XMPPDispatcher` actor, which, like the AMQP actor, is used to handle the low-level details of sending and receiving XMPP information. Next, we need to define some bookkeeping values to hold information about our chats and our roster (list of contacts), as shown in Listing 11-9.

Listing 11-9. Defining Bookkeeping Variables

```
  val chats: Map[String, List[Message]] =
    new HashMap[String, List[Message]]
  val rosterMap: HashMap[String, Presence] =
    new HashMap[String, Presence]
  var roster: Roster = null
  /**
   * @returns an Iterable of all users who are
```

```
   * available along with their Presence
   */
  def availableUsers: Iterable[(String, Presence)] = {
    rosterMap.filter(
    (e) => e._2.getType() != Presence.Type.unavailable)
  }
```

Next, we need to define the actor loop that will handle the various XMPP messages, as shown in Listing 11-10. A set of case classes and objects under `net.liftweb.xmpp` details the various XMPP message types (as well as some state, such as `Start`).

Listing 11-10. Defining the XMPP Actor Loop

```
  def act = loop
  def loop {
    react {
      case Start => {
        xmpp ! AddListener(this)
        xmpp ! SetPresence(
          new Presence(Presence.Type.available))
        loop
      }
      case NewChat(c) => {
        chats += (c.getParticipant -> Nil)
        loop
      }
      case RecvMsg(chat, msg) => {
        println("RecvMsg from: " + msg.getFrom + ": " +
                msg.getBody);
        loop
      }
      case NewRoster(r) => {
        println("getting a new roster: " + r)
        this.roster = r
        val e: Array[Object] =
          r.getEntries.toArray.asInstanceOf[Array[Object]]
        for (entry <- e) {
          val user: String =
            entry.asInstanceOf[RosterEntry].getUser
          rosterMap += (user -> r.getPresence(user))
        }
        loop
      }
      case RosterPresenceChanged(p) => {
        val user = StringUtils.parseBareAddress(p.getFrom)
        println("Roster Update: " + user + " " + p)
        // It's best practice to ask the roster for the
```

```
        // presence. This is because multiple presences
        // can exist for one user and the roster knows
        // which one has priority.
        rosterMap += (user -> roster.getPresence(user))
        loop
    }
      case RosterEntriesDeleted(e) => println(e); loop
      case RosterEntriesUpdated(e) => println(e); loop
      case RosterEntriesAdded(e) => println(e); loop
      case a => println(a); loop
    }
```

We can also define some helper methods for setting up chats and sending messages, as shown in Listing 11-11.

Listing 11-11. Chat Helpers Methods

```
def createChat(to: String) {
  xmpp ! CreateChat(to)
}
def sendMessage(to: String, msg: String) {
  xmpp ! SendMsg(to, msg)
}
```

Finally, Listing 11-12 shows how we would create and start the actor to log in and process messages.

Listing 11-12. Starting the Actor

```
val ex = new ConsoleChatActor(user, pass)
ex.start
ex ! Start...
```

Listings 11-8 through 11-12 show how you can integrate your application with an XMPP server and how messages are processed. We won't be detailing each line of code in this example, as it is generally self-explanatory.

Conclusion

In this chapter, we've covered how you can integrate existing third-party services to handle a variety of tasks for your application. We looked at how you can use the OpenID framework to allow people to use accounts from other sites. We also covered two different approaches to message handling via the AMQP and XMPP protocols, which can be used for everything from asynchronous processing to simple IM messages. We examined how you can use Lift's extensions to access the Facebook API, as well as how to process payments via PayPal. These modules allow you to quickly and easily add support to your application.

Chapter 12: Lift Widgets

In this chapter, we're going to discuss widgets in Lift. A widget is essentially a library of Scala and JavaScript code that together provide packaged XHTML fragments for display on the client browser. In other web frameworks (JavaServer Faces, Struts, etc.), these are sometimes called components. An example of a widget would be small library that automatically embeds a `Calendar` instance (see the "Using Calendar Widgets" section), or a helper library to sort HTML tables (see the "Using the TableSorter Widget" section). Typically, widgets embody dynamic behavior on the client side, which is what makes them so attractive; static client-side content is already dead simple to generate in Lift with snippets, so the extra sauce of JavaScript binding and AJAX callbacks really makes advanced functionality easy.

Lift's widgets are intended to minimize effort on your part. Unlike some other frameworks where widgets, or components, require the use of specific traits or special XML binding, Lift's (and Scala's) inherent flexibility—with XML, JavaScript abstraction, and snippet generators—makes using widgets as simple as dropping in a few lines of code to your existing snippets or views.

Getting to Know the Lift Widgets

To start, we'll cover the current set of widgets included in Lift at the time of this writing. These widgets are contained in the `lift-widgets` module, which means you'll need to add the dependency to your `pom.xml` file if you want to use them (see Appendix A). While this list will likely grow over time, remember that widgets are based on the fundamentals of Scala's XML functionality as well as Lift's JavaScript support (see Chapter 8), so the same general rules apply to all of them. At the end of this chapter, we'll cover writing your own widgets (see the "Building a Widget" section).

Using the TableSorter Widget

The `TableSorter` widget, shown in Figure 12-1, is based on the `TableSorter` jQuery plug-in (`http://tablesorter.com/docs/`).

Figure 12-1. The TableSorter Widget

Last Name	First Name	Email	Due	Web Site
Conway	Tim	tconway@earthlink.net	$50.00	http://www.timconway.com
Smith	John	jsmith@gmail.com	$50.00	http://www.jsmith.com
Doe	Jason	jdoe@hotmail.com	$100.00	http://www.jdoe.com
Bach	Frank	fbach@yahoo.com	$50.00	http://www.frank.com

Basically, the TableSorter widget allows you to take an existing HTML table (THEAD and TBODY tags are required) and add sorting to columns in the table. By default, the widget handles sorting of numeric, currency, and other value types automatically. The full capabilities of the plug-in are beyond the scope of the widget, however; if you need more features, you'll have to set up the JavaScript yourself instead of using the widget.

The first step in using the widget is to call the TableSorter.init function in your Boot class to make Lift aware of the resources used by this widget. Then, you need to set up a table in your page (either statically in the template or via a snippet), as shown in Listing 12-1.

Listing 12-1. The TableSorter Template

```
<lift:surround with="default" at="content">
<lift:TableSorterDemo/>
    <table id="table-id" class="tablesorterv> ... </table>
</lift:surround>
```

Note that you need to have an id attribute on the table and add the tablesorter class to the table element. Next, you simply call the TableSorter widget from a snippet, as shown in Listing 12-2.

Listing 12-2. The TableSorter Snippet

```
class TableSorterDemo {
 def render(xhtml: NodeSeq): NodeSeq = TableSorter("table-id")
}
```

The argument to TableSorter is the HTML element id of the table you want sorted. The TableSorter code relies on a head merge (see Chapter 3) to put the appropriate JavaScript and jQuery functions into the returned page.

Using the Calendar Widgets

There are three calendar widgets corresponding to month, week, and day views. These widgets display calendars with a similar look and feel to Microsoft Outlook or Google Calendar. They provide basic functionality for display, but you can easily customize CSS and JavaScript hooks for calendar items to fit your application requirements. Figure 12-2 shows the widget in month view.

Figure 12-2. The CalendarMonthView Widget

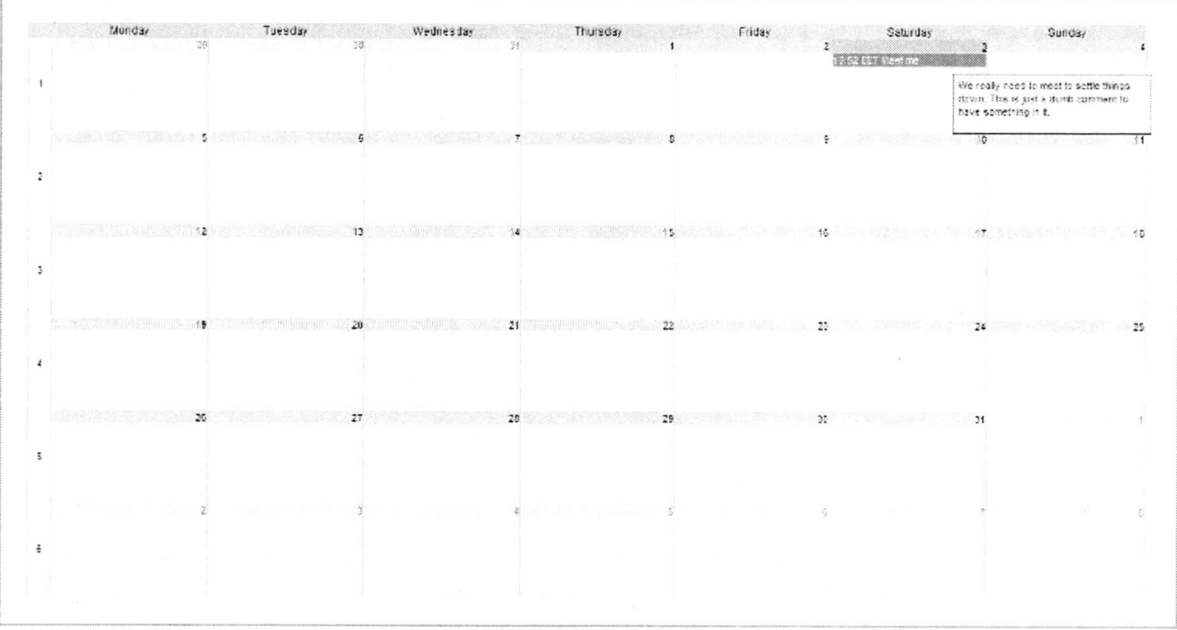

The widget shown in Figure 12-2 allows you to create monthly calendars in your web page, manage your calendar events, and so on. The first thing you need to do is call the `CalendarMonthView.init` function in your `Boot` class. This performs initialization by telling Lift's `ResourceServer` about the paths to JavaScript code and style sheets needed by this widget, since these dependencies are embedded in the same JAR file (we'll cover this topic more in the "Building a Widget" section).

The template for our widget example is relatively straightforward, as Listing 12-3 shows. Basically, we provide a binding element where the calendar will be rendered.

Listing 12-3. The Month View Template

```
<lift:surround with="default" at="content">
    <h2>Calendar Month View Demo</h2>
    <lift:CalendarMonthViewDemo>
      <cal:widget/>
    </lift:CalendarMonthViewDemo>
</lift:surround>
```

In our snippet code, Listing 12-4, we first perform some setup of the widget. The `Calendar` widget takes a `java.util.Calendar` instance and tells it which month to display. Additionally, it takes a set of events (`Seq[CalendarItem]`) to be displayed on the calendar. Finally, it takes three arguments containing optional JavaScript functions to be called when an item, day, or week is clicked. These callbacks can be used to perform any kind of event handling that you need for your calendar. In our example, we're not showing any events or setting up any callbacks to keep the code simple, but we'll be showing how to handle both of those cases in a moment.

Listing 12-4. The Month View Snippet

```
class CalendarMonthViewDemo {
  def render(html: Group) : NodeSeq = {
    val c = Calendar.getInstance;
    c.set(MONTH, 0)
    bind("cal", html,
         "widget" -> CalendarMonthView(c, Nil, Empty, Empty, Empty)
    )
  }
```

In addition, `CalendarMonthView` can also take a `MonthViewMeta` instance as the second argument so that you can control the first day of the week and the locale used for formatting dates and times. For instance, we could set the calendar to use Monday as the first day of the week by modifying our binding:

```
"widget" -> CalendarMonthView(c,
  MonthViewMeta(Calendar.MONDAY, Locale.getDefault),
              Nil, Empty, Empty, Empty)
```

Of course, without anything to display or do, this isn't very useful, so let's look at how you create `CalendarItems`. Listing 12-5 shows how we can create a calendar item for a meeting on June 5 at 2:30 p.m. We have to set up another `Calendar` instance to hold the time of the meeting, and we use the `CalendarItem` helper object to set up the actual item instance. The first parameter is the `id` of the `<div>` that will be created for the item. This can be used from other scripts if necessary. The second argument is the time of the event. The third argument is the `CalendarType` of the event, in this case, a meeting. The optional method on `CalendarItem` allows you to set optional attributes essentially via a sequence of `(CalendarItem) => CalendarItem` functions. This technique is used since `CalendarItems` are immutable and modifying them returns new instances.

Listing 12-5. CalendarItem Example

```
val time = Calendar.getInstance
time.setTime(DateFormat.getDateInstance.parse("June 5, 2009 2:30pm"))
val meeting = CalendarItem("4", time, CalendarType.MEETING) optional (
        _ end(time),
        _ subject("Important Meeting!"))
```

The widget not only renders the XHTML to display the calendar but generates the `<script>` and CSS tags using a head merge to control the display. One common customization of the widget would be to override the CSS used. To do this, provide your own `style.css` file under the `WEB-`

INF/classes/calendars/monthview directory in your project. Because Lift uses the classpath to load resources, your style.css file will be found before the default one bundled in the lift-widgets JAR file. You can use the default style.css (located in GitHub) as a starting point.

The final things we'd like to cover for the month view are the JavaScript callbacks. These callbacks are constructed using the AnonFunc JavaScript artifact, which essentially constructs an anonymous function on the client side. Listing 12-6 shows an example of using the callbacks to redirect to an event view page for the given event when the item is clicked. In this example, we assume that the id of each calendar item is its unique id in the ORM (see Chapter 6) and that we have a rewrite rule set up to handle item viewing (see Chapter 3).

Listing 12-6. A Calendar Callback Example

```
import net.liftweb.http.js.JE._
import net.liftweb.http.js.JsCmds._
val itemClick = Full(
  AnonFunc("elem, param", JsRaw("alert(elem);")))
  Calendar Week-View
```

The CalendarWeekView widget, shown in Figure 12-3, provides a weekly view of the calendar.

Figure 12-3. The CalendarWeekView Widget

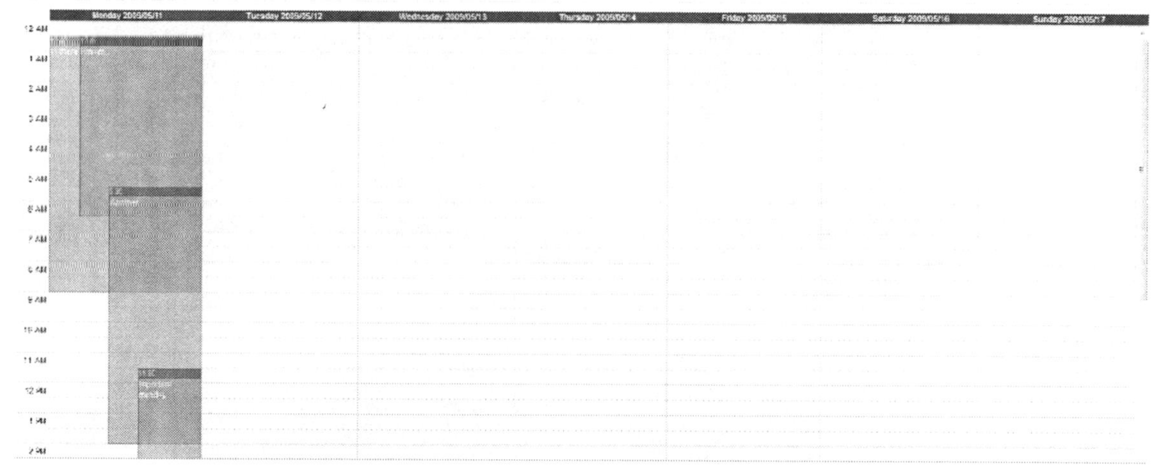

The same general principles apply as for the month view. Again, you need to initialize the CalendarWeekView by calling the CalendarWeekView.init function in your Boot class. Listing 12-7 shows a snippet returning a week view. As you can see, we still use a Calendar instance to set the time, and we also provide a WeekViewMeta in this example to set the first day of the week and the locale. The list argument is a Seq[CalendarItem], constructed exactly the same as for a month view. Finally, we provide a JavaScript item callback. Note that there aren't day or week callbacks available.

Listing 12-7. A Week View Example

```
class CalendarWeekViewDemo {
 import net.liftweb.http.js.JE._
 import net.liftweb.http.js.JsCmds._
 def render(html: Group) : NodeSeq = {
val c = Calendar getInstance
c.set(DAY_OF_MONTH, 17)
 ..... c.set(MONTH, 4)
    bind("cal", html,
         "widget" -> CalendarWeekView(c,
           WeekViewMeta(MONDAY, Locale.getDefault()),
                Nil,
                itemClick))
  }
}
```

The `CalendarDayView` widget, shown in Figure 12-4, renders a calendar for a single day.

Figure 12-4. The CalendarDayView Widget

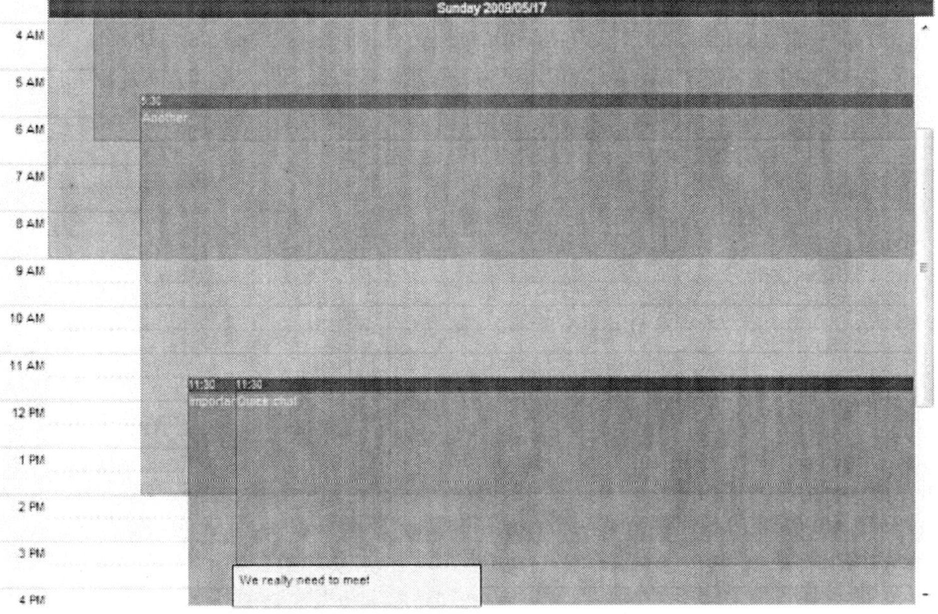

The usage is essentially the same as for the month and week views, as shown in Listing 12-8.

Listing 12-8. A Day View Example

```
class CalendarDayViewDemo { import net.liftweb.http.js.JE._
  import net.liftweb.http.js.JsCmds._
  def render(html: Group) : NodeSeq = {
    val c = Calendar getInstance
    c.set(DAY_OF_MONTH, 17)
    c.set(MONTH, 4)
    bind("cal", html,
         "widget" -> CalendarDayView(c,
           DayViewMeta(Locale.getDefault()),
           Nil, itemClick)
         )
}}
```

The parameters are essentially the same as in the other two calendar views, except that the `Calendar` object represents the day that we want to render, and we pass a `DayViewMeta` containing just the locale for internationalization purposes. Again, only an item click callback is available.

Using the RSS Feed Widget

The RSS feed widget, like its name implies, simply renders RSS feeds; it's shown in Figure 12 5.

Figure 12-5. The RSSFeed Widget

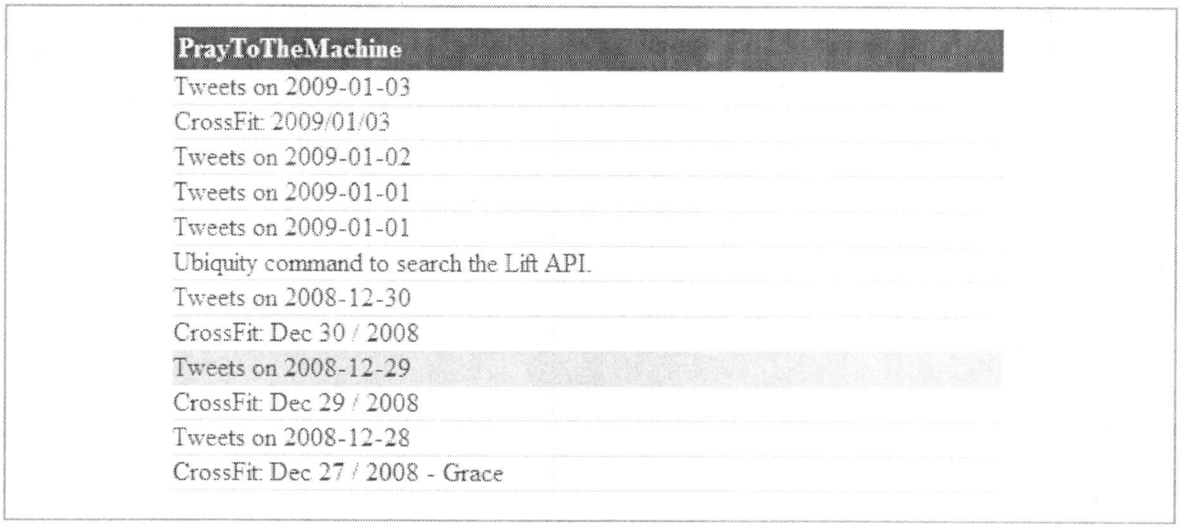

PrayToTheMachine
Tweets on 2009-01-03
CrossFit: 2009/01/03
Tweets on 2009-01-02
Tweets on 2009-01-01
Tweets on 2009-01-01
Ubiquity command to search the Lift API.
Tweets on 2008-12-30
CrossFit: Dec 30 / 2008
Tweets on 2008-12-29
CrossFit: Dec 29 / 2008
Tweets on 2008-12-28
CrossFit: Dec 27 / 2008 - Grace

This widget does not need initialization in Boot, since it has no dependencies on JavaScript, CSS, and so on. In your snippet, you simply use the RSSFeed helper object with the RSS feed URL, as shown in Listing 12-9.

Listing 12-9. An RSSFeed Example

```
class RSSFeedDemo {
  def render(xhtml: NodeSeq): NodeSeq = {
    RSSFeed("http://www.praytothemachine.com/evil/index.php/feed/")
  }
}
```

Although the RSSFeed widget doesn't provide its own CSS, the generated elements do have CSS classes attached to them that you can provide styling for:

- rsswidget: This class is attached to the outer <div> that contains all of the feed elements.
- rsswidgettitle: This class is attached to the <li> that holds the title of the feed.
- rsswidgetitem: This class is attached to each <li> element that holds an RSS item.

Using the Gravatar Widget

Gravatars (http://gravatar.com) are globally recognized avatars. You can add your picture at the Gravatar web site and associate it with one or more e-mail addresses. Sites that interact with Gravatar can fetch your picture and display it, which is what the Gravatar widget does. Listing 12-10 shows an example snippet that will render the Gravatar for the currentUser into a <div>, if a Gravatar is available. The default size of the Gravatar is 42×42 pixels, but you can override this with additional parameters on the Gravatar.apply method. Additionally, you can filter the Gravatar based on its rating (the default rating is "G only").

Listing 12-10. A Gravatar Example

```
class GravatarDemo {
  def render(xhtml: NodeSeq) :NodeSeq = {
   Gravatar(User.currentUser.email)
  }
}
```

Using the TreeView Widget

The TreeView widget transforms an unordered list (<ul>) into a tree-like structure using the TreeView JQuery plug-in (http://docs.jquery.com/Plugins/Treeview). Each nested unordered list gets decorated with a plus or minus sign that allows you to collapse or expand the entire sublist, as shown in Figure 12-6.

Figure 12-6. The TreeView Widget

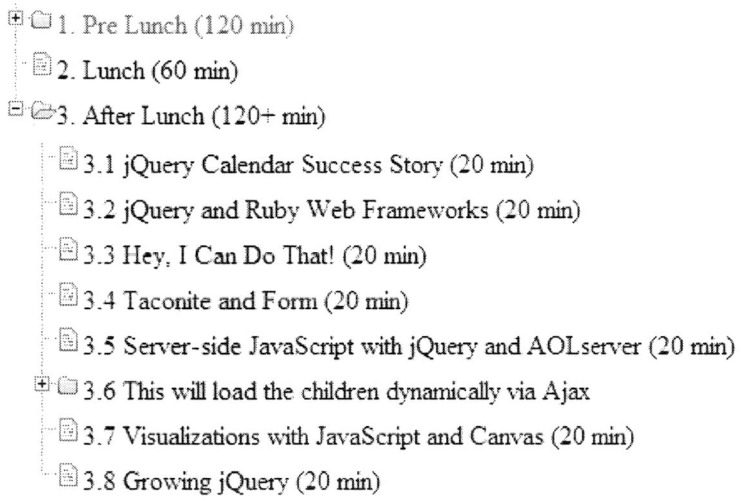

- 1. Pre Lunch (120 min)
- 2. Lunch (60 min)
- 3. After Lunch (120+ min)
  - 3.1 jQuery Calendar Success Story (20 min)
  - 3.2 jQuery and Ruby Web Frameworks (20 min)
  - 3.3 Hey, I Can Do That! (20 min)
  - 3.4 Taconite and Form (20 min)
  - 3.5 Server-side JavaScript with jQuery and AOLserver (20 min)
  - 3.6 This will load the children dynamically via Ajax
  - 3.7 Visualizations with JavaScript and Canvas (20 min)
  - 3.8 Growing jQuery (20 min)

To use this widget, you first need to initialize the widget by calling the `TreeView.init` function in your `Boot` class. The basic snippet looks like Listing 12-11. The first argument is the `id` of the unordered list that you want transformed into a tree. The second argument is a JSON object that is used to configure the tree view. In our example, we're setting the TreeView to animate opening and closing of nodes with a 90-millisecond delay; for more options, see the TreeView jQuery documentation page.

Listing 12-11. A TreeView Snippet

```
class TreeViewDemo {
  import net.liftweb.http.js.JE._
  def render(xhtml: Group): NodeSeq = {
    TreeView("example", JsObj(("animated" -> 90)))
  }
}
```

In addition to transforming static lists into trees, the `TreeView` widget also supports asynchronous loading of trees and nodes via AJAX calls. To do this, you still need to provide an empty `<ul>` element with an `id` attribute; this is essentially modified in place as portions of the tree are loaded. Next, you provide two functions that are used to retrieve the Tree data:

- `() => List[Tree]` loads the initial view of the tree. This is what will be displayed to the client when the page loads, so if you want some nodes to be available without having to make an AJAX call, define them here. We will explain the `Tree` class in a moment.

- (String) => List[Tree] loads the children of a given node (the String argument is the node's id).

The Tree class defines each node in the tree and contains several values that define the appearance and behavior of the node:

- text: This is the text to be displayed in the list item.
- id: This is the optional HTML id of the element.
- classes: This optional string defines CSS classes to be assigned to the element.
- expanded: This Boolean controls whether the element will be expanded initially (it's only valid if hasChildren is true or if the children list is populated).
- hasChildren: If this is set to true when the children value is Nil, the TreeView widget will dynamically load the children of this node as described previously.
- children: This List[Tree] defines the children of this element. Setting this value will prevent AJAX from being used to retrieve the list of children from the server on expansion.

The Tree companion object has a number of overloaded apply methods that make it easy to set one or more of these values without having to set all of them.

To provide a concrete example, Listing 12-12 shows implementations of the loadTree and loadNode functions corresponding to the two AJAX functions used to dynamically construct the tree.

Listing 12-12. A Tree Example

```
def loadTree (): List[Tree] = {
  Tree("No children") ::
  Tree("One static child", Tree("Lone child") :: Nil) ::
  Tree("Dynamic node", "myDynamic", true) :: Nil
}
def loadNode (id : String) : List[Tree] = id match {
  case "myDynamic" =>     Tree("Child one") ::
    Tree("Child two") :: Nil
  case _ => Nil
}
```

In this example, the initial view will show three nodes; the third node ("Dynamic node") will fetch its children via an AJAX call when expanded. The loadNode method will then handle this call by adding two static leaf nodes to the tree.

Using the Sparklines Widget

The `Sparklines` widget is based on Will Larson's excellent Sparklines JavaScript library (`http://www.willarson.com/code/sparklines/sparklines.html`). Sparklines are essentially small, high-resolution charts embedded in text that provide a wealth of information in a compact representation. The term "Sparkline" was introduced by Edward Tufte in his book *Beautiful Evidence*. Dr. Tufte's work is a must read for anyone who is working with visualizing data. Figure 12-7 shows an example Sparkline barchart, complete with percentage lines to assist the user in visually recognizing "normal" values.

Figure 12-7. A Sparklines Bar Chart

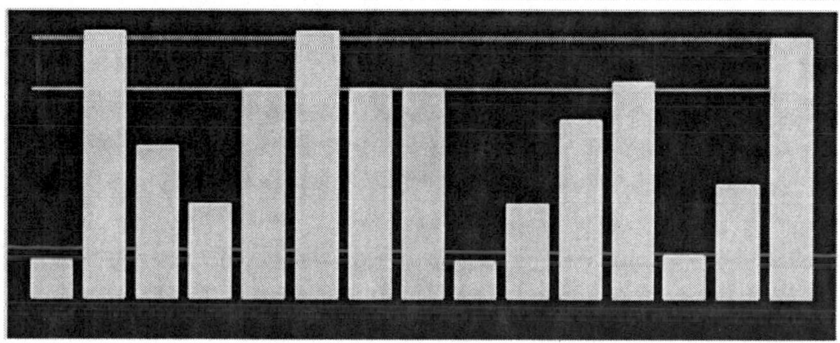

As with our other widgets, you need to initialize the widget in your `Boot` class by calling `Sparklines.init`. Listing 12-13 shows a simple snippet utilizing the widget to produce the graph shown in Figure 12-7. In your template, you need to provide a canvas element with an `id` attribute that will be used by the widget for its content. In our example, we provide a `JsArray` (an abstracted JavaScript array) with our data, as well as a JSON object containing options for the chart; more options for the JSON object can be found on Will Larson's Sparklines web page. We've set our options to draw percentage lines for the bar chart as well as fill in the area between the percentage lines. Finally, we call the `Sparklines.onLoad` method to generate the chart drawing code (the chart will be drawn when the page is loaded). The Sparklines library currently handles bar and line charts, which are chosen via the `SparklineStyle` enumeration.

Listing 12-13. A Sparklines Snippet

```
class SparklinesDemo {
  import net.liftweb.http.js.JE._
  def render(html: NodeSeq): NodeSeq = {
    val data = JsArray(100,500,300,200,400,500,400,400,
                       100,200, 345, 412, 111, 234, 490);
    val opts = JsObj(("percentage_lines" -> JsArray(0.5, 0.75)),
                     ("fill_between_percentage_lines" -> true),
                     ("extend_markings" -> false));
    Sparklines.onLoad("bar", SparklineStyle.BAR, data, opts);
  }
}
```

Building a Widget

As we explained in the introduction, there is no magic formula when building a widget, since Lift and Scala provide so much base functionality without having to resort to restrictions like traits or static XML binding. However, there are a few items to note if you want to design your own widgets.

Generally it's useful to make your widget a self-contained JAR file to simplify dependency management and deployment. Including things like style sheets and JavaScript libraries in your package is quite straightforward if you're using Maven, but the question then becomes, "how do you access these resources from a Lift application?" Fortunately, Lift provides some very simple mechanisms for using class loaders to retrieve resources. The basic functionality is handled through the `net.liftweb.http.ResourceServer` object, which we cover in detail in Chapter 7. This object controls resource loading and, in particular, specifies where resources can be loaded from. Listing 12-14 shows an example `init` method (similar to those that we've previously used for the existing widgets) that tells the `ResourceServer` that it can load resources from the path `/classpath/mywidget`. You would locate these resources under the `mywidget` package in your widget project.

Listing 12-14. Adding ResourceServer Permissions

```
import _root_.net.liftweb.http.ResourceServer
def init() {
  ResourceServer.allow{
    case "iframewidget" :: _ => true
  }
}
```

Once you've set up the appropriate permissions, your widget can generate links or scripts that load from within the classpath, as shown in Listing 12-15. In this example, we've defined a simple (and slightly ridiculous) widget that renders a given URL into an `IFrame` element.

Listing 12-15. Sample Widget Rendering

```
class IFrameWidget {
  def render(url : String) =     <head>
      <link type="text/css" rel="stylesheet"
          href={
            LiftRules.resourceServerPath +
            "/iframewidget/style.css" } />
    </head>
    <div class="iframeDiv">
      <iframe src={url}>
        <p>Your browser doesn't support IFrames</p>
      </iframe>
    </div>
}
```

Note the path that we used uses the `LiftRules.resourceServerPath` variable. It's preferable to use this mechanism instead of hard-coding `/classpath` to keep the code flexible for end users. We also use a head merge to make sure the proper style sheet is loaded for the page.

As you can see, defining your own widget is not much different than writing a snippet. The major difference is in making resources accessible while bundling and making sure that you avoid hard-coding properties that are configurable by the end-users of your widget

Conclusion

In this chapter, we've covered several of the widget modules for Lift that allow you to quickly add functionality to your application simply by embedding some code and/or tags. These widgets include simple functionality for sorting tables, turning an unordered list into a dynamic tree, and retrieving a Gravatar icon based on a user's e-mail address. We also covered some more advanced widgets such as calendar views, RSS feed display, and the Sparkline generator. Finally, we discussed some important tips for writing your own widget so that you can start creating your own reusable components.

Chapter 13: Web Services

In this chapter, we will introduce web services and illustrate how you can easily add this functionality to your Lift application. Using topics that we've already discussed, namely dispatching and pattern matching, we'll show you how easy it is to create an API for your site.

Choosing to Add an API to Your Web Application

Many web applications today now offer an API that allows others to extend the functionality of the service. An API is a set of exposed functions that allow third parties to reuse elements of an application. A number of sites, such as ProgrammableWeb (`http://www.programmableweb.com/`), attempt to catalog all available APIs.

You can combine various APIs to enhance your own application or to create something new. An example of a site that has combined the Google Maps and Flickr APIs is FlickrVision (`http://flickrvision.com/`). FlickrVision allows users to visualize where in the world recent photos have been taken by combining the geolocation information embedded in the photos and the mapping system of Google Maps. This is just one of the countless examples of API mash-ups.

We're going to focus on what it takes to offer a simple RESTful web API for PocketChange.

Reviewing a Little Bit About HTTP

While building our web service, it's going to be helpful to know a few things about HTTP requests and responses. If you're comfortable with the request/response cycle and its details, feel free to jump to the "Defining REST" section and get down to business.

Here's a simplified explanation of how the Web works: clients, typically web browsers, send HTTP requests to servers, which respond with HTTP responses. Let's take a look at an exchange between a client and a server.

We're going to send a `GET` request to the URI `http://demo.liftweb.net/` using the cURL utility. We'll enable dumping the HTTP protocol header information, and we get the result shown in Listing 13-1.

Listing 13-1. A Client Request

```
]> curl -v http://demo.liftweb.net/
* About to connect() to demo.liftweb.net port 80 (#0)
*   Trying 64.27.11.183... connected
* Connected to demo.liftweb.net (64.27.11.183) port 80 (#0)
> GET / HTTP/1.1
> User-Agent: curl/7.19.0 (i386-apple-darwin9.5.0)
  libcurl/7.19.0 zlib/1.2.3
> Host: demo.liftweb.net
> Accept: */*
```

And the corresponding response from the server is shown in Listing 13-2.

Listing 13-2. A Server Response

```
< HTTP/1.1 200 OK
< Server: nginx/0.6.32
< Date: Tue, 24 Mar 2009 20:52:55 GMT
< Content-Type: text/html
< Connection: keep-alive
< Expires: Mon, 26 Jul 1997 05:00:00 GMT
< Set-Cookie: JSESSIONID=5zrn24obipm5;Path=/
< Content-Length: 8431
< Cache-Control: no-cache; private; no-store;
  must-revalidate; max-stale=0; post-check=0; pre-check=0; max-age=0
< Pragma: no-cache
< X-Lift-Version: 0.11-SNAPSHOT
<  <?xml version="1.0" encoding="UTF-8"?> <!DOCTYPE html
PUBLIC "-//W3C//DTD XHTML 1.0 Transitional//EN"
"http://www.w3.org/TR/xhtml1/DTD/xhtml1-transitional.dtd">
<html xmlns:lift="http://liftweb.net"
 xmlns="http://www.w3.org/1999/xhtml"><head>....
```

This process is pretty straightforward: we ask for a resource, and the server returns it to us. Take a look at the HTTP request. We'd like to point out the action, in this case a `GET`, and the URI, which is `http://demo.liftweb.net/`. Actions and addresses are what make the Web work. You can think of the Web as a series of actions on varying resources. Actions, which are also called verbs, are defined as part of the HTTP standard, and we'll use them in our API. In addition to `GET`, the other HTTP actions are `POST`, `DELETE`, `PUT`, `HEAD`, and `OPTIONS`. In this chapter, we will use `GET` and `PUT` in the API.

Just like requests, responses come with a few important pieces of information. Of note are the response code and the entity body. In the preceding example, the response code is 200 (OK) and the entity body is the HTML content of the web page, which is shown as the last two lines starting with `<!DOCTYPE` and is truncated.

This was a quick overview of HTTP, but if you'd like to learn more, head over to the protocol definition. Our intent here was not to make you an HTTP expert; we just wanted to remind you of a few of the relevant parts of the cycle before we got into building a REST API.

Defining REST

Roy Fielding defined REST in his dissertation and defined the main tenet of the architecture to be a uniform interface to resources. "Resources" refers to pieces of information that are named and have representations. Examples include an image, a Twitter status, or a timely item such as a stock quote or the current temperature. The uniform interface is supported by a set of constraints that include the following:

- *Statelessness of communication*: This is built on top of HTTP, which is also stateless.
- *Client-server–style interaction*: Again, just as the Web consists of browsers talking to servers, REST discusses machines or applications talking to servers in the same way.
- *Support for caching*: REST uses the caching headers of HTTP to support the caching of resources.

These features are shared by both the web and by RESTful services. REST adds additional constraints regarding interacting with resources:

- *Naming*: As we mentioned, a resource must be identified, and this is done using URLs.
- *Descriptive actions*: Using the HTTP actions, `GET`, `PUT`, and `DELETE` makes it obvious what action is being performed on the resource.
- *URL addressability*: URLs should allow for the addressing of representation of a resource.

Fielding's goal was to define a method that allowed machine-to-machine communication to mimic that of browser-to-server communication and to take advantage of HTTP as the underlying protocol. You can find Fielding's dissertation at `http://www.ics.uci.edu/~fielding/pubs/dissertation/rest_arch_style.htm`.

You'll see how Lift allows you to create RESTful web services in the rest of this chapter.

Comparing XML-RPC and REST Architectures

So what is the difference between a RESTful architecture and a traditional RPC architecture? An RPC application is more closely related to traditional development. It tends to ignore most of the features offered by HTTP (such as the methods `GET` and `POST`). Rather, the scoping and data for the request are contained in the body of the `PUT`. XML-RPC acts like the Web when it needs to get a resource, but to do everything else, it breaks from those tenets by overloading the `POST` request. You will often see the term "SOAP" (Simple Object Access Protocol) when talking about an XML-RPC setup, as SOAP allows the developer to define the action and the resource and ignore the HTTP details. If you're not familiar with SOAP, please see http://en.wikipedia.org/wiki/SOAP.

RESTful architectures embrace HTTP and use it to their advantage. Since we're using the Web, we may as well act like it.

Creating a Simple API for PocketChange

We're going to start out with a simple example. We'd like to skip some of the more complex steps of a web service at the start, authorization in particular, to keep things simple.

We're going to model two calls to the server, a GET request that responds with the expense details and a PUT action to add an expense. The URLs will be as follows:

- A GET request is sent to the following URL, where expense_id is the expense ID:

  http://www.pocketchangeapp.com/api/expense/<expense_id>

- A PUT request and the XML body are sent to the following URI:

  http://www.pocketchangeapp.com/api/expense

The URLs are almost the same, and as you will see in the next section, we can pattern match on the type of request in addition to the URL.

Pattern Matching for the URLs

Now that we've discussed our design, let's see the code that will handle the routing. In the package com.pocketchangeapp.api, we have an object named RestAPI defined in com/pocketchangeapp/api/RestAPI.scala.

The block of code to handle the routing is shown in Listing 13-3.

Listing 13-3. Dispatch Rules

```
package com.pocketchangeapp.api
object RestAPI extends XMLApiHelper {
  def dispatch: LiftRules.DispatchPF = {
case Req(List("api", "expense", eid), "", GetRequest) =>
  () => showExpense(eid)
case r @ Req(List("api", "expense"), "", PutRequest) =>
  () => addExpense(r)
// Invalid API request - route to our error handler
 case Req(List("api", x), "", _) => failure _
}
}
```

The server will now service GET requests with the showExpense method and will handle PUT requests with addExpense. One thing to note is we are pattern matching on the Req object. In the PUT request, we extract the Req and pass it as a parameter to addExpense, because we're passing in an XML body with the information for the Expense.

As we discussed previously, Lift uses dispatch rules to route requests. We're going to need to update the dispatch rules, since we would like to hook our dispatch under the /api/ path and handle all of the requests.

This is accomplished by adding the code in Listing 13-4 into Boot.scala.

Listing 13-4. Adding Dispatch Rules

```
import com.pocketchangeapp.api
class Boot {
  def boot {
    ...
    LiftRules.dispatch.prepend(RestAPI.dispatch)
    ...
  }
}
```

We'll now be able to intercept incoming requests with /api/ as the start of the URI.

Writing the API Service Code

Now that we're handling the API calls, we'll need to write the code to process and respond to requests. In RestAPI.scala, we'll add the code shown in Listing 13-5.

Listing 13-5. Service Code

```
// reacts to the GET Request
def showExpense(eid: String): LiftResponse = {
  val e: Box[NodeSeq] = for(r <-
    Expense.find(By(Expense.id, eid.toLong)))
    yield {
      wrapXmlBody(<operation id="show_expense"
        success="true">{e.toXML}</operation>)
    }
    e
}


private def getAccount(e: String, n: String): Account = {
  val u = User.find(By(User.email, e))
  val a = Account.findByName(u.open_!, n) match {
    case acct :: Nil => acct
```

```
    case _ => new Account
  }
  a
}

// reacts to the PUT Request
def addExpense(req: Req): LiftResponse = {
  var tempEmail = ""
  var tempPass = ""
  var tempAccountName = ""
  var expense = new Expense
  req.xml match {
    case Full(<expense>{parameters @ _*}</expense>) => {
      for(parameter <- parameters){
        parameter match {
       case <email>{email}</email> => tempEmail = email.text
case  <password>{password}</password> => tempPass = password.text
           case <accountName>{name}</accountName> =>
             tempAccountName = name.text
           case <dateOf>{dateof}</dateOf> =>
             expense.dateOf(new java.util.Date(dateof.text))
           case <amount>{value}</amount> =>
             expense.amount(BigDecimal(value.text))

          case <desc>{description}</desc> =>
             expense.description(description.text)
          case _ =>
         }
       }
       try {
          val u:User = User.find(By(User.email, tempEmail)) match {
         case Full(user) if user.validated &&
user.password.match_?(tempPass) => user
         case _ => new User
}
val currentAccount = Account.find(By(Account.owner,
   u.id.is), By(Account.name, tempAccountName))
     .open_!
   expense.account(currentAccount.id.is)
val (entrySerial,entryBalance) =
 Expense.getLastExpenseData(currentAccount, expense.dateOf)
expense.account(currentAccount).serialNumber(
entrySerial + 1).tags("api")
.currentBalance(entryBalance + expense.amount)
expense.validate match {
  case Nil =>
Expense.updateEntries(entrySerial + 1,
```

```
expense.amount.is)
expense.save
val newBalance = currentAccount.balance.is +
  expense.amount.is
  currentAccount.balance(newBalance).save
CreatedResponse(wrapXmlBody(<operation id="add_expense"
 success="true"></operation>), "text/xml")
   case _ =>
     CreatedResponse(wrapXmlBody(<operation id="add_expense"
     success="false"></operation>), "text/xml")
     }
   }
   catch {
     case e => Log.error("Could not add expense", e);
       BadResponse()
   }
 }
  case _ => Log.error("Request was malformed");
    BadResponse()       }   }
```

Creating a Helper Method for the Expense Model Object

To make it easier to get the name of the Account we care about, we'll add a helper function to our Expense model object, as shown in Listing 13-6.

Listing 13-6. Account Name Helper

```
// look up the account name for the expense
private def getAccountName(id: Long): String = {
  Account.find(By(Account.id, id)) match {
    case Empty => "No Account Name"
    case Full(a) => a.name.is
  }
}

// get a list of tags of the form
// <tag>tagname1</tag><tag>tagname2</tag>
def showXMLTags: NodeSeq = tags.map(t =>
  <tag>{t.name.is}</tag>)

 def toXML: NodeSeq = {
  val id = "http://www.pocketchangeapp.com/api/expense/" + this.id
  val formatter = new java.text.SimpleDateFormat(
    "yyyy-MM-dd'T'HH:mm:ss'Z'")
  val edate = formatter.format(this.dateOf.is)
  <expense>
```

```
    <id>{id}</id>
    <accountname>{getAccountName(account.is)}</accountname>
    <date>{edate}</date>
    <description>{description.is}</description>
    <amount>{amount.is.toString}</amount>
    <tags>{showXMLTags}</tags>
  </expense>
}
```

Setting Up the Request/Response Cycles for Our API

At the beginning of this chapter, we showed you a request and response conversation for `http://demo.liftweb.net/`. Let's see what that looks like for a request to our API; see Listing 13-7.

Listing 13-7. Request and Request of GET for Our API

```
Request:
http://www.pocketchangeapp.com/api/expense/3 GET
Response: <?xml version="1.0" encoding="UTF-8"?>
<pca_api operation="expense" success="true" >
  <operation success="true" id="show_expense">
    <expense>
   <id>http://www.pocketchangeapp.com/api/expense/3</id>
      <accountname>Home</accountname>
      <date>2009-03-26T00:00:00Z</date>
       <description>MacHeist Apps</description>
       <amount>35.00</amount>
       <tags>
          <tag>software</tag>
        <tag>apps</tag>
        <tag>mac</tag>
      </tags>
    </expense>
  </operation>
</events_api>
```

Listing 13-8 shows the output of the `PUT` conversation.

Listing 13-8. Request and Request of PUT for Our API

```
Request:
http://www.pocketchangeapp.com/api/expense -
PUT - addEntry(request) + XML Body
Request Body:
<expense>
  <email>tyler.weir@pocketchangeapp.com</email>
```

```
    <password>******</password>
    <accountName>Home</accountName>
    <dateOf>2009/03/26</dateOf>
    <amount>45.00</amount>
    <desc>I buy food</desc>
</expense>

Response:
HTTP/1.1 201 Created
<?xml version="1.0" encoding="UTF-8"?>
<pca_api>
  <operation success="true" id="add_expense" />

</pca_api>
```

Extending the API to Return Atom Feeds

What if you'd like to return your data in a different format than XML? For this example, we'll add support for Atom (`http://tools.ietf.org/html/rfc4287`). Atom is a simple publishing standard for content syndication. To change the data output format, you'll have to do two things. First, define the helper or helpers that are common across output formats. After that, update the dispatch rules to allow users to request the alternate data formats.

In our case, we'll first add `toAtom` to the model as shown in Listing 13 9.

Listing 13-9. Request and Request of PUT for Our API

```
def toAtom = {
  val id = "http://www.pocketchangeapp.com/api/expense/" + this.id
  val formatter = new  SimpleDateFormat("yyyy-MM-dd'T'HH:mm:ss'Z'")
  val edate = formatter.format(this.dateOf.is)
  <entry xmlns="http://www.w3.org/2005/Atom">
    <expense>
      <id>{id}</id>
      <accountname>{getAccountName(account.is)}</accountname>
      <date>{edate}</date>
      <description>{description.is}</description>
      <amount>{amount.is.toString}</amount>
      <tags>{showXMLTags}</tags>
    </expense>
  </entry>
}
```

And we'll have to modify the dispatch rules to add a format selection in the URI. We'll leave plain XML as the default response, and we'll add a way for users to select XML or Atom.

The URIs for `GET` will now be as shown in Listing 13-10.

Listing 13-10. Updated URLs for Our API

```
http://www.pocketchangeapp.com/api/expense/<eid>
http://www.pocketchangeapp.com/api/expense/<eid>.xml
http://www.pocketchangeapp.com/api/expense/<eid>.atom
And these are the additions to the dispatch:
object RestAPI extends XMLApiHelper {
  def dispatch: LiftRules.DispatchPF = {
case Req(List("api", "expense", eid), "", GetRequest)
  => () => showExpenseXml(eid) // old
    case Req("api", "expense", eid), "xml", GetRequest)
  => () => showExpenseXml(eid) // new
    case Req("api", "expense", eid), "atom", GetRequest)
  => () => showExpenseAtom(eid) // new
    case r @ Req("api", "expense", eid), "", PutRequest)
  => () => addExpense(eid, r)
// Invalid API request - route to our error handler
    case Req("api" :: x :: Nil, "", _) => failure _   }
  }
```

Finally, as shown in Listing 13-11, we'll add `showExpenseAtom`, and rename `showExpense` to `showExpenseXml`.

Listing 13-11. Atom Request Handler

```
def showExpenseXml(eid: String): LiftResponse = {
  val e: Box[NodeSeq] = for(e <- Expense.find
    (By(Expense.id, eid.toLong)))
yield {
XmlResponse(<operation id="show_expense_xml"
success="true">{r.toXML}</operation>)
}  e
}

def showExpenseAtom(eid: String): AtomResponse = {
val e: Box[Node] = for(e <- Expense.find(By(Expense.id, eid.toLong)))
   yield {
     e.toAtom
    }
  AtomResponse(e.open_!)
}
```

Let's take a look at a request for an Atomized entry in Listing 13-12.

Listing 13-12. Request and Request for Atom

```
Request:
GET - http://localhost:8080/api/expense/10.atom
Headers and Response:
ExpiresThu, 01 Jan 1970 00:00:00 GMT
Set-CookieJSESSIONID=1bq219bmoevv1;Path=/
Content-Length 353
Content-Typeapplication/atom+xml
X-Lift-Version0.11-SNAPSHOT
Server Jetty(6.1.15.rc3)
<entry xmlns="http://www.w3.org/2005/Atom">       <expense>
  <id>http://www.pocketchangeapp.com/api/expense/10</id>
  <accountname>Home</accountname>
  <date>2009-03-26T00:00:00Z</date>
  <description>I buy food</description>
  <amount>45.00</amount>
  <tags>
    <tag>api</tag>
   </tags>
</expense>
</entry>
```

Conclusion

In this chapter, we outlined a RESTful API for a web application and showed how to implement one using Lift. We then extended that API to return Atom in addition to XML.

If you want to expand the API beyond what we've done here, some logical extensions would be a full authentication layer or transforming the data to another format, such as JSON.

Copyright

The Definitive Guide to Lift: A Scala-Based Web Framework

ISBN-13 (electronic): 978-1-4302-2422-8

ISBN-13 (paperback): 978-1-4302-2421-1

Distributed to the book trade in the United States by Springer-Verlag New York, Inc., 233 Spring Street, 6th Floor, New York, NY 10013, and outside the United States by Springer-Verlag GmbH & Co. KG, Tiergartenstr. 17, 69112 Heidelberg, Germany.

In the United States: phone 1-800-SPRINGER, fax 201-348-4505, e-mail orders@springer-ny.com, or visit http://www.springer-ny.com. Outside the United States: fax +49 6221 345229, e-mail orders@springer.de, or visit http://www.springer.de.

For information on translations, please contact Apress directly at 2855 Telegraph Ave, Suite 600, Berkeley, CA 94705. Phone 510-549-5930, fax 510-549-5939, e-mail info@apress.com, or visit http://www.apress.com.

LaVergne, TN USA
03 September 2009
156630LV00008B/33/P

9 781430 224211